# The British Empire's Regulars 1880–1914

*Soldiers of Britain, India and Africa*

---

Wendell Schollander

**Helion & Company**

Helion & Company Limited
Unit 8 Amherst Business Centre
Budbrooke Road
Warwick
CV34 5WE
England
Tel. 01926 499 619
Email: info@helion.co.uk
Website: www.helion.co.uk
X, Formerly Twitter: @helionbooks
Visit our blog https://helionbooks.wordpress.com/

Published by Helion & Company 2025
Designed and typeset by Mach 3 Solutions (www.mach3solutions.co.uk)
Cover designed by Paul Hewitt, Battlefield Design (www.battlefield-design.co.uk)



ISBN 978-1-804515-62-4

British Library Cataloguing-in-Publication Data.
A catalogue record for this book is available from the British Library.

# Contents

## List of Abbreviations

5th LI – 5th Light Infantry
A&E – Artillery and Engineers
AWOL – absence without leave
BEF – British Expeditionary Force
C&I – Cavalry and Infantry
CAR – Central African Rifles
CARgt – Central African Regiment
CGS – Chief of the General Staff
CIGS – Chief of the Imperial General Staff
CO – commanding officer
DCM – Distinguished Conduct Medal
DSO – Distinguished Service Order
EAR – East African Rifles
EIC – East India Company
FK – *Feld-Kompanie*
GR – Gurkha Rifles
H&EPM – Hindustani and Eastern Punjabi Muslims
HM – Hindustani Muslims
IDSM – Indian Distinguished Service Medal
IOM – Indian Order of Merit
KAR – King's African Rifles
KGO – King George's Own
KOSB – King's Own Scottish Borderers
LNL – Loyal North Lancashires
M&G – Magar and Gurung
MC – Military Cross
MP – member of Parliament
NCO – non-commissioned officer
OTC – Officers' Training Corps
PM – Punjabi Muslim
POW – prisoner of war
PSC – passed Staff College
TB – tuberculosis
UR – Uganda Rifles
VC – Victoria Cross
VCO – viceroy's commissioned officer
WAFF – West African Frontier Force

# 1

# British Officers

The British officer is brave. The British officer has been criticised over the years for many failings, particularly after the Boer War and the First World War.[1] But, by and large, his courage in battle has never been doubted. In the First World War, only two British army officers were found guilty of cowardice or desertion in the face of the enemy.[2] This includes prisoners of war (POWs), who, after the war was over, were required to explain the circumstances of their capture. The goal of these inquiries was to uncover any instances of cowardliness or desertion under the guise of being captured.[3]

However, being granted a Queen's or King's Commission does not automatically make a person a superman. Down through the years, a few officers have been cashiered for failure to show sufficient bravery in the face of the enemy. In the First World War, letters home gave accounts of officers, mostly from Kitchener New Army divisions, of men deserting their posts and running back when they came under heavy fire.[4]

This is true even though the makeup of the officer corps has changed over the years. Prior to the Cardwell Reforms of 1871–1872, the officer corps had many nobles and wealthy landowners (landed gentry) who mixed freely with them. A good example of this ongoing movement towards middle-class officers is that only 15 percent of cadets had ridden before enlisting.[5] See Table 1 for a percentage breakdown of the different status groups in the army over the years.

1 C. E. Montague, *Disenchantment* (London: Chatto and Windus, 1922).
2 John Lewis-Stempel, *Six Weeks: The Short and Gallant Life of the British Officer in the First World War* (London: Orion Publishing Group, 2010), p.207.
3 Lewis-Stempel, *Six Weeks*, p.301.
4 Tim Travers, 'Learning the Art of War: Junior Officer Training in the British Army from the Eighteenth Century to 1914', in E. Converse III (ed.), *Forging the Sword: Selecting, Educating, and Training Cadets and Junior Officers in the Modern World* (Chicago: Imprint Publications, 1998), p.22.
5 Nick Evans, '"Sport and Hard Work." Tactics, Reform and Equestrianism in the British Cavalry 1900–1914', *Journal of the Society for Army Historical Research*, 89:358 (2011), p.151, <https://www.jstor.org/stable/44231835>.

**Table 1 Officer Status Groups in the British Army**[6]

| Year | Aristocracy | Landed Gentry | Middle Class | Sample Size* |
|---|---|---|---|---|
| 1780 | 24% | 16% | 60% | 100 |
| 1830 | 21% | 32% | 47% | 100 |
| 1875 | 18%† | 32% | 50% | 100 |
| 1912 | 9% | 32% | 59% | 100 |

* Samples taken from army lists for the named years.
† The drop in the numbers for 1875 and after is probably due to the end of the purchase system.

Up until 1871, men could purchase their ranks. This allowed men with money to advance much faster than those without it. In addition, the general rule was that the more money, the faster the advancement. The best known of this breed is the Earl of Cardigan, who led the charge of the light brigade. He paid between £35,000 and £40,000 (£3,318,400–£3,792,500 or $3,905,500–$4,463,400 in current money) to buy the lieutenant colonelcy of the 15th Hussar Regiment in 1832.[7] In 1834, he was found unfit to command, and, upon the orders of the King, he was removed from command.[8] However, his family was able to use connections at court and in Parliament to reverse the findings of the court martial.[9] Then, in 1836, he bought command of the 11th Light Dragoons. He is said to have paid over £40,000 (£3,869,100 or $4,553,600 in current money) for the 11th.

But this went on at all levels. One of the last purchases was by Sir Hugh McCalmont, who bought the rank of captain in 1869 for £5,125 (£516,600 or $608,000 in current funds). This enabled him to become a captain in less than four years after joining the army. He went on to become a major general.[10] To achieve a rapid rise in rank, officers would need to buy higher ranks as they became open, normally in another regiment. This led to jokes about officers not knowing the name of their regiment, only the colour of its facings and what train one would take to reach it. With some officers moving between regiments like that, it was hard to develop a regimental *esprit de corps* among the officers.

The Cardwell Reforms changed all that. It abolished the purchasing of ranks. Who could become an officer was limited by requiring tests. This gave rise to a new type of officer, one who had attended a public school. The public school catered to the upper middle classes. They were quite expensive and taught subjects that helped their students pass the officer's and civil service tests of the time.

6 Peter E. Razzell, 'Social Origins of Officers in the Indian and British Home Army: 1758–1962', *British Journal of Sociology*, 14:3 (1963), p.253, Table 7.
7 Cecil Woodham-Smith, *The Reason Why: The Story of the Fatal Charge of the Light Brigade* (London: Penguin Books, 1958), p.38.
8 Woodham-Smith, *Reason*, pp.50–51.
9 Woodham-Smith, *Reason*, p.51.
10 John M. Brereton, *The 7th Queen's Own Hussars* (London: Leo Cooper, 1975), p.133.

## Public Schools

Officer – hussars.

In time, public school largely took over the job of preparing students to join the military. During the Boer War, some 62 percent of the regular officers came from public schools, with 41 percent from the 10 great public schools and 11 percent from Eton alone.[11] So close was the connection between the public schools and the officer corps that, when the First World War began, the military authorities drew up a list of public schools. In the first rush of volunteers, men who wanted to try and become officers could only do so if they had attended a school on that list. If a person had attended a school, no matter how old and venerable, that was not on the list, he was not eligible. One candidate who had attended Kingston Grammar School, founded by Queen Elizabeth I in 1567, was turned down because the school was not on the magic list.[12]

The pre-First World War public schools were Spartan places where the students were cold and hunger was the norm.[13] The schools severed the boys' ties with home, which made the students perfect to go out and serve in the far-flung empire. They stressed a muscular Christianity through the required chapel and games. In most public schools, chapel was required every morning and evening (and three times on Sunday). All this time, listening to sermons did not impart a deep knowledge of the doctrines of Christianity.[14] Boys' minds will wander. But it did give a good idea of the contents of the Bible. Officers and civilians would use references to Bible verses as a code when telegraphing each other. Rhodes did it with Jameson when the latter was organising for his raid into Transvaal, and it was done as late as Dunkirk.

This is not to say that the officers were not religious. The entire British society was probably much more religious than it is today, despite what cynics say. For example, consider the actions of the soldiers wounded on the first day, or days, of the Battle of the Somme. It is said that,

11 Edward M. Spiers, 'The Regular Army of 1914', in I. F. W. Beckett and K. Simpson (eds), *A Nation in Arms: A Social Study of the British Army in the First World War* (Manchester: Manchester University Press, 1985), p.41.

12 Lewis-Stempel, *Six Weeks*, pp.37–38.

13 J. A. Mangan, 'Social Darwinism and Upper-Class Education in Late Victorian and Edwardian England', in J. A. Mangam and J. Walvin (eds), *Manliness and Mortality: Middle-Class Masculinity in Britain and America, 1800–1940* (Manchester: Manchester University Press, 1987), p.151.

14 Lewis-Stempel, *Six Weeks*, pp.20–21.

after the battle, officers came upon their bodies in shell holes. They had crawled into them for shelter, wrapped their waterproof sheets around them, taken out their army-issued field bibles, and died.[15]

The public schools required all types of sports; cross-country runs were required at many schools. Boxing and track-and-field events were offered. It is claimed that, after the sports programmes at school, many found army physical training and route marches a relative breeze.[16]

The schools also stressed team sports, such as rugby and soccer. They were believed to teach discipline, teamwork, sublimation of the individual to the needs of the group, the art of decision-making under pressure, leadership, discipline, and unselfishness.[17] In short, the qualities an officer would need.

The flipside of muscular Christianity was said to be possible ambivalence towards the intellect and making heroes of the athletes.[18] The charge of anti-intellectualism had been made by academic writers about the pre-First World War officers of every army. At bottom, this seems to be more of a complaint that the officers are not like us academics attracted to intellectual matters. But officers need a different skill set. They need an outdoor athletic life. They need to lead and teach men who are often not very intelligent and often do not want to be in the army. Academicians have trouble teaching students who have paid money, or their families have, to be in the classes and should be motivated to learn.

Officers must work together. So most maintained good relations with each other. Consequently, in every army, they tended to have friendly, outgoing personalities. On the other hand, academicians are famous for their feuds. There is a saying that emphasises how poorly scholars interrelate: 'Academic disputes are so vicious because the stakes are so small.'[19]

The schools taught a moral code that included taking responsibility for one's actions and looking after those under one's charge. Honesty and loyalty were stressed. The German officer corps is roundly criticised for stressing character, honesty, taking responsibility, and loyalty. But it was also stressed in the British army. The military authorities placed great emphasis on character and rather less on technical skills.[20]

Perhaps responding to what the army wanted, the public schools stressed building character through sports and gave short shrift to the sciences or, indeed, the students' general intellect.[21]

15 Adam Hochschild, *To End All Wars: A Story of Loyalty and Rebellion, 1914–1918* (New York: Houghton Mifflin Harcourt, 2011), p.207; Robert and Isabelle Tombs, *That Sweet Enemy: Britain and France: The History of a Love-Hate Relationship* (London: Random House, 2006), p.490. I have read many accounts of these wounded men in the shell holes, and they all use essentially the same wording. This would seem to point to just one text or oral account as the source for this account, a *Somme Q* document, if you will. Tombs' book has one of the most chilling passages I have ever read about the scale of losses on that day. Numbers, being so abstract, are hard to grasp emotionally. It contains a quote that states that reinforcements approaching the front lines heard a sound like 'wet fingers screeching across an enormous plate of glass'. It was the screams of thousands of wounded men.

16 Lewis-Stempel, *Six Weeks*, p.15.

17 Lewis-Stempel, *Six Weeks*, p.16.

18 Lewis-Stempel, *Six Weeks*, pp.143, 149.

19 This proverb takes many forms, each slightly different from the other one quoted. It also has many possible origins. Today, in a slightly different form, it is normally attributed to Henry Kissinger, who was a Harvard professor as well as the American Secretary of State (1973–1977).

20 David French, *Military Identities: The Regimental System, the British Army, and the British People c. 1870–2000* (Oxford: Oxford University Press, 2008), p.149.

21 French, *Military*, p.32.

In 1913, Brigadier General Braithwaite, commandant of the Staff College at Quetta, gave a lecture stating, 'For the conduct of an army character weighs more than knowledge or science.' This phrase was taken from Prussia's von Moltke.[22]

Public school students spent as much as half their time studying Greek and Latin.[23] It is said that, during the Indian Mutiny, British officers sent each other secret messages not in Latin, which they feared educated Indians might be able to read, but in Greek learned in public school.

Another important attribute the public-school graduate possessed was comfort and confidence in giving orders. Since almost all of them came from well-to-do families, when they were still at home, they would have seen their parents giving orders to the household servants. When they went off to public school, at first, they were fags receiving orders. Then, as they got older and climbed the ranks, they were able to give commands.[24] By the time they graduated, giving orders was second nature to them, and, importantly, they believed they had every right to do so and that would be followed. Attitude is all important in giving orders, as those receiving them are quick to spot self-doubt.

The public-school boys paid dearly in the First World War for the right to be officers. Most came out and became junior officers, captains, and down. The general death rate among British soldiers who served in the First World War was 12 percent. In contrast, the death rate among officers from public schools was much higher (see Table 2). These cold percentages do not fully reflect the random heavy losses suffered. One man found that half of the students who had been with him in his house at Rugby in 1910 were dead.[25]

**Table 2 Death Rate for Selected Public Schools[26]**

| School | Percent Killed |
|---|---|
| Harrow | 22% |
| Charterhouse | 22% |
| Eton | 21% |
| Uppingham | 20% |
| Rugby | 20% |
| Sedbergh | 20% |
| Cheltenham | 19% |
| Wellington | 18% |
| Monmouth | 13%* |

* The percentage for Monmouth is low because about half of its old boys served in the ranks.

In peacetime, young men, age 17 or 18, would need to choose a career. Why did some choose one as an officer in the army? Their motives for doing so varied widely. Some were attracted by the glamour; others by the chance to travel. One man said he looked at the wars of the period as a sort of superior hunting. After the Cardwell Reforms, a growing proportion of young men

22 Walter Braithwaite, 'For the Conduct of an Army Character Weighs More Than Knowledge or Science', *Journal of the United Service Institution of India*, 42 (1913), p.351.
23 Lewis-Stempel, *Six Weeks*, p.18.
24 Lewis-Stempel, *Six Weeks*, p.21.
25 Lewis-Stempel, *Six Weeks*, p.26.
26 Lewis-Stempel, *Six Weeks*, pp.25–26.

entering the officer's ranks were following their fathers as officers. Others were fulfilling their fathers' frustrated ambitions. For these young men, it had been assumed all their short lives that they would be army officers, and they just went along with what was planned for them. One man, Archibald Wavell, who came from a military family and went on to become a field marshal, Viceroy of India, and an earl, said that it would have taken more independence of character than he possessed at the time to avoid the army career his father expected.[27]

Others thought of the military based on the atmosphere in their public schools. These schools had a heavy God, Empire, and Duty ethos, and this led naturally to thoughts of serving Britain by becoming an officer, all the more so since the schools had military training in the form of cadet corps.[28]

Another factor was that there was a limited number of careers a young man could take up without losing status. He, of course, did not want to go into trade. That left the clergy, the law, the navy, and the army. If he did not have a calling for the clergy or the funds and intelligence for the long, challenging years of training to become a barrister, he was left with the navy or the army.

## Sandhurst

Once an army career was decided on, most serious young men elected to attend Sandhurst. During the period 1876–1914, Sandhurst produced 55 percent of the non-technical regular officers (engineers and artillery). Most of the balance came through the 'backdoor' of Militia service until this option was removed in 1908.

To attend Sandhurst, a prospective cadet needed to pass entrance tests. These tests covered the same subjects that had been taught at public school, which is one reason a public-school education was so useful. For years, one could even elect to be tested on Greek as well as the more normal Latin. In addition, drawing skills were tested.[29] The schools would teach this, but this was not something the average teenager who did not attend public school would be skilled at doing.

Besides determining who could matriculate at the military college, the test's scores performed a number of other functions. Between 1873 and 1878, if a candidate's test score on the entrance test for Sandhurst was among the six highest, he did not have to attend the school and could enrol directly in his regiment.[30] This is how Robert S. S. Baden-Powell, the father of Boy Scouting, came to the 13th Hussars. He was a brainy young man. In 1876, he passed the entrance test for Sandhurst, and, without using a crammer, he placed second for cavalry and fifth overall, thereby earning the exemption from attending Sandhurst. However, he had failed entrance tests to two colleges at Oxford.

The entrance test scores would also control whether one went into infantry or cavalry. Because serving in the infantry cost less money, there was more interest in entering that branch of

27 Spiers, 'Regular Army', p.40.
28 French, *Military*, pp.30–31, 39–40, 42.
29 Emory Upton, *The Armies of Asia and Europe: Embracing Official Reports on the Armies of Japan, China, India, Persia, Italy, Russia, Austria, Germany, France, and England* (Cranbury, NJ: Scholar's Bookshelf, 2006), p.257.
30 Travers, 'Learning', p.16; Upton, *Armies*, p.260. However, an American officer who made a study of Sandhurst in 1877–1878 said that the top six still had to attend Sandhurst.

service. Thus, a higher test score was required to be assigned to Sandhurst's infantry programme.

Winston Churchill ran into this when he took the tests. He failed the entrance tests several times. At last, with the help of a special tutor, known as a 'crammer', he was able to pass the test. He was not alone in using a crammer. It was common to use them to pass the difficult Sandhurst entrance test. For example, in 1858–1863, 65 percent of the candidates for Sandhurst were tutored by crammers. In 1889, of the successful candidates, 70 percent had been helped by crammers.[31] Churchill entered ninety-second on a list of 102. This was only good enough to become a cavalry cadet. His father had been pulling strings to let him into the prestigious King's Royal Rifle Corps. Since they were infantry and his test scores blocked him from the infantry course, the regiment was out. To add insult to injury, as a cavalry student, it would cost his father an extra £200 (current values of £21,760 or $25,610) a year in fees to send him to Sandhurst.[32] But then, his luck changed. A few boys who had infantry cadetships elected not to go to Sandhurst. This opened infantry slots, and Winston got one.[33] Once he got into Sandhurst, he worked hard. He had come into Sandhurst ranked ninety-second, but he placed twentieth in a class of 130 when he passed out.[34]

Officer – fusiliers.

The entry tests served another function. Prior to 1903, entry into the Indian army was decided by the candidate's placement on the entrance examinations. For example, in 1902, Auchinleck stood forty-eighth coming in and got the last Indian army vacancy. In 1903, Indian army appointments were changed to be based on placement in the final tests at the end of the Sandhurst course.[35] In 1906, additional ways to become Indian officers opened. See the section on British Indian officers for a discussion of them.

31 Byron Farwell, *Mr. Kipling's Army: All the Queen's Men* (New York: W. W. Norton and Company, 1987), p.144.
32 Randolph S. Churchill, *Winston S. Churchill: Youth, 1874–1900* (Boston: Houghton Mifflin Company, 1966), vol. 1, p.197.
33 Churchill, *Churchill*, vol. 1, p.194.
34 Churchill, *Churchill*, vol. 1, p.233.
35 Alun A. G. J. Chalfont, *Montgomery of Alamein* (New York: Atheneum, 1976), p.54.

If one did not think they could pass the difficult Sandhurst entrance examinations and still wanted to attend Sandhurst, there was a method that could be used if there was sufficient money available. Douglas Haig used it. He attended Oxford before attending and graduating from Sandhurst. It has been suggested that Haig went to Oxford not because of a love of learning but because it offered a loophole around passing the hard entrance tests for Sandhurst, which he stood little chance of passing even if he used a crammer. Oxford's colleges had a simpler entrance examination, which was relatively easy to pass and all the more so if one used a crammer. Once in one of Oxford's colleges – Haig was in Brasenose – the student needed only to read for a 'pass' degree, which was not demanding. The real magic of the loophole was that a college student could then, up to age 23, transfer to Sandhurst without having to take an entrance exam. Haig did this after three years without gaining a degree from Brasenose, Oxford.[36]

Once at the Royal Military College at Sandhurst, the gentlemen cadets faced a school term that was normally 18 months during the period 1880–1914. Earlier, it had been one year,[37] and, in 1905, a two-year term was tried.[38]

Tuition at Sandhurst was on a sliding scale. In the 1870s, the sons of private citizens paid a fee of £125 per year (£12,214 or $14,375 in current funds). By 1907, this had risen to £150 per year (£15,281; $17,984). Sons of officers paid a lower amount and received an allowance. In the 1870s, it was £20–£80 annually (£1,954–£7,817 or $2,300–$9,200 in current money). The sons of officers who had been killed in service or died from wounds within six months of being wounded (King's or Queen's cadets) were given free tuition and granted an allowance. Pages of Honour were exempt from the entrance examinations. There were also Indian cadets, who were the sons of officers in the Indian military or civil service. They were treated as the sons of officers.[39]

The schools did not make any effort to teach leadership, assuming that had been learned at the cadet's public school. The syllabus consisted of military engineering, topography (map making), administration and military law, tactics, French or German, mathematics, drill, gymnastics, riding for everyone, and fencing.[40] The school also did not make any effort to give its students education beyond military matters, and it was sometimes claimed that the vast majority of officers never read a book again once they left public school.[41]

After 1903, the lessons of the Boer War were taken to heart, and the training at Sandhurst was made more practical. The emphasis was placed on outdoor work, tactics, engineering, and topography. To make cadets apply themselves while in school, places in the Indian army were changed to being granted based on standing in the final order of merit.[42] This final standing would also affect, to a certain degree, the order in which cadets could select regiments in the British army.

While at the Royal Military Academy, the students at the school hazed other students who did not conform to the public-school norms. These 'outsiders' could come in because of the open entrance examination system. Once in, the other students would bully them until they learned how to conform to the desired norm or dropped out of the school. In 1877, three or four cadets who had

36 Phillip Warner, *Field Marshal Earl Haig* (London: Bodley Head, 1991), pp.17–18.
37 Upton, *Armies*, p.259.
38 Travers, 'Learning', p.17.
39 Farwell, *Mr. Kipling's Army*, p.145; Upton, *Armies*, p.258.
40 Chalfont, *Montgomery*, p.52; French, *Military*, p.69.
41 Farwell, *Mr. Kipling's Army*, p.149.
42 French, *Military*, p.70.

dined with the commandant's cook were thrown into a lake, an action that met with the approval of the commandant.[43]

In 1907, Bernard Law 'Monty' Montgomery, who would go on to become a field marshal and the 1st Viscount Montgomery of Alamein, set fire to an undressing cadet's shirttails while the cadet was held in place with a bayonet. The young man was badly burned and had to go to the hospital.[44] At other times, the gentlemen-cadets acted like thugs. In Montgomery's time, companies fought one another in the halls at night with hockey sticks and pokers. Often, participants in these battles ended up in the hospital.[45]

Soon, the bright school days ended, and the cadets were faced with moving to a regiment. For many, this decision had been made long before graduation day.

Senior line officer.

## Regiment Selection

The British did not use anything so crass as the black ball system in the regiments. In most cases, placement was done more informally on an old-boy system. Conversations might be held between regimental officers and the boy's father about his interest in the regiment if the two adults knew each other. These often took place before the young man went to Sandhurst. In some cases, there were strong ties between a given public school and a regiment, such as the ties between Eton and the King's Royal Rifle Corps, which had a large number of Eton old boys in its officer corps.

The regiment's colonel would often meet the potential officer to determine his suitability, and, in addition, normally, the cadets would often visit the regiment or the officers' mess. If the colonel rejected the candidate, he had little hope of getting into the regiment. On the other hand, if he was won over, often nothing else was needed.[46]

43 Chalfont, *Montgomery*, p.52.
44 Chalfont, *Montgomery*, pp.53–54.
45 Chalfont, *Montgomery*, p.53.
46 French, *Military*, pp.53–57.

The path Winston Churchill took to become an officer in the 4th Hussars shows this British system of personal contacts in regimental placement. Winston's father wanted him to join the 60th Rifles (the King's Royal Rifle Corps), a very elite regiment. His father did not have a military background, but he moved in rarified political circles. He was able to obtain the blessings of the Duke of Cambridge, the commander-in-chief of the British army, for this placement.

As Churchill neared graduation from Sandhurst, the best-laid plans of his father ran afoul of the muddle-headedness of youth. Winston decided he wanted to go for the flash and join a cavalry regiment. He somehow set his heart on the 4th Hussars, a regiment much lower on the status pecking order than the King's Royal Rifle Corps that his father had gamed the system for him to join.[47] In addition, it would cost more to be in the 4th Hussars. While he was alive, his father would never agree to such a change in his plans, but his father was dying.[48]

After his father's death, Churchill moved to join the cavalry. He had his mother write letters to the Duke of Cambridge. She also wrote to Colonel Brabazon about Winston joining the 4th Hussars. The duke agreed, and the colonel found room for Winston in the regiment.[49]

When it came to getting into the 4th, Churchill may have had, unknown to him, an advantage. Randolph S. Churchill, a descendant of the Churchill family, wrote that Colonel Brabazon of the 4th had known Lord and Lady Randolph Churchill for many years.[50] However, Ralph G. Martin, who wrote an extensive biography of Sir Winston's mother, Jennie, blandly referred to a brief love affair between Jennie and Brabazon.[51] After the affair, there remained a solid friendship. It was Colonel Brabazon who told Jennie whom to write and what to say to get her son into the 4th Hussars at that late date.[52] By the time Sir Winston was trying to change to the 4th, it was February, and the regimental postings were mostly settled. But, by obtaining the acquiescence of both the regimental commander and the army's commander-in-chief, Winston's assignment to the 4th Hussars went through even at the late date without any problem.

Another example of contacts leading to officer placement is that of Julian Byng and how he came to join the 10th Hussars in the 1880s. He would rise to command an army in the First World War, become a field marshal, the governor general of Canada, and the 1st Viscount of Vimy, but his start in life was not auspicious. He was the youngest of 13 children of the Earl of Strafford. This entitled him to be called 'Honourable', and he attended Eton, where he did not do well. His father was short on money to pay for a place in the cavalry. Byng was the product of a military family. One ancestor, Admiral John Byng, had been shot for his failure to relieve Minorca during the Seven Years' War.[53] Others were generals under Wellington, and one was even a field marshal. His father's large family and high lifestyle had drained the family's wealth. His older brothers had enjoyed good starts in life. One had gone into Parliament and was an under-secretary for Foreign Affairs. One was in the 1st Life Guards, another was in the Blues, and a third was in the 7th Hussars. Yet another was in the Coldstream Guards, and his brother, Francis, was chaplain at Hampton Court.[54] When it came to Julian, the family was so short on

47 Churchill, *Churchill*, vol. 1, p.219.
48 Churchill, *Churchill*, vol. 1, pp.226–31.
49 Churchill, *Churchill*, vol. 1, p.234.
50 Churchill, *Churchill*, vol. 1, p.216.
51 Ralph G. Martin, *Jennie: The Life of Lady Randolph Churchill* (Naperville, IL: Sourcebooks, 2008).
52 Martin, *Jennie.*
53 Jeffery Williams, *Byng of Vimy: General and Governor General* (London: Leo Cooper, 1983), pp.1–2.
54 Williams, *Byng*, pp.4, 6.

money that they thought about sending him into business. But the earl, it would seem, could not bring himself to undergo that humiliation, so Julian's life just drifted.[55]

His life was changed by a chance meeting between his father and the Prince of Wales, who knew each other. In the course of small talk, the prince offered young Byng a place in the 10th Hussars. It was an offer that could not be refused, whether or not the family had the money to keep him up in what was probably the most expensive line regiment in the British army, where at least £600 a year was needed (current value of £61,120 or $71,940) and most officers had double that amount.[56]

What Byng did to earn the money he needed to take a full part in regimental life casts an interesting light on the Victorian and Edwardian mindset. If he undertook business transactions or trade, he would lose status, so that was out. Instead, he bought horses, trained them for polo, and resold them at a profit.[57] British officers often sold their trained horses to either make money or to carry them over when money was tight.[58] This was not considered business or a trade, and so it did not involve any loss of status. This enabled him to make up the monetary shortfall, and he was able to stay and thrive in the regiment. He became friends with both sons of the Prince of Wales. He went to Staff College in 1892 and made more contacts. From there, he had commands in both the Boer War and the First World War. Gaining them was doubtlessly helped by the contacts he had required in the 10th Hussars.

Not every cadet had the contacts to have his way smoothed into a regiment. Those who did not would be assigned a regiment by the military secretary. He tried to consider the cadet's desires, and the cadet's class standing also played a part in where the cadet was placed.[59]

## Militia Backdoor

Sandhurst was not the only way for a young gentleman to become an officer. There was the so-called 'backdoor' of the Militia, which over the period 1876–1914 provided much of the balance of the officer corps.[60] It has been estimated that, between 1885 and 1906, more than a third of incoming young officers came from the Militia. It has been said that they chose the Militia backdoor because they and their families could avoid the costs of hiring a crammer and the fees at Sandhurst, to say nothing of the risk of failing the Sandhurst entrance tests.[61]

The Cardwell–Childers Reforms had tried to link the regular regiments with local geographical areas. As part of this effort, local Militia units were tied to the regular regiments. To attract more men to take commissions in the Militia and to make a reality of the link between the Militia and the regulars, each Militia regiment was, from 1872 on, allowed to nominate one of its subalterns for a regular commission. Each nominee had to be between the ages of 19 and 22, have attended at least two annual training camps, and then pass an officer's examination.[62] The

55 Williams, *Byng*, p.6.
56 Williams, *Byng*, p.7.
57 Williams, *Byng*, p.9.
58 Denzil Holder, *Hindu Horseman* (Chippenham: Picton Publishing, 1986), pp.97, 109.
59 French, *Military*, p.55.
60 Keith Simpson, 'The Officer', in T. Bartlett and K. Jeffery (eds), *A Military History of Ireland* (Cambridge: Cambridge University Press, 1996), p.64.
61 French, *Military*, p.214.
62 French, *Military*, p.207.

men coming in via the Militia backdoor did not change the social composition of the regular army, as they (and the Yeomanry) came from the same social classes as the regular officers.[63]

As it turned out, when the Militia men went into the army, they often did not go into the regiment that the Militia regiment was linked to, so this part of the reform did not work. For example, the Militia Battalion of the Somerset Light Infantry sent 45 men to the regular army between 1874 and 1908 (the year the exchange system was terminated). Only 11 of them joined the linked regiment.[64]

Junior line officer in overseas dress.

The backdoor was closed in 1908 by the Haldane Reforms. But a side door was created in those reforms in the form of a revised Officers' Training Corps (OTC) for public schools and universities. A certificate from them would allow a man to join a regular army regiment after a reduced period of training.[65] In 1914, 15 percent of officers coming into the regular infantry and cavalry came directly from university OTC programmes. Another 15 percent came from a Special Reserve Territorial Unit where they had gone through OTC training.[66]

The cadet or Militia officer transferring in and their families, in thinking about what regiment the young man might try to join, had to consider the costs of life in the regiments. Different regiments required different levels of expenditure from their officers, and these could vary greatly.

## Cost

### *Cavalry*

It took a great deal of money to serve as a cavalry officer. The government's pay did not come close to covering an officer's expenses. A British hussar officer in a crack regiment needed a private income of between £600 and £700 per year, with £700 being better.[67] At current values, £600

63 French, *Military*, p.206.
64 French, *Military*, p.208.
65 Spiers, 'Regular Army', p.42.
66 Simpson, 'Officer', p.64.
67 Committee on Military Education [CME], *Minutes of Evidence Taken before the Committee Appointed to Consider the Education and Training of Officers of the Army* (London: HMSO, 1902), pp.67, 305–06.

is about £62,450 or $73,500, and £700 is about £72,860 or $85,750.[68] This amount was in the upper range of the annual income for a doctor, solicitor, or barrister.[69] Lancers were close behind, with Dragoon Guards and Dragoons falling off a bit in what the officer or his family needed to provide to be a cavalry officer. In some cavalry regiments, a man could live on an income of £350–£400 per year, current values being about £36,430–£41,630 or $42,870–$49,000.[70]

Some of this money went for elaborate uniforms. It cost one young officer's family £1,100 to set him up with his first set of uniforms and first two chargers. This is currently about £114,500 or $134,800.[71] But a more normal cost range was the £450 range, approximately £46,840 or $55,120 in current value.[72] Officers' horses normally cost around £100–£150 (£10,410–£15,610 or $12,250–$24,840 in current prices) or even £200 each (£20,280 or $24,840 in current prices).[73] Cavalry uniforms were a good bit more expensive than infantry uniforms.[74]

The need for a large amount of money meant that fewer men could become officers and even fewer could become cavalry officers. Basically, almost anyone who wanted to become a cavalry officer could if he or his family had the money. The supply was not equal to the demand.[75] The army commission that studied the education and costs required of cavalry officers noted the interplay between cavalry officers and money: 'We may require from the candidates either money or brains; the supply of men is most unlikely to meet the demand, if we endeavour to exact both.'[76] General Evelyn Wood said that a man needs test marks of 72–74 percent to get into the infantry, only 50 percent to get into the cavalry, and 25 percent to get into the Household Cavalry.[77]

The cavalry officers had to buy at least two horses. These cost, as noted above, between £100 and £200 each. Most of the cavalry officers played polo. Polo ponies were highly trained and, thus, very expensive. They cost about £150–£200 or more each.[78] In some cases, these could range as high as £400–£500 apiece (£41,630–£52,040 or $49,000–$61,250 in current values).[79] It took a minimum of four ponies to play in a match, and more was far better.

Having horses meant they also had to employ grooms to take care of the horses. A groom would earn between £15 and £30 a year.[80] This is about £1,560–£3,120 or $1,840–$3,670 at

68 Current values were computed using the Bank of England inflation calculator (<https://www.bankofengland.co.uk/monetary-policy/inflation/inflation-calculator>) and the United States Department of Labor's consumer price inflation calculator (<www.bls.gov.data.inflation_calculator.htm>) for November 2023. The year 1913 was used as the changeover point from pounds to dollars, as this was the first year for the American consumer price inflator. A pound was worth about $4.867 prior to the First World War.
69 Sally Mitchell, *Daily Life in Victorian England* (Westport, CT: Greenwood Press, 1996), p.34.
70 CME, *Minutes*, p.299.
71 CME, *Minutes*, p.318.
72 CME, *Minutes*, p.298.
73 CME, *Minutes*, pp.68, 298–99.
74 CME, *Minutes*, pp.61, 298; War Office [WO], *Report of the Committee Appointed by the Secretary of State for War to Enquire into the Nature of the Expenses Incurred by Officers of the Army* (London: HMSO, 1903), pp.7–8.
75 Committee on Military Education [CME], *Report of the Committee Appointed to Consider the Education and Training of Officers of the Army* (London: HMSO, 1902), p.35.
76 CME, *Report*, p.36.
77 CME, *Minutes*, p.1.
78 CME, *Minutes*, p.298.
79 CME, *Minutes*, p.319.
80 Mitchell, *Daily*, p.55.

current values.[81] This amount assumes room and board were provided. Much more would have to be paid if room and board were not provided to the groom. This is consistent with the £20 cost for servants given in a government study of army officers' expenses in 1902.[82]

Taking part in fox hunting was encouraged for cavalry officers. It was thought to develop horsemanship and quick thinking. But, of course, it added to a man's expenses. This extra cost was estimated to be at least £100 a year.[83]

### *Infantry*

Life in the infantry regiments was, on average, much cheaper. In 1903, a parliamentary committee stated that infantry subalterns who were paid just over £95 per year (£9,782 or $11,512 in current monies) would need a private income of between £60 and £150 per annum (£6,178–£15,445 or $7,271–$18,177 in current funds), and this could go as high as £200 (£20,594; $24,237), to meet their mess bills and other expenses.[84] But the committee seemed to always underestimate what it would take an officer to live.

In addition, just as in the cavalry, there were wide variations between the regiments in what level of private income was required. In 1882, an officer with a private income opted to serve in the East Yorkshire Regiment, as it was an inexpensive line regiment, and then, to make his money stretch further, he asked to be posted to India.[85] In the 1870s, a subaltern of the Gordon Highlanders, Ian Hamilton, in India, said he needed a private income of £200 per year (£19,543; $23,000) for that high-living regiment.[86]

At the turn of the twentieth century, an officer in the Royal Welch Fusiliers could not make ends meet because his family was only giving him £200 a year (£20,594 or $24,265 in current money). And this was in India, where the cost of living was lower.[87]

Montgomery joined the Royal Warwickshire Regiment, he said, because he liked its cap badge and it had a good reputation, but probably because the regiment did not require much in the way of private income. His family gave him £100 a year (£10,187 or $11,989 in current money), which was £8.33 a month (£849 or $998). His pay was £9 a month (£917; $1,079), and his mess bill was about £11 or £12 (£1,121 or £1,222; $1,318 or $1,439 in current monies). The regiment was in India, where living costs were lower, but Monty still did not have enough money to take a full part in regimental life.[88] He did buy a racehorse for £8 – it had once been a baggage horse – far less than what other officers paid for theirs, and, through constant training, it was able to win at least one race.[89]

81 Mitchell, *Daily*, gives wages for 1861; they would be slightly lower in 1900, as there was deflation during this period. A wage of £30 was equal to £29.05 in 1900.
82 WO, *Expenses*, p.10.
83 WO, *Expenses*, p.10.
84 French, *Military*, p.52; Farwell, *Mr. Kipling's Army*, p.58.
85 French, *Military*, p.52.
86 Farwell, *Mr. Kipling's Army*, p.59.
87 Frank Richards, *Old Soldier Sahib* (London: Faber and Faber, 1945), pp.274–75.
88 Chalfont, *Montgomery*, pp.55–57.
89 Chalfont, *Montgomery*, p.57.

## Officer's Background

The background of the officers who passed through Sandhurst and entered the army in the early 1890s is shown in Table 3. There is no reason to believe that the mix of social backgrounds in the officer corps would be different for any other time between 1880 and 1914, except that the number of private gentlemen may drop as one gets closer to 1914.

**Table 3 Social Background of Sandhurst Cadets Going to the British Army, 1890–1895[90]**

| | | Number | Percentage |
|---|---|---|---|
| *Military Officers* | British Army | 540 | 42.8% |
| | Indian Army | 37 | 2.9% |
| | Navy | 39 | 3.1% |
| | *Total in the Services* | *616** | *49.6%* |
| *India Services* | Indian Civil Services | 72 | 5.8% |
| | Others Employed in India | 4 | 0.32% |
| | *Total Connected to India* | *76* | *6.12%* |
| *Legal Professions* | Judges | 7 | 0.56% |
| | Barristers | 27 | 2.1% |
| | Solicitors | 29 | 2.3% |
| | Stipendiary Magistrates and Recorders | 6 | 0.48% |
| | *Total Legal Professions* | *69* | *5.5%* |
| *Private Gentlemen* | *Total Private Gentlemen* | *170* | *13.7%* |
| *Traditional Professions* | Clergymen | 86 | 6.9% |
| | Medical Profession | 23 | 1.8% |
| | Landowners | 6 | 0.45% |
| | Diplomats | 4 | 0.32% |
| | *Total Traditional Professions* | *119* | *9.47%* |
| *High-Status Employment* | Merchants | 36 | 2.9% |
| | Civil Servants | 19 | 1.5% |
| | Bankers | 10 | 0.81% |
| | Manufacturers | 8 | 0.64% |
| | *Total High-Status Employment* | *73* | *5.85%* |
| *Other Employment* | Engineers | 17 | 1.3% |
| | Brewers | 9 | 0.72% |
| | Stockbrokers | 8 | 0.64% |
| | Teachers | 5 | 0.41% |
| | Shipowners | 4 | 0.32% |
| | Farmers | 4 | 0.32% |
| | Tradesmen | 4 | 0.32% |
| | Other | 64 | 5.12% |
| | *Total Other Employment* | *115* | *9.15%* |
| | Grand Total | 1,238 | 99.39% |

* The fathers of these cadets tended to be very successful officers. Among them, there was one field marshal, 124 generals of various grades, and 223 lieutenant colonels or colonels. The 39 naval fathers included nine admirals.[91]

90 T. A. Heathcote, *The Indian Army: The Garrison of British Imperial India, 1822–1922* (London: David and Charles, 1974), p.142.

91 Heathcote, Indian, p.140.

As more and more middle-class officers came into the army, the aristocracy tended to retreat into a small number of regiments. As the number of nobles in these regiments increased, they became elite regiments. In the British army, the nobles became more and more concentrated in the Guards regiments as purchases were done away with and one moves closer to 1914. Table 4 shows the process over a 130-year time span.

**Table 4 Officers with Inherited Titles in Various Regiments and Branches of the Army**[92]

| | 1780 | 1810 | 1830 | 1852 | 1875 | 1912 |
|---|---|---|---|---|---|---|
| 1st Life Guards | 0% | 4% | 15% | 24% | 34% | 42% |
| 2nd Life Guards | 17% | 15% | 21% | 24% | 27% | 21% |
| Royal Horse Guards | 6% | 3% | 15% | 27% | 33% | 33% |
| Grenadier Guards | 15% | 17% | 13% | 20% | 23% | 23% |
| Coldstream Guards | 15% | 15% | 16% | 28% | 33% | 12% |
| Scots Fusilier Guards | 8% | 15% | 15% | 21% | 24% | 19% |
| Artillery | 0.5% | 0.5% | 2.5% | 1.5% | 1% | 0.5% |
| Engineers | 0% | 1.5% | 1% | 1% | 1% | 0% |
| Royal Marines | 1% | 0.5% | 1% | 0% | 0% | 0% |
| Total Army | 2.5% | 2% | 2.5% | 2% | 2.5% | 2% |

## Protestant Ascendancy

In considering the British officer corps, consideration needs to be given to the so-called 'Protestant Ascendancy' of southern Ireland. In 1911, there were 256,700 Protestants in a sea of 2,551,800 Catholics.[93] They, as a class, at one time owned most of the land in southern Ireland and held most of the political power. As time moved towards 1914, they lost political power, their income from land rents fell, and their land was taken in government purchase programmes.

The Ascendancy produced many officers for the army across the years. A line from a novel, *Diana of the Crossways*, is often quoted about the situation: '… 't is Ireland gives England her soldiers, her generals too'.[94]

They were often referred to as 'Britain's Junkers'. The men of the Ascendancy would refer to themselves this way until bad relations with Germany prior to the First World War made the German Junkers very unpopular.

The roster of well-known Ascendancy officers is long and includes, in no particular order, Napier, Nicholson, Lawrence, and Henry Wilson.[95] To this can be added the Duke of Wellington, Montgomery, Wolseley, Roberts, French, field marshal and first commander of

92 Razzell, 'Social Origins', p.255, Table 10.

93 Patrick Buckland, *The Anglo-Irish and the New Ireland, 1885–1922* (Dublin: Gill and Macmillan, 1972), p.xiv.

94 George Meredith, *Diana of the Crossways: A Novel* (Revised edition, New York: Charles Scribner's Sons, 1900), p.17.

95 R. T. Stearn, 'A Great Philanthropist: Sir James Gildea and the Soldiers' and Sailors' Families Association', *Soldiers of the Queen: Journal of the Victorian Military Society*, 142 (2010), p.3.

the British Expeditionary Force (BEF) in the First World War, and the Gough family, which includes a field marshal, three Victoria Cross (VC) recipients (two brothers earned VCs in the Indian Mutiny and one of their sons earned a VC in Somaliland in 1903), and the commander of the 5th Army in the First World War in their ranks.

It is estimated that Irish, which almost by definition means Ascendancy, officers were 17.5 percent of all British officers in 1878. It was further estimated that the percentages were similar for senior officers in 1854, 1868, and 1899.[96] These officers were not spread evenly throughout the army. In 1878, they were more concentrated in the line cavalry (20.2 percent) and infantry (20.1 percent), whereas the engineers had 10.4 percent, the Household Cavalry 11.6 percent, and the Guards 6.7 percent. In 1878, they were not a majority in any regiment, not even the Irish regiments.[97]

## Hazing and Initiations in the Regiment

Before a young man could settle down into regimental life, he had to be accepted by the officers of the regiments. When he first came in, he was a bit of an unknown commodity, and acceptance was not always automatic. The written memoirs of regimental life exhibit a survivors' bias. Only the officers that were accepted are the ones that write about regimental life.

However, we have the actions of Winston Churchill in the 4th Hussars to throw light on what might happen to an unacceptable young man. In 1895, a young man named Allan Bruce, who had been at Sandhurst with Churchill, was set to join the regiment. Churchill and several other subalterns had an unfavourable opinion of Bruce and tried to dissuade him from joining the 4th Hussars. Over a dinner, they told him the £500 a year (£55,674; $65,523) his father was giving him was not enough to maintain the lifestyle to which the 4th was accustomed. This was at a time when Churchill had an allowance of £300 a year.

Bruce went ahead and joined the regiment. It was soon rumoured that he was using abusive language towards the non-commissioned officers (NCOs). In addition, it was said that he forced his way into the sergeants' mess and stayed there drinking for an hour. Bruce was asked to resign from the army for not understanding 'what was the proper position of an officer toward non-commissioned officers'.

Bruce and his father strongly objected to these allegations and went to a newspaper that specialised in exposing minor service scandals. The paper wrote a sensational account of Bruce's problems. It was also reported that, in the year before, 1894, a young officer named Hodge had been so mistreated in the 4th that he resigned his commission. Among the rough handling he suffered was being dunked in a horse trough.

The actions of the subalterns became a *cause célèbre* and were debated in the House of Commons, and, after that, they were investigated by the Under-Secretary of State for War.[98] In the 18th Hussars, any young officer who failed to meet regimental standards found a wet bed every night. Everything he possessed was broken, and he sometimes found himself in a horse

96 Edward M. Spiers, 'Army Organisation and Society in the Nineteenth Century', in T. Bartlett and K. Jeffery (eds), *A Military History of Ireland* (Cambridge: Cambridge University Press, 1996), p.341.
97 Spiers, 'Army Organisation', p.341.
98 Churchill, *Churchill*, vol. 1, pp.238–42.

trough to cool his brain. He had his luggage packed and left at the station. One chap was shut up in a room full of hay, which was set on fire. At that, he left.[99]

Driving out a new officer was clearly the exception. Normally, the new subaltern was merely subject to some type of initiation ritual. The Royal Welch Fusiliers took no notice, outside of the interaction required by duty, of a newly joined officer for six months.[100] Other regiments had less drastic rituals, usually at the newcomer's first regimental Guest Night (Guest Night is a formal meal full of ceremonies with the regimental silver laid out). These allowed the regimental officers to get a feel for the newcomer, his table manners, ability to hold liquor, and conversational fluency, and, most importantly, how he reacted to friendly ragging. They usually tried to get the new officer drunk. The Dorsetshire Regiment had the newcomer crawl while the other subalterns spanked him with billiard cues. He then downed an alcoholic drink in the Dorsetshire colours, red, yellow, and green. In the 2nd Battalion of the Seaforth Highlanders, the newcomer downed a drink made up of all the different drinks in the mess in the regiment's liquor supply. In the King's Liverpool Regiment, the newcomer, after a good number of drinks on his first Guest Night, was induced to conduct the band.[101]

## Officer's Style of Command

The British officer's style of leadership and operation in the period between 1871 and 1914 was a distinctive mix of two elements: first, a cheerful, larky amateurishness, a survival of the cavalier strain with enough Cromwellians to prevent it from getting out of hand.[102] The second was benevolent paternalism.

The larky amateurishness of the officers was the despair of the sober-sided senior officers. Officers would tend to business in the mornings, but, in the afternoons, they spent their time playing polo or engaging in other sports. It was basically impossible to induce them to study the science and art of war, as keenness was somewhat looked down on.[103] It was fine to do well, but one should not be seen trying too hard to do well in either studies or sports.

The paternalism of the officers appeared in many ways. One of the more vivid images of the First World War was of officers inspecting the feet of their men. By the twentieth century, this ritual had been institutionalised by the army, and officers had to sign certificates that their men's feet had been rubbed with grease, their socks changed, and that they had eaten a hot meal.[104] Officers saw that their men had eaten before they ate. During the First World War, one colonel even went out into no man's land between battling forces, a dangerous place to be, to obtain dry socks for his men by looting the knapsacks of dead Germans. Robert Graves went out to collect German overcoats for his men to use as blankets.[105] The officers would go out of their way to obtain extra supplies, food, or tea for the men when otherwise they would

99 Farwell, *Mr. Kipling's Army*, p.71.
100 Lewis-Stempel, *Six Weeks*, p.82.
101 Richard J. Dickinson (ed.), *Officers' Mess: Being a History of Mess Origins and Customs: From a Wealth of Military Records* (London: Midas Books, 1973), pp.12–15.
102 John Connell, *Wavell, Scholar and Soldier* (San Diego: Harcourt, Brace and World, 1965), p.75.
103 Chalfont, *Montgomery*, p.56.
104 Lewis-Stempel, *Six Weeks*, p.151.
105 Lewis-Stempel, *Six Weeks*, pp.151–52.

have gone without.[106] Often, they would spend their own money to help their men or their families. In 1852, officers of the Foot Guards raised £9,000 (£1,064,000 or $1,252,200) to build housing for married privates so at least some of the wives would no longer have to live in the barracks.[107]

On marches, officers carried the same packs and equipment as their men and, in addition, had revolvers, field glasses, and other items carried only by officers. To help their men, officers would often carry two or even three of their rifles or an exhausted man's pack.[108] This seems strange to us today, as we assume a working-class man is tougher and stronger than a toff. However, before 1914, an upper class young man was normally larger than a youth brought up in the urban slums because he was fed better as a child. Fee-paying public-school boys in Edwardian Britain were on average 12.7cm (five inches) taller than their state-educated fellows and generally healthier.[109] The lower-class boys that became the army's other ranks would, in turn, be shorter than average. In the 1st Battalion of the Black Watch, which was 92 percent Scottish and had a small number from the slums, the average officer was a little more than 5.72cm (2.25in) taller than the average man of the rank and file in 1914.[110]

A prewar survey of Cambridge undergraduates (who were almost all from public schools) found that 70 percent were in Grade I physical fitness. But, in Britain as a whole, only about 34 percent of the male population was in that category. Again, the number would be smaller in the slums, which supplied the army's enlisted men. In Leeds in 1904, 50 percent of schoolchildren suffered from rickets because of their poor diet. Add the heavy physical conditioning that took place in public schools, which made the officers strong and gave them endurance, and one can see how officers could be in a position to help weaker enlisted men.

Officers learned the names of all the men under their command. In the 2nd Scottish Rifles, and probably in all the regiments, the officers took infinite pains to sort out every problem brought to them by the enlisted men.[111] They might also help with letters home or to girlfriends.[112] There were limits as to how far the officers were to go in caring for their men. The army's officer training manual informed platoon commanders that they were to stand as 'a father to their men, but not be a dry nurse'.[113]

A couple of examples of an officer's level of concern about his men can be seen in their actions during cholera outbreaks. In 1883, there was a severe outbreak of cholera in Egypt, affecting the civilian population and the British and Egyptian troops. The British Medical Service was fully occupied treating the British troops, and no civilian medical personnel could be spared from treating the civilian sick.

The Egyptian army medical service proved more interested in avoiding infection than treating and nursing the Egyptian army sick. One Egyptian doctor examined cholera victims

106 Lewis-Stempel, *Six Weeks*, p.152.
107 Farwell, *Mr. Kipling's Army*, p.233.
108 Lewis-Stempel, *Six Weeks*, p.81.
109 Lewis-Stempel, *Six Weeks*, p.14.
110 A. G. Wauchope (ed.), *A History of the Black Watch (Royal Highlanders) in the Great War, 1914–1918, Volume One: Regular Army* (East Sussex: Naval and Military Press, 2016), p.3.
111 John C. M. Baynes, *Morale: A Study of Men and Courage* (New York: Avery Publishing Group, 1988), p.120.
112 Lewis-Stempel, *Six Weeks*, p.152.
113 Lewis-Stempel, *Six Weeks*, p.151.

from a distance through binoculars. The Egyptian officers in the army disappeared. The British officers serving in the Egyptian army stepped into the breach and took care of the infected soldiers.[114]

In his 1888 book *Under the Deodars*, a book that was widely read by the youth of Britain, Kipling had a young subaltern, Bobby Wick, die while nursing one of his men in a cholera epidemic.[115]

British officers seem to have been unique, in that they often engaged in team sports, such as cricket, soccer, and rugby, with the enlisted men. Not all officers did this, and, most of the time, they were not good enough to make regimental teams. But there were inter-regimental matches they could take part in, and, most important of all, they were mixing with the men under their command on a somewhat equal basis while on the playing field.[116]

Middle-aged line officer in overseas dress.

This care and concern made for close officer–men relationships. There were many times in which officers and men risked and sometimes sacrificed their lives for each other in battle.[117] When their officers were killed, the men under him went to the trouble to write to his family to tell them what a good officer he was and how much he meant to the men.[118] Keown-Boyd, who studied and wrote extensively on British soldiers and campaigns, felt that a good part of the soldiers', most of whom had grown up in Dickensonian slums and lived harder lives before the army, attachment to their officers lay in this background. Some officers anonymously paid out of their own pockets the funds needed for extra comforts for soldiers' families left behind when their regiment went on campaign.[119] For most of the men, the officer's care was the only kindness and generosity they had ever known.[120]

But, for all their concern about their men, the officers could have blind spots when it came to their privileges. It did not occur to the officers that they should go without their luxuries when campaigning, even if this meant less room in the baggage train for necessities for the men.

114 Henry Keown-Boyd, *A Good Dusting: A Centenary Review of the Sudan Campaigns, 1883–1899* (London: Leo Cooper, 1986), p.101.
115 Lewis-Stempel, *Six Weeks*, p.20.
116 French, *Military*, pp.118–19.
117 Keown-Boyd, *Good Dusting*, p.36.
118 Lewis-Stempel, *Six Weeks*, p.154.
119 Lewis B. Oatts, *The Highland Light Infantry (the 71st H.L.I. and 74th Highlanders)* (London: Leo Cooper, 1969), p.47.
120 Keown-Boyd, *Good Dusting*, p.36.

In the summer of 1884, a force under two British officers was sent with 550 Bedouins as escorts on a reconnaissance march of 500 miles (804.67km) into the desert. On at least one occasion, the entire group nearly died of thirst. But the two officers never quite had to drink their last two dozen small bottles of champagne and kept their blue silk smoking jackets.[121]

Usually, the men just accepted their lot, but, occasionally, the unequal treatment was so bad they commented on it. A young trooper in the 20th Hussars wrote home during the 1885 Campaign, which largely took place in the deserts of the Sudan, about the disparity of treatment: 'It was alright for the officers with champagne, ice, soda-water, potted tomatoes and peaches and potted strewed steaks, Liebeg's extract and a thousand different other kinds of stuff… and yet they begrudge us a drink of water with salty corned beef.'[122]

This was the equivalent of the woman in the officer's family who would exhaust herself doing charity work but expected her own household help to arise at 5:00 or 6:00 a.m. and work until the family went to sleep, ideally seven days a week.[123]

## Speech

Cavalry officers, around the turn of the twentieth century, affected a speech pattern where they pronounced the letter 'r' as a 'w'. This made them sound like Elmer Fudd of cartoon fame.

## Bets

Officers prided themselves on being physically hard and tough. This often showed up in the bets they would make about physical feats of endurance to be accomplished. This custom is thought to go back to the Regency days. In 1809, Captain Barclay of the Royal Welch Fusiliers won a bet of 1,000 guineas (£71,820 or $84,526 in current money) by walking 1,000 miles (1,609.34km) in 1,000 successive hours.[124] Bets on an officer's ability to walk and run a long distance in a fairly short period of time often occurred: in 1880, Bagot of the Grenadier Guards, 54 miles (86.90km) in 12 hours; in 1905, Carton de Wiart of the 4th Dragoon Guards, 30 miles (48.28km) in 10 hours;[125] and in the 1820s, Booth of the 21st Infantry (later Royal Scots Fusiliers) in St Vincent, 50 miles (80.47km) in under 12 hours.[126]

Most of the time, the bets were between the officers. But, in 1877, Lieutenant Lord Grimston of the 1st Life Guards wagered £25 (£2,468 or $2,904 in current funds) that he could outwalk

121 Keown-Boyd, *Good Dusting*, p.106.
122 Keown-Boyd, *Good Dusting*, p.84.
123 Wendell Schollander and Wes Schollander, *Forgotten Elegance: The Art, Artifacts, and Peculiar History of Victorian and Edwardian Entertaining in America* (Westport, CT: Greenwood Press, 2002), p.218; Baynes, *Morale*, pp.166–67; Pamela Horn, *Life as a Victorian Lady* (Gloucestershire: The History Press, 2007), pp.59–72.
124 'Our Sporting Heroes', *Royal Welch Fusiliers Museum*, <https://www.rwfmuseum.org.uk/downloads/our-sporting-heroes.pdf>, accessed 1 Sept. 2023, p.21.
125 Farwell, *Mr. Kipling's Army*, pp.66–67.
126 John Buchan, *The History of the Royal Scots Fusiliers, 1678–1918* (East Sussex: Naval and Military Press, 2015), p.187.

any man in the regiment. This challenge was accepted by Corporal Maxwell, and the two men set out on a 22.5-mile (36.21km) course. The corporal won by 40 minutes.[127] In 1910, an officer of the 2nd Scottish Rifles bet he could ride a mile (1.61km), swim a mile, and row a mile within an hour. He won by seven minutes.

Sometimes, the officers made other types of bets, some very silly. In the 15th Foot (later West Yorkshire Regiment), officers bet on who could stand on one leg the longest. The winning time, by Lieutenant Wilkinson, was two hours.[128]

Veteran officer – Black Watch.

## Regimental Life

Once in the regiment, life settled down to a routine. For British officers of the period 1879–1914, this likely meant going on periodic campaigns against one foe or another. They saw far more fighting than the typical officer of any other power. In 1879, there was the Zulu War. The Second Afghan War lasted from 1878 to 1880. The First Boer War took place in 1880–1881. Egypt was invaded in 1882, and, from 1885 on, there was fighting in the Sudan, which went on past 1899. There were innumerable campaigns in Burma and on the Northwest and Northeast Frontiers of India during the entire period. A second Ashanti War on the west coast of Africa was fought in 1896, and a third in 1900. During the years 1899–1902, the Second Boer War ('Boer War') took place.

These campaigns offered the chance for medals, promotions, and other honours. If an officer's regiment was not assigned to the campaign, the individual officer did everything he could to obtain a place among the men taking part in the campaign. This included having men and women of influence write letters on their behalf.[129] Churchill was one of the worst at doing this.

This type of life and outlook is captured in an exchange that took place in 1900 during a local truce between the British and the Boers to recover the dead and wounded from a battlefield on the Tugela River. A Boer soldier talking with a British officer remarked that everyone had been having a rough time. The officer replied, 'Yes, I suppose so, but for us, of course it's nothing. This is what we're paid for. This is the life we always lead…' The flabbergasted Boer, who was probably a civilian in uniform, could only reply, 'Great God.'[130]

127 Farwell, *Mr. Kipling's Army*, p.67.
128 Farwell, *Mr. Kipling's Army*, p.67.
129 Farwell, *Mr. Kipling's Army*, pp.239–40.
130 Jan Morris, *Farewell the Trumpets: An Imperial Retreat* (London: Faber and Faber, 2010), p.72.

Promotion was calculated within the regiment, and the speed of promotion could vary greatly between the regiments. Generally, the Guards regiments and cavalry officers had fast promotion rates, as those regiments often had young nobles or sons of rich men who resigned their commissions when they inherited their father's property. Other regiments, mostly infantry, had sons of poorer men, and they had long waits for promotion.[131]

While they waited for their promotions, the officers led fairly pleasant lives. They worked with their men only in the mornings and had the afternoons free to pursue sports. Many of them played polo, especially in India. Other regiments developed specialties in other sports.

Leave was generous. In the 1880s, it was possible for cavalry officers to be absent on leave or hunting for 250 days of the year.[132] But that was hunting, which was considered good training for a cavalry officer. Leave for other officers and to do other things was limited to two to three months a year as one got closer to 1914.[133] The Guards had better arrangements, as they did for most things; subalterns could obtain four months of leave a year, and captains could earn six.[134]

## Field Marshals and Generals

The senior leaders of the army, the field marshals, generals, lieutenant generals, and major generals, were fixed in numbers between 1881 and 1914. They were as follows:

**Table 5 Number of Officers in Senior Leadership Ranks, 1881–1914, Drawn from the Cavalry and Infantry[135]**

| | |
|---|---|
| Field Marshals* | 6 |
| Generals | 7 |
| Lieutenant Generals | 22 |
| Major Generals | 65 |

* Field marshals could come from any branch.

**Table 6 Percentages from Different Regiment Branches in Army Senior Leadership[136]**

| | 1890 | 1910 |
|---|---|---|
| Household Brigade* /King's Royal Rifle Corps / Rifle Brigade | 21% | 17.8% |
| Line Cavalry (28 regiments)† | 8% | 10.8% |
| Line Infantry (70 regiments)‡ | 19% | 17.0% |
| Passed Staff College (PSC)§ | 7% | 39% |

* Guard cavalry and infantry regiments.
† Cavalry regiments had fewer officers than infantry regiments.
‡ Counting the West India Regiment.

131 French, *Military*, pp.149–50.
132 Farwell, *Mr. Kipling's Army*, p.206.
133 Farwell, *Mr. Kipling's Army*, p.68.
134 Farwell, *Mr. Kipling's Army*, p.68.
135 French, *Military*, p.168.
136 French, *Military*, pp.168–69.

§ Passed Staff College – one can be a PSC and in one of the other groups. This entry is to show the growth in the number of PSC officers.

## Staff Work

One way to avoid the trap of slow promotion was to go to the Staff College. The Staff College was first formed in 1799 and moved to Sandhurst in 1820. It made very little impression on the army. Napier, in 1817, thought the course was impractical and the instructors were incompetent.[137]

In 1858, the Staff College was revamped. Four years later, it moved to Camberley. With the establishment of the Staff College, in theory, no other channel of admission to the staff would be allowed, except for officers who have proven in the field their fitness for staff work.[138]

Attending the Staff College was not overly popular. The school took in 20 students a year. Normally, an average of over 40 a year applied, but 33 applied in 1878, and only 27 in 1879.[139] This drop in applications led to the formation of a study commission. They found some men only went to the college to escape their regiments or disagreeable foreign stations. The training was poor for its purpose and overly theoretical. In addition, passed Staff College (PSC) certificates were given out too freely. The accuracy of some of these points was shown by the fact that an officer with PSC by his name was assumed by other officers to not be practical unless he proved he was.[140]

There was another problem with the intake of officers. Most regimental officers were discouraged from leaving their regiments to go to a questionable venture such as the Staff College. An officer of the Suffolk Regiment, W. N. Nicholson, was told by his commander in 1910, 'Why do you want to leave the battalion? … The regiment should be good enough; only wasters go away'. Even in the 1930s, some infantry regiments were said to boast that none of their officers had even been encouraged to leave the regiment in order to attend the Staff College.[141] In addition, the officers themselves saw no reason to change their pleasant lifestyle. D. E. Hawes of the Royal Fusiliers wrote to a friend in 1901, 'I feel I never want to leave this jolly battalion, and the thought of one day perhaps doing so, to work for the Staff College and then afterwards living alone outside a mess fills me with horror.'[142] In the Gordon Highlanders, no one, as of 1875, had ever attended the Staff College. As of 1879, in the Coldstream Guards, only one officer had applied to go to the college. When Edmund Allenby of the 6th Dragoons went to the school in 1896, he was the first man in his regiment to do so.[143]

The regiments that produced students for the Staff College tended to be the infantry regiments. By the end of the nineteenth century, all of the Foot Guards and all but five regiments of the line infantry had sent at least one officer through the Staff College. On the other hand, none

137 Brian Bond, *The Victorian Army and the Staff College, 1854–1914* (Fakenham: Eyre Methuen, 1972), p.53.
138 Bond, *Victorian*, pp.73, 82.
139 Bond, *Victorian*, p.134.
140 Bond, *Victorian*, pp.134–35, 143.
141 French, *Military*, p.153.
142 Farwell, *Mr. Kipling's Army*, p.61.
143 Farwell, *Mr. Kipling's Army*, p.148.

of the household cavalry regiments and only 17 of the 28 line cavalry regiments had an officer who had passed through the college.[144]

As of 1905, there were 483 officers who could put PSC after their names.[145] There were also 57 officers with the rank of captain or above who were qualified for staff appointments in spite of not having PSC. They had served as staff in the field, and this made them eligible under Section V, Paragraph 74, of the regulations.[146]

Relatively few of these men served with the regiments. These numbers would have the benefit of additional output of PSC officers by Deolali and then by Quetta in India at 12 per year between 1905 and 1914.[147]

The reason for these high numbers is that, in the late 1870s and then in the 1880s, PSC men began to be used more on campaigns. Wolseley, who was to become a towering military figure in the late Victorian period, used a large number of Staff College-trained men in his Ashanti campaign of 1873. Four of the headquarters staff were Camberley men, as were six out of the other 22 of the officers specially employed.[148] A third of the men being PSCs is very high given the questionable status of the college during this period. However, one naysayer did say it was like 'cutting blocks with a razor to send highly instructed officers into the bush to fight savages'.[149]

Wolseley again made heavy use of Staff College men in his Egyptian campaign of 1882 and on the Gordon Relief Expedition. He also urged able young officers to compete for Camberley, as it was 'the surest avenue to professional advancement'.[150]

Candidates had to have five years of service and, after 1885, be under the age of 37.[151] But, in fact, many of the officers entered in their twenties.[152] Up to 1884, there were 20 students per class. In 1884, class sizes rose to 24 and in 1886 to 32, where it stayed until 1914. Admittance was partly by examination, but seven came in by nomination, and, every other year, an eighth man was added.[153] This opened the school up to political and social favouritism. Haig, after a 'near pass' in 1893, received a nomination in 1896.[154] Haig had ties with the court because his older sister, Henrietta, was married to the keeper of the Prince of Wales' racing yachts.[155] It also allowed the higher-ups to favour certain types of officers in their appointments. Neville Lyttleton, Chief of the General Staff (CGS) 1904–1908, is said to have favoured officers from the rifle regiments, and William Nicholson, CGS 1908–1909 and Chief of the newly formed Imperial General Staff (CIGS) 1909–1912, favoured men from the Indian army.[156]

144 Farwell, *Mr. Kipling's Army*, p.148.
145 H. G. Hart, *Hart's Annual Army List, Militia List, and Imperial Yeomanry List, for 1914* (London: John Murray, 1914), pp.127–28a.
146 Hart, *Annual*, p.129.
147 Bond, *Victorian*, p.204.
148 Bond, *Victorian*, pp.128–29.
149 Bond, *Victorian*, p.128.
150 Bond, *Victorian*, pp.129–31.
151 French, *Military*, p.160; Bond, *Victorian*, p.138.
152 Bond, *Victorian*, p138.
153 Bond, *Victorian*, p.138–39.
154 Tim Travers, 'The Hidden Army: Structural Problems in the British Officer Corps, 1900–1918', *Journal of Contemporary History*, 17:3 (1982), p.536, <http://www.jstor.org/stable/260559>.
155 Denis Winter, *Haig's Command: A Reassessment* (London: Penguin Books, 1992), p.29.
156 Travers, 'Hidden', p.536.

By the late 1880s and early 1890s, the Staff College was drawing more applications as it was losing its reputation as a dangerous experiment and instead was opening the doors to speedy advancement and coveted appointments.[157] In 1890, a captain in the 1st Suffolks thought it worthwhile to spend the whole of his life savings on studying for the entrance examination. It is not clear whether or not he was successful.[158]

By the early 1900s, the Staff College graduates had been able to move into positions of authority where they could log-roll for each other. John French, riding high after doing well in the Boer War in 1904 while in command at Aldershot and I Corps, came into conflict with them over one of his protégés. He wanted the man, Major Algernon Lawson, to be named brigade major for the 1st Cavalry Brigade. This was turned down by the Army Council. The PSC men would not allow a man who had not gone to Staff College to have such a staff job. French, who did not have a PSC after his name either, had to threaten to go to the king and resign to get his way. The same dispute took place in 1905 over an officer named Maurice Brett. That time, French took his case and resignation all the way to the king's private secretary for submission to the king before the PSC men gave way.[159]

It has been reported that, by 1904, there were four candidates for each Staff College vacancy.[160] But this is misleading because entries were divided into quotas by branch. Table 7 lists the annual breakdown.

**Table 7 Number of Students Allowed per Service Branch in 1884[161]**

| | |
|---|---|
| Cavalry and Infantry | 18 |
| Indian Army | 3* |
| Royal Marines | 1 |
| Nominated by the Commander-in-Chief (later by the CGS or CIGS) | 4 |
| **Total** | **32** |

* Every other year, a fourth Indian army student would be nominated by the commander-in-chief or his successors, the CGS or CIGS, and would attend.[162]

The quota system had a bad flaw. The Artillery and Engineers (A&E) applicants generally scored better on the entrance test than the other branches, and the Cavalry and Infantry (C&I) applicants generally scored worse. In 1886, the artillery officers had the top seven scores, and an engineer the eighth. On the other hand, only 13 C&I officers received a passing score. The school then admitted five C&I officers who had failed to make a qualifying grade. An artillery officer who placed seventh and was denied entrance was given a grace nomination and was thus allowed to attend.[163] But for the nomination, he would have been excluded with a test score of 2,407. On the other end, the infantry officer, a rifleman who had failed the exam, had a score of

157 Bond, *Victorian*, pp.142, 153.
158 French, *Military*, p.160.
159 Richard Holmes, *The Little Field-Marshal, Sir John French* (London: Jonathan Cape, 1981), pp.127–28.
160 French, *Military*, p.160.
161 Bond, *Victorian*, p.139.
162 Bond, *Victorian*, p.139.
163 Bond, *Victorian*, p.139.

1,585 but was the last man let in because of a lack of qualified C&I officers. In 1887, the same thing happened. The A&E officers occupied 10 of the first 12 places, and four of them were turned away.[164]

The PSCs were required to return to their regiments for only a year before becoming eligible for staff posts, and, by 1900, an officer's best career move was to obtain a staff appointment as soon as possible. This meant that many staff officers had little experience with regimental soldiering. This caused problems since staff officers were favoured in obtaining promotions. For example, in 1908, of the seven infantry generals at the War Office, only one had ever commanded a battalion.[165]

In 1914, there were 400 PSC men serving in staff positions around the world and 317 serving with the line regiments (38 with the cavalry and 279 with the infantry). Of the 400 serving in staff slots, 91 served as staff in the War Office, 172 in the British Isles, and 101 in India. In addition, the Mediterranean had 16 PSC men serving. Furthermore, the dominions, colonies, and protectorates contained another 20 PSCs. Table 8 gives a breakdown of the branch background of the PSC men serving in staff posts.

**Table 8 Background of PSC Men Serving in Staff Positions[166]**

| **Background** | **Number of PSCs** | | | | | | | | | | | | | |
|---|---|---|---|---|---|---|---|---|---|---|---|---|---|---|
| | **War Office[*]** | **UK** | **India[†]** | **Med.[‡]** | **Dominions, Colonies, and Protectorates[§]** | | | | | | | | **Egyptian Army[**]** | **Total** |
| | | | | | **Africa[††]** | **Bermuda** | **Canada** | **Ceylon** | **China[¶]** | **Jamaica** | **Mauritius** | **Straits** | | |
| General | 0 | 1 | 1 | 0 | 0 | 0 | 0 | 0 | 0 | 0 | 0 | 0 | 0 | 2 |
| Lieutenant General | 1 | 4 | 1 | 1 | 1 | 0 | 0 | 0 | 0 | 0 | 0 | 0 | 0 | 8 |
| Major General | 6 | 15 | 2 | 3 | 0 | 0 | 0 | 0 | 0 | 0 | 1 | 1 | 0 | 28 |
| Artillery | 16 | 19 | 3 | 2 | 1 | 1 | 0 | 0 | 2 | 0 | 1 | 0 | 0 | 45 |
| Engineer | 5 | 6 | 5 | 0 | 0 | 0 | 0 | 0 | 0 | 0 | 1 | 0 | 0 | 17 |
| British Cavalry | 4 | 9 | 2 | 0 | 0 | 0 | 0 | 0 | 0 | 0 | 0 | 0 | 0 | 15 |
| British Infantry | 33 | 67 | 13 | 6 | 1 | 1 | 1 | 1 | 2 | 1 | 0 | 1 | 0 | 127 |
| Royal Marines | 0 | 1 | 0 | 1 | 0 | 0 | 0 | 0 | 0 | 0 | 0 | 0 | 0 | 2 |
| Unknown | 18 | 48 | 11 | 3 | 2 | 0 | 0 | 0 | 0 | 0 | 0 | 1 | 0 | 83 |
| Indian Cavalry | 2 | 1 | 21 | 0 | 0 | 0 | 0 | 0 | 0 | 0 | 0 | 0 | 0 | 24 |

164 Bond, *Victorian*, p.139.
165 French, *Military*, p.162.
166 War Office [WO], *The Monthly Army List: August, 1914* (London: HMSO, 1914), pp.7–94, <https://digital.nls.uk/british-military-lists/archive/103627418>.

| Background | Number of PSCs | | | | | | | | | | | | | |
|---|---|---|---|---|---|---|---|---|---|---|---|---|---|---|
| | War Office* | UK | India† | Med.‡ | Dominions, Colonies, and Protectorates§ | | | | | | | | Egyptian Army** | Total |
| | | | | | Africa†† | Bermuda | Canada | Ceylon | China¶ | Jamaica | Mauritius | Straits | | |
| Indian Infantry | 1 | 1 | 23 | 0 | 0 | 0 | 0 | 0 | 0 | 0 | 0 | 0 | 0 | 25 |
| Corps of Guides†† | 0 | 0 | 2 | 0 | 0 | 0 | 0 | 0 | 0 | 0 | 0 | 0 | 0 | 2 |
| Gurkha | 2 | 0 | 10 | 0 | 0 | 0 | 0 | 0 | 0 | 0 | 0 | 0 | 0 | 12 |
| Indian Army (Unspecified) | 0 | 0 | 7 | 0 | 0 | 0 | 0 | 0 | 0 | 0 | 0 | 0 | 0 | 7 |
| Royal Canadians | 1 | 0 | 0 | 0 | 0 | 0 | 0 | 0 | 0 | 0 | 0 | 0 | 0 | 1 |
| New Zealand Staff Corps | 1 | 0 | 0 | 0 | 0 | 0 | 0 | 0 | 0 | 0 | 0 | 0 | 0 | 1 |
| Army Service Corps | 1 | 0 | 0 | 0 | 0 | 0 | 0 | 0 | 0 | 0 | 0 | 0 | 0 | 1 |
| Total | 91 | 172 | 101 | 16 | 5 | 2 | 1 | 1 | 4 | 1 | 3 | 3 | 0 | 400 |
| | | | | | 20 | | | | | | | | | |

* Includes the departments of Chief of the Imperial Staff, Adjutant General to the Forces, Quartermaster General to the Forces, Master General of the Ordnance, Civil Member of the Army Council, Finance Member of the Finance Council, and Secretary of the War Office, as well as the Inspector General of the Home Forces, Inspector General of the Overseas Forces, and the Military Attachés to Embassies and Legations at Foreign Counts. The departments of the Master General of the Ordnance, Finance Member of the Army Council, and Secretary of the War Office had no PSC officers on their staff.

† Includes India, the Burma Division, and the Aden Brigade.

‡ Includes Cyprus, Gibraltar, Malta and its dependencies, and the British army in Egypt. Cyprus had no PSC officers on its staff.

§ Dominions, colonies, and protectorates not listed include Australia, the Bahamas, Barbados, British Guiana, British Honduras, the Falkland Islands and their dependencies, the Fiji Islands, the Leeward Islands, Newfoundland, the Dominion of New Zealand, St Helena, the Seychelles, Trinidad and Tobago, and the Windward Islands. These locations had no PSC officers on their staff.

†† Includes South Africa and West Africa. East and Central Africa had no PSC officers on their staffs.

¶ Includes both North and South China.

** Officers seconded to the Egyptian army.

†† The Guides were a regiment that consisted of a cavalry regiment and an infantry battalion.

## General Staff

When the Duke of Cambridge left the office of commander-in-chief in 1895, there began to be talk of creating the office of Chief of the General Staff and a true General Staff under him. Politics and personal rivalries among the senior generals blocked this at that time.

Following the Second Boer War and its problems, a committee, the War Officer (Reconstitution) Committee, was formed under Viscount Esher to look into the training and performance of Britain's officers. One of the outcomes of the commission's work was the creation in 1904 of an embryonic General Staff. The General Staff was not to operate on the German model; the country's political systems, defence problems, and armies were too different. This opened the question of how the General Staff should function and what its duties would be. It took several years to work this out.

It was only when Richard Haldane took over as War Secretary in 1906 that the General Staff was transformed from a blueprint into a workable machine. This took most of the years 1906–1909.[167]

In 1905, at the urging of Kitchener, who was commander-in-chief in India, a Staff College was opened in India. In 1906, it moved to its permanent home at Quetta. It provided for 24 officers, approximately one-third belonging to the British army in India and two-thirds from the Indian army. After 1909, two Australians also attended.[168]

In 1909, the name of the General Staff was changed to the 'Imperial General Staff' to recognise Britain's far-flung empire. However, they did not make military plans for the entire empire. The Indian army staff, which included 101 PSC men, made the plans for campaigns east of Suez.[169] Table 9 gives a breakdown of these officers' branch backgrounds.

**Table 9 Background of PSC Men in Indian Staff Positions[170]**

| **Background** | **Number of PSCs** |
|---|---|
| General | 1 |
| Lieutenant General | 1 |
| Major General | 2 |
| Artillery | 3 |
| Engineer | 5 |
| Indian Cavalry | 21 |
| Indian Infantry | 23 |
| Corps of Guides | 2 |
| Gurkha | 10 |
| Indian Army* | 7 |
| British Cavalry | 2 |
| British Infantry | 13 |
| Unknown | 11 |
| **Total** | **101** |

* Infantry or cavalry was not specified.

167 Bond, *Victorian*, pp.212–35; Correlli Barnett, *Britain and Her Army, 1509–1970: A Military, Political and Social Survey* (London: Allen Lane, 1970), pp.362–63.
168 Bond, *Victorian*, pp.199–206.
169 WO, *August, 1914*, pp.65–77.
170 WO, *August, 1914*, pp.65–77.

## Promotion Tests

To be promoted within a regiment, officers had to pass promotion tests. The first test was for lieutenant to captain, and the second was for captain to major. If an officer should go far enough to be considered for the rank of lieutenant colonel, a third examination had to be taken.[171] In 1912, 38 percent of candidates who took promotion exams to command a unit (the lieutenant colonel test) failed.[172] The officers resented the pressure placed on them by these tests, and some made their feelings known by writing articles for professional journals, the popular press, and other means.[173]

## Souvenirs in the Mess

The officers, when it came to collecting souvenirs to take home to display in their regimental mess, acted like magpies. They would grab whatever they could find as a memento. A few examples will give an idea of the scope of the items. The Lancashire Fusiliers had a lock of Napoleon's hair, a piece of Napoleon's coffin (the old 20th, a predecessor regiment, guarded Napoleon on St Helena), and a silk sash worn by Wolfe when killed.[174] The Berkshire Regiment had a Russian drum captured in the Crimea (it also captured a German drum to go with it in the First World War).[175] The 1st Battalion of the King's Royal Rifle Corps kept a ship bell from the 1897 wreck of the troop ship *Warren Hastings*, and, even today, the battalion sound ship's time on it throughout the day. This is done in memory of the discipline shown by all ranks on that day, which saved the lives of over 1,000 people on the ship.[176] The 1st Battalion of the Black Watch had a 71.12cm (28in) brass gong captured from the mutineers of the Gwalior Contingent during the Indian Mutiny.[177] The Cornwall Light Infantry kept a musket ball that had lodged in a damaged regimental silver soup tureen. The packing crates holding the regiment's silver had been used as part of the defensive works by the old 32nd Infantry at the siege of the Lucknow Residency during the Indian Mutiny. Several other pieces of their regimental silver, also badly damaged by enemy fire, were also kept by the regiment.[178] The 3rd Guard Dragoons, the 1st Battalion, King's (Lancashire Regiment), and the 1st Battalion, Duke of Wellington's Regiment, all held in their mess part of a silver drum that belonged to Emperor Theodore III, captured when his Abyssinian (Ethiopian) stronghold was stormed in 1867. The Duke's Regiment also brought back to its mess Theodore's throne cloth and his shirt.[179] The final example is perhaps the best known: the silver chamber pot taken from the carriage of King

171 French, *Military*, p.155.
172 French, *Military*, p.158.
173 French, *Military*, p.157, footnote 70.
174 Benjamin Smyth, *A History of the Lancashire Fusiliers (Formerly XX Regiment)* (Sheridan, WY: Creative Media Partners, 2017), pp.283: note, 297: footnote 2.
175 Dickinson (ed.), *Officers' Mess*, p.20.
176 Thomas J. Edwards, *Military Customs* (4th edition, Aldershot: Gale and Polden, 1954), p.22.
177 Edwards, *Military*, p.22.
178 John Masters, *Bugles and a Tiger: My Life in the Gurkhas* (London: Cassell, 2002), p.19.
179 James D. Lunt, *The Duke of Wellington's Regiment (West Riding): The 33rd/76th Regiment of Foot* (London: Leo Cooper, 1971), p.55.

Joseph Bonaparte, King of Spain and Napoleon's brother, after the Battle of Vittoria in Spain.[180] This was held by the 14th Hussars, and several regimental ceremonies have developed using it.

## Marriage

The British army discouraged marriage among both enlisted men and officers. Both needed the permission of their regiment's commanding officer (CO) to marry. John Baynes' book *Morale* lends support for a low percent of other ranks being allowed to marry. It repeats the requirements as to length of service, good conduct badges, and money saved.[181]

### *Officers*

Before 1914, officers were strongly discouraged from marrying before they were age 30.[182] Normally, they could not afford to do so anyway before they reached the rank of captain. There was a saying in the army that lieutenants may not marry, captains might marry, majors should marry, and lieutenant colonels must marry.[183]

Sometimes, the field officers took steps to keep young officers away from temptation. Ian Hamilton recalled that he and the other subalterns of the Gordon Highlanders were told not to dance with unmarried girls at a ball.[184]

One officer in the 2nd Scottish Rifles remembered that, as a fresh subaltern, he was required, quite against regulations, to sign a document stating he would pay a fine of £50 (£4,886 or $5,750 in current funds) if he married before he was captain.[185] In fact, many of the officers never married while they were in the army. For example, in the 2nd Scottish Rifles in 1914, out of 28 officers, only two were married. The CO and his four company commanders were all bachelors. None were homosexuals.[186] This was an unusual ratio, but it does not show that many officers did not marry, and those that did marry often did so in their late thirties or forties. Prior to that, they concentrated on building their careers.[187]

### *Other Ranks*

There are conflicting accounts of whether or not men in the other ranks were allowed to marry during the period 1880–1914. One states that all staff were allowed to marry. In addition, 50 percent of other sergeants and 40 percent of the other ranks could marry. The other ranks that wished to marry had to have seven years of service, two good conduct badges, and £5 (current value of £536 or $619).[188] The number allowed to marry prior to the Crimean War was four, or, in some cases, six, per 100.[189]

180 Lewis B. Oatts, *Emperor's Chambermaids: The Story of the 14th/20th King's Hussars* (London: Ward Lock, 1973), pp.167–68.
181 Baynes, *Morale*, pp.149–50, 268.
182 French, *Military*, p.128.
183 Farwell, *Mr. Kipling's Army*, p.233.
184 Farwell, *Mr. Kipling's Army*, p.234.
185 Baynes, *Morale*, p.211.
186 Baynes, *Morale*, p.212.
187 Farwell, *Mr. Kipling's Army*, pp.235–36.
188 Veronica Bamfield, *On the Strength: The Story of the British Army Wife* (London: Charles Knight, 1974), p.25.
189 Bamfield, *Strength*, p.14.

Another source, published in 1901 and which purports to cover the British army from within, states that three percent of an infantry battalion and four percent of a cavalry regiment or a battery of artillery could marry. The book goes on to give the requirements of seven years of service, two good conduct badges, and £5 in savings. It also says the soldier must show his intended bride is a woman of reputable character.[190]

### *Wives*

Eventually, many officers did marry. The wives came into the regiments and were fitted into a regimental pecking order according to their husband's rank.[191] For example, the CO's wife, or, if he was unmarried, the wife of the next most senior officer, would be given the position of honour at teas, that of pouring tea, and the wife of the next senior officer would pour the coffee. The wives would also go into dinner by order of their husband's rank, except when sometimes the honour of going first would be given to a new bride at her first dinner after her honeymoon.[192] To a large extent, her husband's rank would also control whom she socialised with. A captain's wife would not socialise daily with the CO's wife.

After the Crimean War, the government began providing housing for married families of both enlisted men and officers. Being built by the government, they were mostly built to a standard pattern and had little architectural merit. But they got the job done. Government-issued housing also came with government-issued furniture. Often, this was put into storage. But it had to be accounted for when the officer moved to another station.[193] Many married officers preferred to collect a lodging allowance and find housing on their own.[194]

In Victorian times, the home of a genteel married family could not operate without servants. All officers were entitled to a personal servant, a batman, drawn from the soldiers of their regiment. The CO of the regiment was also entitled to a gardener and a groom. Other servants were paid for by him personally. This normally included a cook, a parlour maid, and, if there were children, a nanny.[195] The household of lower-ranking officers would require the same range of servants as his CO and would engage more if the officer had the money. He would also need to hire his own gardener and, if he kept a horse (most infantry officers did not), a groom.

All of this, of course, took extra money. This is why officers, unless they were one of the relatively few who had a good private income above what it took to pay his mess bills, buy his uniforms, and so on, looked carefully at a prospective wife's financial condition. Most simply avoided getting into a serious relationship with a young woman who could not bring money into the marriage.[196]

Often, the officer's wife became a semi-official part of the functions of the regiment. In many regiments, the wife of the company commander visited all of the company's families, both on and off the strength, about once a month.[197] This allowed them to inspect the living arrangements and keep up to date on the men and their families. When a major event happened in an

190 William E. Cairnes, *The Army from Within* (London: Sands and Co., 1901), p.116.
191 Richards, *Old Soldier*, p.159.
192 Schollander and Schollander, *Forgotten*, pp.143, 147, 250.
193 Bamfield, *Strength*, p.25.
194 Bamfield, *Strength*, pp.25–26.
195 Bamfield, *Strength*, pp.25–26.
196 Bamfield, *Strength*, p.26; Farwell, *Mr. Kipling's Army*, pp.233–35.
197 Bamfield, *Strength*; Richards, *Old Soldier*, p.159.

enlisted man's family, for example, a death or birth, his CO's wife was expected to be first on the scene with condolences or congratulations.[198]

The wives of senior officers in some regiments also ran a sort of unofficial marriage counselling service for the enlisted men under their husband's command.[199] Soldiers who were bad husbands were liable to be given a dressing-down by the CO or even posted to another unit. Wives who misbehaved were subject to the same type of treatment, with their husbands being transferred out as a last resort.[200]

Many wives also organised social events, such as Christmas parties for men's wives and children, taught classes on different subjects, and set up and ran charities that benefited the enlisted men of their regiments and their families.[201]

The wives were a distant second behind their husband's career and regimental duties. They were expected to wait and keep the household intact while the officer attended mess dinners, worked with the regiment, and went off to as many wars as he possibly could.[202] In one seven-year period, Evelyn Wood spent only 14.5 months at home, and much of that time was spent fox hunting.[203] Lady Wolseley once wrote her husband, 'You have no time for God or me. I don't say that unkindly, but it is a fact – is it not?'[204] Ian Hamilton praised his wife by saying that she had never tried to keep him from going off into the wars: 'She never said one word to hold me back – not one.'[205]

## Officers in the First World War

The army and the officers, even after the Second Boer War, still had a traditional outlook. One of the steps on the officer's checklist for preparing for war in France was to have his sword sharpened. Then, in the first fight, at least some of the officers carried their swords into battle. Montgomery, leading his platoon into battle, drew his sword, ran six paces, and tripped over his scabbard. This embarrassing accident likely saved his life. By the time he caught up with his men, he found most of them had been killed.[206]

In August 1914, a photograph of the officer of the 1st Battalion of the Black Watch just prior to its embarkation for France was taken. By December 1914, of the 25 men pictured, nine were dead, 12 wounded, two invalided home, and one captured. Only one remained unscathed.[207] The dead included CO Lieutenant Colonel Duff, a major, a captain, and five lieutenants. Two more lieutenants who were promoted sergeants were also killed in 1914. The six-week life span of subalterns was already starting to bite. Of the group of 29, only 11 were still serving in the 1930s.[208]

198 Bamfield, *Strength*, p.25.
199 Richards, *Old Soldier*, p.161; French, *Military*, pp.131–32.
200 French, *Military*, pp.131–32.
201 French, *Military*, p.131.
202 Bamfield, *Strength*, p.26.
203 Farwell, *Mr. Kipling's Army*, p.237.
204 Farwell, *Mr. Kipling's Army*, p.237.
205 Farwell, *Mr. Kipling's Army*, p.236.
206 Travers, 'Learning', p.21.
207 Ian F. W. Beckett and Keith Simpson (eds), *A Nation in Arms: A Social Study of the British Army in the First World War* (Barnsley: Pen and Sword Select, 2004), p.vi.
208 Personal correspondence from J. MacMillan, 17 January 1990, Black Watch Regimental Museum.

The 2nd Battalion of the Cameronians (2nd Scottish Rifles) had a group photo of its officers made in 1913. There were 27 officers in this regiment, and five were not shown.[209] The colonel retired shortly thereafter, but the balance of the officers stayed on to serve in the First World War. They were stationed in Malta when the war began and did not reach Britain until 22 September 1914 and then France on 5 November 1914 as part of the 8th Division.[210] During the war, they had 15 killed (two of whom died later of wounds in 1915 and 1918), four left the regiment for other commands, one was invalided home, two were wounded, and two retired (this includes the colonel mentioned above).[211] However, given the high casualty rate of the First World War, which greatly reduced the number of competitors, if an officer survived the war, he had a good chance of having a good career. Of the group in the photograph who survived the war, one became a brigadier general in the Second World War and two became lieutenant generals (one of the two retired as a general in 1947).[212]

## Jewish Officers

Many Jews in the army felt anti-Semitism could interfere with promotions and cause unpleasant personal encounters. One example of the casual anti-Semitism common in the army is a comment by an officer in the Gordon Highlanders in the late 1870s. His name was Billy Isaacs, and his nickname was 'Jew' because of his name and features. Despite this, he was a Christian. He would say that 'one of his female ancestors got mixed up in a money-lending affair with a Hebrew... and thus hampered a decent fellow with a hooked proboscis and an ikey name'.[213]

One author said such prejudices resulted in no British Jewish generals.[214] However, this is incorrect. Between 1880 and 1914, there were at least six Jewish generals in the British and Indian armies. The First and Second World Wars brought additional generals. There was another general in the Royal Marines. In addition, one Jewish family, the Schombergs, had five admirals in the late 1700s and the 1800s.[215]

There were, of course, officers who did not make the rank of general. The path of Jewish men becoming army officers was not hampered by prejudice so much as it was by finances. There were two classes in the Jewish community. The first group included the old, small core that had been in the country for generations and had almost as much chance as any other Britain to be able to afford the cost of becoming an officer. The other group were the immigrants, mostly from the Russian Empire, who were very poor. They had almost no hope of affording an officer's life. Thus, the pool of Jewish men who could become officers was much smaller than the total Jewish population would suggest.

It is claimed that the Duke of Wellington said there were at least 15 Jewish officers at the Battle of Waterloo.[216] One author, E. Rubin, reported that, in 1893, there were 61 Jewish officers in

209 Baynes, *Morale*, Photograph No. 2 after p.136.
210 E. A. James, *British Regiments, 1914–1918* (East Sussex: Naval and Military Press, 2001), p.70.
211 Baynes, *Morale*, pp.261–63, Appendix B.
212 Baynes, *Morale*, pp.261–63, Appendix B.
213 Farwell, *Mr. Kipling's Army*, p.110.
214 Farwell, *Mr. Kipling's Army*, p.110.
215 Eli Rubin, *140 Jewish Marshals, Generals & Admirals* (London: De Vero Books, 1952), pp.220–53.
216 Rubin, *140 Jewish*, p.223.

the regular army, the Militia, the Yeomanry, and the Volunteers. He also claimed that, by 1900, the number within these four groups had risen to 204, with 42 of them serving in the regular army.[217] This seems to be the type of overstatement made by many Jewish authors, writing before Israel's military triumphs, who seem to have felt they needed to counteract negative stereotypes about Jews and the military and to emphasise Jewish participation in their society.

*The Jewish Year Book* for 1900 lists 29 officers in the regular army and another 94 serving in the other three military groups. This number includes medical officers and men holding honorary rank.[218] Today, the Israeli soldier, after outstanding victories in mid-eastern wars, is often viewed as a type of super-warrior, and Jewish soldiers everywhere benefit from this new stereotype.[219] The author who stated 42 also said it probably should be higher, as being known to be Jewish could hurt promotion chances.[220] The author also made the claim that appears to have been made by about every Jewish community in every country during this period: the proportion of Jewish men serving in the army was higher than their proportion in the entire population. He went on to say that, in times of peace, only a few Jewish men take up the military profession.[221]

The 1900 *Jewish Year Book* attempts to list by name officers in the regular army, the Indian army, the Royal Navy, Militia, and Yeomanry, and Volunteers. The man who compiled the list remarked that it was difficult to make a reliable list for officers because official statistics were not kept on officers' religion, and he felt a considerable number of officers, in addition to those listed, had Jewish origins that had not been picked up in making the list.[222]

As noted above, the 1900 *Year Book* lists 29 Jewish officers in the regular army. It also shows four in the Indian army and a captain in the Royal Marine Light Infantry.[223] Of these men, the majority served in the technical and support arms. This was common in every army that accepted Jewish officers.[224] Aristocratic officers and men who tried to live their lifestyle generally did not want to serve in these branches. However, in 1914, this was no longer the case, as is shown by the table below.

**Table 10 Number of Jewish Officers in Different Branches**[225]

| Branch | 1900 | 1914 |
|---|---|---|
| British Cavalry | 2 | 9** |
| British Infantry | 8* | 11¶ |
| India Army | 3† | 10† |

217 Rubin, *140 Jewish*, p.224.
218 Isadore Harris (ed.), *The Jewish Year Book: An Annual Record of Matters Jewish, #5661, 24th September, 1900 – 13th September, 1901* (London: Greenberg and Company, 1901), pp.190–92.
219 A good balance to the new super-warrior view is *The 188th Crybaby Brigade* by Joel Chasoff, an American Jewish man who voluntarily joined the modern Israeli army.
220 Rubin, *140 Jewish*, p.224, opinion cited.
221 Rubin, *140 Jewish*, p.225.
222 Harris, *Jewish #5661*, p.189.
223 Harris, *Jewish #5661*, p.190.
224 See Derek J. Penslar, *Jews and the Military: A History* (Princeton: Princeton University Press, 2013), p.85, for an example.
225 Harris, *Jewish #5661*, p.190; Isadore Harris (ed.), *The Jewish Year Book: An Annual Record of Matters Jewish, #5674-75, 1st January – 31st December, 1914* (London: Greenberg and Company, 1914), vol. 18, pp.177–78.

| Branch | 1900 | 1914 |
|---|---|---|
| Artillery | 6‡ | 7‡ |
| Engineers | 8§ | 10 |
| Service Corps | 3 | 2 |
| Pay Department | 1 | – |
| Medical | – | 1 |
| Jewish Chaplain | 1 | – |
| Assistant Adjutant General | 1 | – |
| Marine Light Infantry | 1 | 3 |

* Includes an officer in West India Regiment.
† In all branches.
‡ Of all types. Includes one officer in the Malta artillery.
§ Includes a civil engineer.
** These men were in the 3rd and 5th Dragoon Guards, 6th Dragoons, 16th and 17th Lancers, and 13th, 14th, 18th, and 20th Hussars.

One man was in the King's Royal Rifle Corps and another in the Rifle Brigade, two very high-status regiments. The others were in the following regiments: Queen's (Royal West Surrey), Northumberland Fusiliers, Royal Fusiliers, Somerset Light Infantry, East Yorkshire, Yorkshire, Middlesex (2), and Royal Irish Fusiliers.

In 1900, the Jewish chaplain for Aldershot made an estimate of the number of Jewish enlisted men in the regular army. He said it was hard to produce reliable numbers because Jews, like many of the men who belong to the other smaller religious bodies, 'follow the big drum' and declare for the Church of England.[226] He then estimated that there were 450 Jewish enlisted men in the regular army, while only 82 were shown on the official records as of 1 January 1899.[227] By 1907, after the Boer War was well over, the numbers were estimated at 400, while official records had the number at 188 as of 1 January 1906.[228]

In addition to service in the regular army, large numbers of Jewish men served in the Militia, the Yeomanry, and the Volunteers. The British *Jewish Year Book*s attempt to list the names of all Jewish men so serving. For 1905, after the effects of the Boer War had passed, the *Year Book* lists 106 men serving in these branches. They were Reserve of Officers (6), Militia and Yeomanry (16), and Honourable Artillery Company and Volunteers (84).[229]

In 1908, Richard Haldane, Secretary of State for War (1905–1912), changed the organisation of the supplemental forces and created reserves, special reserves, and Territorials. Jewish men continued to serve in large numbers in the auxiliary forces. For 1914, the British *Jewish Year Book* states there were 118 Jewish officers in them. The breakdown was Reserve of Officers: 15; Special Reserve: 10; and Territorial Forces: 93.[230]

226 Harris, *Jewish #5661*, p.189.
227 Harris, *Jewish #5661*, p.189.
228 Isadore Harris (ed.), *The Jewish Year Book: An Annual Record of Matters Jewish, #5668-9, 9th September, 1907 – 31st December, 1908* (London: Greenberg and Company, 1907), p.271.
229 Isadore Harris (ed.). *The Jewish Year Book: An Annual Record of Matters Jewish, #5666, 30th September, 1905 – 19th September, 1906* (London: Greenberg and Company, 1905), pp.258–60.
230 Harris, *Jewish #5674-75*, vol. 18, pp.178–80.

Jewish men probably joined these supplemental units for the same reasons as the general population: patriotism, fellowship, recreation, or stepping up in status, either to respectability for the lower ranks or to a higher class for the officers.[231]

However, the status issue was very tricky. Infantry Volunteer officers normally suffered from low status. It was hard to induce noblemen, the gentry, and land proprietors to join these units. Although in large cities such as London, they might hold nominal command.[232] This meant the unit's officers were in the main professions: businessmen and employees.[233]

Things were different in the countryside. Leading squires and gentlemen normally did come forwards to provide officers for the mounted units,[234] the Yeomanry. In 1849, the Leicestershire Yeomanry had three members of Parliament (MPs) in its ranks. In the 1880s, the officer corps of the Queen's Own West Kent Regiment had six MPs and two peers.[235]

The Yeomanry, full of high-status officers, could provide an introduction to other high-status individuals and country society.[236] This would have been partially attractive to emerging Jewish families, who likely found so many other social organisations, such as clubs, closed to them.

## Jewish Legion

During the First World War, it was decided to form several all-Jewish fighting units. In the end, three combat battalions were raised. The three battalions were raised under the umbrella of the Royal Fusiliers Regiment to fight in Palestine. They were designated as the 38th through 40th Battalions. Another two battalions, the 41st and 42nd Battalions, were raised to provide replacements for the fighting battalions. The 38th was composed of men from the United Kingdom. Many of them were Russian Jews living in Britain who joined to avoid being drafted and sent to serve in the Russian army. (The draft had been introduced in Britain in 1916.) The 38th was known as the 'tailors', a common occupation among the immigrant Jewish community. When Russia withdrew from the war, most of the men soldiered on to gain British citizenship in exchange for their military service.[237] The 39th consisted of men from North America, mostly the United States, and the 40th consisted of volunteers from Palestine, Egypt,[238] and other areas in the Middle East.

The 38th was formed on 20 January 1918, shipped out on 5 February, and was in a combat division in Palestine on 1 June. The other two were slower to form and reach combat readiness in Egypt and Palestine. The 39th and 40th were formed in January 1918. The 39th did not reach a fighting division until September. The 40th was formed as a unit in Egypt in August but never joined in the fighting.[239] Some of them originally seemed to have been intended to be labour battalions.[240]

231 Hugh Cunningham, *The Volunteer Force: A Social and Political History 1859–1908* (Hamden, CT: Archon Books, 1975), pp.103–04, 109–10, 117–22.
232 Cunningham, *Volunteer*, p.55.
233 Cunningham, *Volunteer*, pp.56–59.
234 Cunningham, *Volunteer*, p.55.
235 Ian F. W. Beckett, *Discovering British Regimental Traditions* (New York: Bloomsbury USA, 2008), p.189.
236 Cunningham, *Volunteer*, p.55.
237 Penslar, *Jews*, p.197.
238 Penslar, *Jews*, pp.197–98.
239 James, *British*, p.50.
240 John B. M. Frederick, *Lineage Book of the British Army: Mounted Corps and Infantry, 1660–1968* (Kingston, NY: Hope Farm Press, 1969), p.253.

The reason the 38th was slow to go overseas was that recruiting was slow.[241] The explanation given by the Christian officer in charge of the 38th was that some factions of the British Jewish community were against the creation of the Jewish battalions and went to young civilian Jews and Jewish men already in the army, advising them not to join the Jewish battalions.[242] The established Jewish community did not trust Russian Jews and their descendants who had recently immigrated to Britain and feared they would bring discredit to Jewry.[243] Undoubtedly, less sympathetic people said the low enlistment rate merrily confirmed suspicions about Jewish reluctance to serve in the military, especially in the combat branches. On the other hand, they may not have wanted to sign up to be labourers. It was the hard, unglamorous end-of-the-war work.

The reluctance of the British Jewish community to volunteer was partially offset by Jews from other countries volunteering. For example, in December 1918, some 2,000 American Jews from the United States arrived at a base on the Egyptian–Palestine border.[244] They came from Britain and should have received some training. But Lieutenant Colonel Patterson, the commander of the 38th Battalion, which received 800 of them, considered them untrained.[245] However, they were thrown into front-line duty in their raw, untrained states with unfortunate results.[246] Efforts were also made to recruit Jews from other countries, such as Russia, Poland, other neutral countries, and, of course, those of the 40th Battalion who came from the Middle East. It must have worked, because Lieutenant Colonel Patterson mentioned in passing that some of his Jewish soldiers enlisted did not speak English.[247] At the end of the war, there were 5,000 Jewish men serving in the battalions in the Middle East.[248] A research paper by the Board of Deputies of British Jews lists 6,500.[249] This source goes on to say that 31 men of this number were killed.[250]

There was a joke about the 38th that reflected the general mild anti-Semitic tone of the time. It was said that their motto was 'No advance without security.'[251] It is claimed that some of the military terms of the Jewish legion have made their way into the modern Israeli army, probably by way of the men of the 40th Battalion.[252]

241 John H. Patterson, *With the Judeans in the Palestine Campaign* (London: Macmillan, 1922), p.25.
242 Patterson, *Judeans*, p.25.
243 Patterson, *Judeans*, p.26.
244 Vladimir Jabotinsky, *The Story of the Jewish Legion*, as translated by Shmuel Katz (New York: B. Ackerman, 1945), p.21.
245 Patterson, *Judeans*, p.175.
246 Patterson, *Judeans*, pp.220–22.
247 Patterson, *Judeans*, p.32.
248 Patterson, *Judeans*, p.27.
249 Barry A. Kosmin, Stanley Waterman, and Nigel Grizzard, 'The Jewish Dead in the Great War as an Indicator for the Location, Size and Social Structure of Anglo-Jewry in 1914', *Immigrants & Minorities: Historical Studies in Ethnicity, Migration and Diaspora*, 5:2 (1986), p.185, DOI 10.1080/02619288.1986.9974631.
250 Kosmin, Waterman, and Grizzard, 'Jewish', p.185.
251 Patterson, *Judeans*, p.96.
252 Penslar, *Jews*, p.199.

2

# British Men

If Britain held the world's largest empire in 1914, she did so because her other ranks – the men Wellington had called 'the scum of the earth' – had won and held it in many a bloody battle. Furthermore, the soldiers had done this against every type of foe in every type of terrain and climate while often desperately outnumbered.

Wellington notwithstanding, the British officers appreciated the worth of their other ranks. The official history wrote of the ordinary soldiers of the Old Contemptibles' staunchness, patience, indomitable cheerfulness under incessant hardship, and their calm, cool courage.[1]

This type of comment is repeated over and over. 'The British soldier took war and soldiering not seriously but with mock humour', and 'the British soldier would fight with unflinching doggedness while absolutely necessary and then break off for tea'.[2]

Writer after writer has written about the British soldiers not knowing when they were beaten, delivering devastating volley fire, and showing steadiness under fire. One French officer, Villars, gave this description in 1731 of the English soldiers: 'He is slow and heavy and must have his belly full but he fights like a bull dog, and never gives in. I saw the red coats to my cost at Malplaquet; they were the best of the enemy's troops in the field. I prefer 20,000 Englishmen to 30,000 Germans.'[3]

In 1846, during the Sikh Wars in India, a Sikh soldier likened the British infantry to demons bent on the Sikhs' destruction. To paraphrase what he said:

> ... the British came steadily as if on parade and in unnerving unnatural perfect silence. When the Sikhs at last fired their cannons, he expected the demons to be destroyed and indeed half were down. But, they still advanced in perfect order and silence. The guns fired again and again each time making large gaps in the British ranks, but they still came in that awful silence. They were ordered to stop a short distance from the cannons to catch their breath, and they did so under heavy fire. Then, with a shout such as only angry demons could give, they rushed the guns. In ten minutes, they had defeated our Sikh infantry

1 Michael Barthorp, *The Old Contemptibles* (New York: Bloomsbury USA, 1989), p.55.
2 Barnett, *Britain*, p.474.
3 Maurice N. Hennessy, *The Wild Geese: The Irish Soldier in Exile* (London: Sidgwick and Jackson, 1973), pp.78–79.

> and gunners who fought bravely. But, who could withstand such fierce demons, with those awful bayonets, which they preferred to their guns. They did not fire a shot the whole time.[4]

Lancer.

Another Indian soldier thought the answer to such courage in battle may lie in part in the grog ration given to the soldiers. The other part was that they did not worry about defeats:

> Four times I have seen a (British) regiment driven back with terrible slaughter, and yet their fifth attempt was as fierce as the first.
>
> I hardly know why the (British) soldiers love fighting as much as they do, unless it is for grog. They would fight ten battles in succession for one bowl of spirits. Their pay is negligible, so it cannot be for that. They also love looting, but I have seen them give a cap full of rupees for one bottle of brandy.
>
> I have been told that the English doctors have discovered some kind of essence which is mixed with the soldiers' grog. Great care has to be taken not to mix too much, since otherwise the men would all kill themselves in battle by their rashness… Whenever I have seen them discouraged, or fighting half-heartedly, it has always been on occasions when they were deprived of their usual ration (of) spirit.[5]

Brave as they were, little faith was placed in the ability of the other ranks to do things correctly. If two soldiers were needed to empty dustbins (garbage cans), a lance corporal accompanied them to supervise the work. When a soldier went on furlough, an NCO would take him to the station.[6]

The Boer War brought out several deficiencies in the British soldier. He was found to lack resourcefulness and the ability to look after himself in the field. In addition, he was usually

4 Richard Holmes, *Sahib: The British Soldier in India, 1750–1914* (Hammersmith: HarperCollins, 2005), pp.10–11.

5 James D. Lunt (ed.) and James T. Norgate (trans.), *From Sepoy to Subedar: Being the Life and Adventures of Subedar Sita Ram, a Native Officer of the Bengal Army Written and Related by Himself* (Hamden, CT: Archon Books, 1970), pp.37–38.

6 Farwell, *Mr. Kipling's Army*, pp.137–38.

Life Guards trooper.

too dependent on his officers and lacked individuality.[7] It was also felt that there was a shunning of responsibility from the corporals up the ranks.[8]

The army felt it needed to closely watch its men because it had found that many showed no sense of responsibility when left on their own. John Baynes, in his book *Morale*, examined the other ranks of the Cameronians (Scottish Rifles) in the pre-1914 period. But his findings are probably applicable to all regiments. The recruits came to regiments undernourished and having never had any mental stimulation. He estimated that the majority of recruits, those from the lower end of the lower class, came into the army with a mental age of about 10.[9] Training, instruction, and experience would raise this to around 12 or 13, but few of them ever developed a truly adult approach to life.[10] One of the results of this was irresponsibility. They might go a long time doing everything correctly, even earning promotions, then go off the tracks and have a major drinking session. This would cause a loss of trust, punishment, and the loss of any rank they had obtained.

Baynes estimated the background of the men who joined the Cameronians as follows:

7 Barnett, *Britain*, p.343.
8 Barnett, *Britain*, p.343.
9 Most witnesses to a parliamentary committee examining what went wrong in the Boer War thought the British rank and file was inferior in intelligence to the Boers and the British colonial soldiers. One witness also thought that the British soldiers' mental qualifications were not up to those of the average European soldier.
10 Baynes, *Morale*, p.157.

**Table 11 Backgrounds**[11]

| | |
|---|---|
| Lower Middle Class | 5% |
| Working Class | 25% |
| Lower Low Class | 70% |

He cited a study of the city of York by Seebohn Rowntree, a social investigator, who said that 90 percent of recruits in 1900 belonged to the working classes, seven percent were shopmen or clerks, three percent were boys under 17, and only one percent belonged to the servant-keeping class (gentlemen rankers). His working-class group would cover Baynes' working-class and lower-low-class groups, so there is a rough agreement between the two.[12]

Between 1874 and 1911, the number of recruits who described themselves as unskilled labourers ranged from 61 to 65 percent.[13] That left a large number who knew a skill or trade.

## Prior Occupations

In the mid-1800s, the British army still drew a fair number of its men from rural areas. Table 12 shows the background of British soldiers in 1860.

**Table 12 Previous Occupations of Soldiers in the British Army on 1 January 1860**[14]

| Occupation | Number | Percent |
|---|---|---|
| Rural Workers | 31,802 | 15.5% |
| Industrial Workers | 74,305 | 37.6% |
| Semi-Skilled Tradesmen | 30,894 | 14.8% |
| Artisans | 26,959 | 13.1% |
| Domestic Workers | 12,942 | 6.3% |
| Professional/Semi-Professional | 4,922 | 2.4% |
| Other | 20,684 | 10.1% |
| **Total** | **202,508** | **100.0%** |

As can be seen, just under a third – 30 percent – had learned some type of trade before enlistment (artisans, professionals, so on, and semi-skilled tradesmen). These categories, while not broken down into specific trades and skills, covered a wide range of backgrounds.

After 1862, the army continued to keep records of the previous occupations of volunteers accepted for military service. These records broke down the prior occupations into somewhat different categories and no longer differentiated between rural and factory workers. However, about a third had learned a trade or a profession before joining the army.

11 Baynes, *Morale*, p.134.
12 Baynes, *Morale*, p.134.
13 French, *Military*, p.33.
14 Alan R. Skelley, *The Victorian Army at Home: The Recruitment and Terms and Conditions of the British Regular, 1859–1899* (London: Croom Helm, 1977), p.296, Table 6–8.

**Table 13 Previous Occupations of Recruits, 1862–1898**[15]

| Year | Labourers* | Mechanics† | Artisans‡ | Shopmen/Clerks | Professionals | Boys§ |
|---|---|---|---|---|---|---|
| 1862 | 52.8% | 22.9% | 9.9% | 7.5% | 1.3% | 5.6% |
| 1871 | 63.9% | 18.2% | 8.0% | 7.7% | 0.8% | 1.4% |
| 1880 | 62.5% | 16.7% | 12.8% | 6.7% | 1.0% | 2.2% |
| 1892 | 65.9% | 11.2% | 13.1% | 5.3% | 1.1% | 3.4% |
| 1898 | 65.7% | 9.5% | 12.9% | 7.0% | 0.9% | 3.9% |

* Labourers include rural and urban workers. The urban factory worker would become larger as time passed. It also included day workers and the underclass.

† Mechanics were workmen who were at least semi-skilled, toolmakers, apprentices, tinsmiths, pipefitters, and so on.

‡ Artisans were non-industrial craftsmen, locksmiths, painters, and so on who had some skill and training.

§ The enlistment of boys was a traditional method to augment recruiting. They were enrolled at age 15 and served as musicians (drummer and buglers – 75 percent) or tailors and shoemakers (the others). On reaching the age of 18, they formally joined the regiment they had been serving with.[16]

## An Army of Veterans

When accounts are written about the soldiers of Queen Victoria and the Old Contemptibles of 1914, there is always a loose assumption that these regiments consisted of experienced veterans who had honed their skills through long years of military service. This led to the belief that, while the British army may have been small, the long experience of its soldiers made it an incomparable fighting instrument.

It may be well to examine just how many years the Queen's men served. The army did not give out long-service awards as such. Rather, it gave out badges for years of good conduct to privates only. They were not worn by corporals and above.[17] This can serve as a rough proxy for years of service. But it should be realised that there were men who had drinking problems and, because of that, would commit acts that would prevent them

Hussar – other rank.

15 Skelley, *Army at Home*, p.297, Table 6–9.
16 Skelley, *Army at Home*, p.262.
17 Brian L. Davis, *British Army Uniforms and Insignia of World War Two* (London: Arms and Armour Press, 1983), p.14.

from maintaining a record of good conduct. But they could still spend many long years in the army and gain steady experience in battle.

**Table 14 Percent of Privates in Possession of Long Service Badges (Stripes) for Select Years**[18]

| Year | Years | | | | | |
|---|---|---|---|---|---|---|
| | **2** | **5** | **12** | **18** | **23** | **28** |
| 1870 | 22.2% | 18.9% | 6.9% | 2.0% | 0.5% | 0.1% |
| 1874 | 25.7% | 14.0% | 10.6% | 4.0% | 0.1% | 0.004% |
| **Year** | **Years** | | | | | |
| | **2** | **6** | **12** | **16** | **18** | **21** |
| 1878 | 20.9% | 15.5% | 5.7% | 5.9% | 0.2% | 0.007% |
| 1882 | 27.6% | 11.4% | 4.9% | 2.2% | 0.4% | 0.02% |
| 1890 | 36.4% | 10.3% | 1.2% | 1.1% | 0.2% | 0.06% |
| 1898 | 38.1% | 12.6% | 1.5% | 0.6% | 0.8% | 0.06% |

In addition to long service stripes, from 1833 on, the army also gave a medal for long service and good conduct (the 'Rooti Gong'). In 1870, the time to earn the medal was reduced to 18 years.[19] This medal was often referred to as a medal for 18 years of undetected crime.

Another way to look at the experience of the men in the army is to look at their age. Table 15 shows the percentages of different age groups at different years. As can be seen, the percentage of men over 30 fell markedly during the period 1871–1898, while the percentage for those 20–25 grew. All in all, at the turn of the century, the British army was much younger than it had been 30 years earlier, making its age profile closer to that of the continental armies with their young draftees.

**Table 15 Ages of NCOs and Men in the Regular Army, 1866–1898**[20]

| Year | Ages | | | | | |
|---|---|---|---|---|---|---|
| | **Under 18** | **18–20** | **20–25** | **25–30** | **30–40** | **Over 40** |
| 1866* | 1.8% | 11.5% | 27.5% | 35.6% | 22.5% | 1.1% |
| 1871 | 2.9% | 16.1% | 27.3% | 21.7% | 30.0% | 2.0% |
| 1883 | 1.5% | 7.4% | 42.7% | 27.8% | 19.2% | 1.4% |
| 1891 | 1.7% | 14.1% | 49.3% | 25.5% | 8.4% | 1.0% |
| 1898 | 1.8% | 14.9% | 48.1% | 25.7% | 8.9% | 0.6% |

* Infantry of the line only.

18 Skelley, *Army at Home*, p.320, Table IVA–1.
19 R. M. Barnes, *Military Uniforms of Britain and the Empire* (London: Sphere Books, 1972), p.108; Guido Rosignoli, *Ribbons of Orders, Decorations and Medals* (New York: Arco Publishing Company, 1977), p.119, Plate 29. It had a ribbon the crimson colour that was later used for the VC. This led to white stripes being added to the ribbon during the First World War.
20 Skelley, *Army at Home*, p.284, Table 6–2.

## *Birkenhead* Drill

They could be self-sacrificing in a noble way. When the HMS *Birkenhead* was sinking off South Africa in 1852, the group of replacements from 10 different regiments being sent out to join their regiments was ordered to stand at attention in rows in order to allow the women and children on the ship to board the insufficient number of lifeboats. About 360 soldiers and officers (some nine army officers) stood and went down with the ship.[21] The incident deeply impressed everyone. Kipling popularised the phrase '*Birkenhead* Drill', courageous behaviour in the face of hopeless circumstances. King Frederick William IV of Prussia had an account of the soldiers' actions read to every regiment in the Prussian army.

## Flogging

To maintain order and discipline, the British army traditionally relied on flogging. This was done by a team of regimental drummers, each giving 25 strokes at a time with a cat-o'-nine-tails. The 'cat' consisted of six strips of leather, each two or three times the thickness of ordinary whip cord. Each line had several knots tied into it. The knotted lines bruised and lacerated the victim's naked flesh, often disabling him for days and sometimes for weeks. Many flogging victims, in fact, ended up in the hospital.[22] Army returns from foreign stations in 1818 show that about 12 percent of the men flogged were hospitalised.[23]

Flogging was meant to punish the erring soldier and set an example for other soldiers. For the latter reason, the punishment was carried out before the miscreant's entire regiment.[24]

Coldstream Guards – other rank.

21 Albert C. Addison and William H. Matthews, *A Deathless Story: Or, the 'Birkenhead' and Its Heroes: Being the Only Full and Authentic Account of the Famous Shipwreck Extant, Founded on Collected Official, Documentary, and Personal Evidence, and Containing Narratives and Lives of Actors in the Most Glorious Ocean Tragedy in History* (London: Hutchinson, 1906), pp.12–36. This has details on the regiments and the number of officers and men from each regiment involved.

22 Sylvia R. Frey, *The British Soldier in America: A Social History of Military Life in the Revolutionary Period* (Austin: University of Texas Press, 1981), p.90.

23 Edward M. Spiers, *The Army and Society, 1815–1914* (London: Longman, 1980), p.63.

24 Spiers, *Army Society*, p.63.

The number of strokes the erring soldier could be sentenced to was astounding. Over 50 sentences of 1,000 lashes were issued during the Peninsular War. As late as 1825, a soldier was sentenced to 1,900 lashes, of which he actually received 1,200.[25] In these jumbo sentences, the number of lashes was administered in a way that had the lashes applied at different times over several weeks under the supervision of a regimental surgeon who was held responsible for the death or permanent injury of the victim.[26]

Sentences in the 1,000-stroke range were rare. But those in the 25–100 range were fairly common.[27] Regardless of the size of the sentence and the presence of medical care, sometimes the man being flogged would die. A man in 1867 died after 50 lashes.[28]

Two old regiments of line foot, the 57th and the 58th, gained the nickname the 'Steelbacks' for the stoicism with which their men endured their frequent flogging. Upon the amalgamation of the regiments in 1881, the 57th brought this nickname to the Middlesex Regiment. The 58th in 1881 likewise carried its nickname to the Northamptonshire Regiment.[29]

An element of public opinion was firmly against flogging, both civilian and military. Under this pressure, the number of soldiers flogged and the number of lashes that could be awarded slowly fell during the nineteenth century. At the end of the 1820s, about two percent of army soldiers were being flogged each year. By 1833, the percent was less than one, and, by 1846, it was around one-half of one percent. Then, in 1859, the military command made what seemed to be a major concession. Troops would be divided into two categories. The 90 percent of the army who had good character would not be flogged in peacetime except for mutiny. They could be flogged during war service. The other 10 percent were always subject to flogging. This was changed to no flogging in peacetime in 1868 after a soldier died from flogging in 1867. These amorphous guidelines produced wildly varying flogging counts from year to year, depending on whether a military campaign was underway someplace around the world.[30] Finally, in the 1881 army reforms, flogging was abolished.[31]

**Table 16 Number of Corporal Punishments in the British Army in Various Years[32]**

| Year | Number of Corporal Punishments* |
|---|---|
| 1847 | 42 |
| 1858 | 218 |
| 1859 | Year new rule was adopted. |
| 1860 | 651 |

25 Spiers, *Army Society*, pp.62–63.
26 Frey, *British Soldier*, p.91.
27 Spiers, *Army Society*, p.63.
28 Spiers, *Army Society*, p.63.
29 Tim Carew, *How the Regiments Got Their Nicknames* (London: Leo Cooper, 1974), p.84; Anon., *Regimental Nicknames and Traditions of the British Army* (5th edition, London: Forgotten Books Publishing, 2018), pp.87, 91.
30 Skelley, *Army at Home*, pp.147–52; J. R. Dinwiddy, 'The Early Nineteenth-Century Campaign against Flogging in the Army', *English Historical Review*, XLVI:CLXXXIII (1931), p.331, note 1, DOI 10.1093/ehr/XLVI.CLXXXIII.308.
31 Frey, *British Soldier*, p.93.
32 Skelley, *Army at Home*, p.151, Table 3–8.

| Year | Number of Corporal Punishments* |
|---|---|
| 1865 | 233 |
| 1867 | 54 |
| 1869 | 1 |
| 1872 | – |
| 1876 | 2 |
| 1879 | 545† |
| 1880 | 25 |

* Up to 1871, this included branding.[33]
† As a result of the Anglo-Zulu War in 1879.

While the percentage of soldiers being flogged was falling, the army was also responding to outside pressure by reducing the number of lashes that could be awarded by different levels of court martial. The maximum punishment that general and district court martials could award was capped at 300 lashes in 1829. This was progressively reduced to 200 lashes in 1832 and 100 in 1837. Then, in 1846, it was reduced to 50 but was used with a decreasing frequency after a soldier died from being flogged. Then, in 1879, the maximum number of lashes that could be given in wartime was set at 25. As noted above, flogging ended in 1881.[34]

In considering flogging, it should be remembered that, in addition to being a method of controlling soldiers prior to military crimes, it was also a way to protect the fairly defenceless good soldiers in the ranks against the misbehaving men.[35] It should also be remembered that a soldier was flogged because of his own actions. One guard NCO noted he was never afraid of the lash: 'No man comes to that but through his own conduct.'[36]

## Drink

Drinking in the British army was an ongoing problem in the nineteenth century. The soldiers that fought in the Napoleonic Wars were said to consist of Irish peasants, who, while hardy and brave, were also mad for drink, violent, and without self-discipline. The jails of England supplied drunks, felons, debtors, and psychopaths. Added to this was a sprinkling of 'respectable' and intelligent men who had enlisted because of getting a girl pregnant, other legal peccadilloes, or because of visions of military glory.

These men, when the steel restraints of discipline were removed, could and did run wild. Witness the drunken rapes, looting, and general destruction that occurred in captured Spanish fortress towns during the Peninsular War or at Delhi in the Indian Mutiny. Appeals to their better nature often simply did not work. On the retreat to Corunna in 1808–1809, it was the floggers who best held their regiments together, while Moore's appeals to the other soldiers' better nature failed (except in the light infantry that Moore had trained).[37]

33 Skelley, *Army at Home*, p.147.
34 Spiers, *Army Society*, p.63; Dinwiddy, 'Campaign', p.331, note 1.
35 Barnett, *Britain*, p.243.
36 Barnett, *Britain*, p.242.
37 Barnett, *Britain*, pp.241–42; Spiers, *Army Society*, p.131.

During the Victorian period, which is more or less equal to the nineteenth century, the army relied with decreasing frequency on the Irish and increasingly on the English and Scottish urban poor. Drunkenness was a recurrent problem within the Victorian army because it was also a problem for civilian society, the Irish, and the urban poor, which supplied the bulk of its soldiers. John Baynes, writing on the Scots urban underclass, stated it was not unusual to find men who spent over half their tiny income on drink, leaving wives and children to go hungry.[38]

Drunkenness was not only in itself a military crime, but it was also a contributing factor to many other crimes, such as insubordination, desertion or absence without leave (AWOL), violence or disrespect towards superior officers, and venereal disease. Some claimed that drinking was responsible for 75 percent of the crimes in the army.[39] Soldiers were paid four times a month, and, inevitably, payday at least meant brawls in the taverns and rowdy behaviour in the barracks.[40]

But change was on the way. In 1861, social centres began opening in garrisons as an alternative to regimental canteens and taverns. The first centres were sponsored by evangelical Christians, and soon churches followed their example. The main goal of these homes was the saving of souls. As part of doing that, they prohibited the consumption of liquor within their premises. By the 1890s, the churches were actively trying to reduce drunkenness in the army. An Army Temperance Association was formed in 1893. By 1895, it had some 8,641 members, and the membership increased to a claimed 20,000 a few years later.[41]

Drunkenness, in fact all crimes, decreased in the late Victorian army. In 1872, some 51,500 fines for drunkenness were levied. This dropped to 9,230 in 1912–1913.[42] However, judging by the comments scattered through Frank Richards' autobiography on life in the regular army in India at the turn of the twentieth century, the temperance organisations were as subject to hypocrisy and backsliding by their leaders and members as any other human organisation.[43] Therefore, their numbers should be taken with a grain of salt. But the overall trend does show the programmes probably did work, as drinking was down.

## Ethnic Makeup of Army

The ethnic background of Britain was as complicated as any of the continental countries. A 10-year study between 1996 and 2006 of the DNA makeup of England, Scotland, and Wales conducted by researchers at Oxford University shows that the old wisdom gained from language studies and ancient accounts is largely wrong.[44] It is no longer proper to talk of an Anglo-Saxon core and a Celtic fringe.

38 Baynes, *Morale*, p.145.
39 Skelley, *Army at Home*, p.143.
40 Spiers, *Army Society*, pp.60–62.
41 Spiers, *Army Society*, pp.66–67.
42 Spiers, *Army Society*, p.67.
43 Richards, *Old Soldier*.
44 Bryan Sykes, *Saxons, Vikings, and Celts: The Genetic Roots of Britain and Ireland* (New York: W. W. Norton and Company, 2006), p.110. This book was somewhat groundbreaking and therefore was the subject of several published reviews in Britain (under its British title, *The Blood of the Isles*) and the United States. These reviews were almost uniformly favourable, and the science involved in the DNA testing was not questioned.

The studies of the DNA of both the maternal and paternal lines of ancestry tell slightly different stories, as normally invading war bands and armies have few, if any, women among them. On the maternal side, the maternal population base is Celtic everywhere. In Scotland, England, and Wales, Celts make up about 45 percent of the ancestry of the female population, which is quite high given that there are 13 groupings. In the Danelaw area, which was north of a line that ran from London to Chester, Norse maternal DNA is about 10 percent in the east and five percent in the north, which shows that the Vikings who were given this land brought their families with them to establish settlements.[45]

Finally, there are microscopic traces of maternal DNA from Sub-Saharan Africa and the Syria–Jordan area found in the south of England.[46] Could these be from women who came to England with the Roman legions?

On the paternal side, the DNA tells the same story. There is a solid Celtic base everywhere, even in England. Table 17 breaks down the percentages of the different DNA types.

Grenadier Guards – other rank.

**Table 17 Estimated Ethnic Groups by DNA among Men[47]**

| | Scotland | England | Wales |
|---|---|---|---|
| Celts | 72.9% | 64% | 83.2% |
| Germanic and Norse | 24.2% | 27% (Total of A, B, and C below) | 12.4% |
| (A) Saxons/Danes in South England | | 10% | |
| (B) In Danelaw | | 15%* | |
| (C) Norman | | 2% | |
| Other | 3.0% | 8.4% | 4.5% |
| Total | 100.1% | 99.4% | 99.7% |

* Goes up to 20 percent in East Anglia.

45 Sykes, *Saxons*, pp.282–83.
46 Sykes, *Saxons*, p.283.
47 Sykes, *Saxons*, pp.286, 290.

The very smallest of traces of a DNA line that goes back to southern Europe, including Italy, was found. It was found only in southern England.[48] Could this be a remainder from the Roman legions?

Ireland is the archetypal Celtic area. Ireland was not in the Oxford study, but studies were made in Ireland of their DNA. The following results were obtained:

**Table 18 Percent of Paternal Celtic DNA in Different Areas of Ireland[49]**

| Province | Percentage |
|---|---|
| Leinster* | 73% |
| Ulster*† | 81% |
| Munster | 95% |
| Connacht | 98% |

* These are the ancient provinces of Ireland.
† This Celtic percentage has a high number of Lowland Scots and maybe Viking DNA.

Tough-looking other ranks – Argil and Southerland Highlanders.

It should be remembered that Ireland was also subject to Viking raids and some settlements on her east coast. There was also an Anglo-Norman invasion and occupation in the twelfth century, which began in Leinster.

Considering the above, it is probably improper to speak of Anglo-Saxon phlegmatic steadiness and Celtic impetuousness when assigning fighting characteristics to the English, Scots, Welsh, and Irish. Differences between the groups are more likely to be cultural.

### *Irish*

Following the support that the Irish had given James II in his effort to win back his crown, a ban on Catholic Irish men serving in the English army was instituted by the Whigs. The ban was not formally lifted until 1799, when the danger from France seemed greater than what the Irish rank and file might do.[50]

Even prior to the lifting of the ban, some Catholic Irish recruits had found their way to British regiments. In 1771, the 15th Foot was said to be almost all Irish. It is said that as many as 50 percent of the East India Company's (EIC's) recruits in the 1770s and 1780s were of Irish

48 Sykes, *Saxons*, p.286.
49 The maternal DNA was about the same in all provinces. Sykes, *Saxons*, p.160.
50 Peter Karsten, 'Irish Soldiers in the British Army, 1792–1922: Suborned or Subordinate?', *Journal of Social History*, 17:1 (1983), p.52, <http://www.jstor.org/stable/3787238>.

extraction, and most of them were Catholics.[51] In addition, between 1825 and 1850, 48 percent of all recruits for the British Bengal regiments of the EIC were Irish.[52]

Another historian, Peter Stanley, put the Irish component drafts going out to serve in all of John Company's European regiments at between one-third and three-quarters and felt they were a majority in the late 1830s to late 1840s, the later years being the time of the potato famine.[53] With numbers such as these, it is easy to see how the following saying became common: 'The Empire was conquered by the Irish in the name of the English for the benefit of the Scots.'

Royal Horse Guards – other rank.

Following the lifting of the official ban on recruiting Catholic Irish, a large portion of the army was from that group. Table 19 shows the percentage of Irish soldiers in the army at different dates as compared to the percentage of Irish in the population.

51 Karsten, 'Irish Soldiers', pp.72–73, footnote 20.
52 Keith Jeffery, 'The Irish Military Tradition and the British Empire', in K. Jeffery (ed.), *'An Irish Empire'? Aspects of Ireland and the British Empire* (Manchester: Manchester University Press, 1996), p.94.
53 Holmes, *Sahib*, p.235.

**Table 19 Ireland's Share of the British Army by Year Compared against Emigration Numbers[54]**

| | Ireland's Percentage of UK Population | Ireland's Percentage of Army | Roman Catholic Percentage | Presbyterian Percentage | Irish Passengers to Extra-European Countries* | Decade | Irish Immigration Numbers to US‡ |
|---|---|---|---|---|---|---|---|
| 1795–1810 | | 42.0%† | | | | 1820–1830 | 54,338 |
| 1830 | 32.2% | 42.2% | | | 32,000 | | |
| 1831 | | | | | 56,000 | | |
| 1832 | | | | | 55,000 | | |
| 1833 | | | | | 28,000 | | |
| 1834 | | | | | 44,000 | | |
| 1835 | | | | | 23,000 | | |
| 1836 | | | | | 43,000 | 1831–1840 | 207,381 |
| 1837 | | | | | 46,000 | | |
| 1838 | | | | | 13,000 | | |
| 1839 | | | | | 33,000 | | |
| 1840 | 31.0% | 37.2% | | | 55,000 | | |
| 1841 | | | | | 32,000 | | |
| 1842 | | | | | 41,000 | | |
| 1843 | | | | | 38,000 | | |
| 1844 | | | | | 54,000 | | |
| 1845 | | | | | 75,000 | | |
| 1846 | | | | | 106,000 | 1841–1850 | 780,719 |
| 1847 | | | | | 220,000 | | |
| 1848 | | | | | 181,000 | | |
| 1849 | | | | | 219,000 | | |
| 1850 | | N.A. | | | 214,000 | | |
| 1851 | | | | | 255,000 | | |
| 1852 | | | | | 225,000 | | |
| 1853 | | | | | 193,000 | | |
| 1854 | | | | | 150,000 | | |
| 1855 | | | | | 79,000 | | |
| 1856 | | | | | 72,000 | 1851–1860 | 914,119 |
| 1857 | | | | | 86,000 | | |
| 1858 | | | | | 43,000 | | |
| 1859 | | | | | 53,000 | | |
| 1860 | | N.A. | | | 61,000 | | |
| 1861 | | | | | 36,000 | | |
| 1862 | | | 28.2% | 10.5% | 50,000 | | |
| 1863 | | | | | 116,000 | | |
| 1864 | | | | | 115,000 | | |
| 1865 | | | | | 101,000 | | |
| 1866 | | | | | 99,000 | 1861–1870 | 435,778 |
| 1867 | | | | | 89,000 | | |
| 1868 | | | 28.4% | 9.6% | 65,000 | | |
| 1869 | | | | | 73,000 | | |
| 1870 | 17.4% | 27.9% | | | 74,000 | | |

54 Except for the first line, Spiers, *Army Society*, pp.50–51.

| | Ireland's Percentage of UK Population | Ireland's Percentage of Army | Roman Catholic Percentage | Presbyterian Percentage | Irish Passengers to Extra-European Countries* | Decade | Irish Immigration Numbers to US‡ |
|---|---|---|---|---|---|---|---|
| 1871 | | | | | 71,000 | 1871–1880 | 436,871 |
| 1872 | | | | | 73,000 | | |
| 1873 | 16.6% | 23.6% | 22.8% | 8.8% | 84,000 | | |
| 1874 | | | | | 60,000 | | |
| 1875 | | | | | 41,000 | | |
| 1876 | 15.9% | 22.7% | | | 26,000 | | |
| 1877 | | | | | 23,000 | | |
| 1878 | | | 23.0% | 7.8% | 29,000 | | |
| 1879 | 15.4% | 20.3% | | | 41,000 | | |
| 1880 | | | | | 94,000 | | |
| 1881 | | | | | 76,000 | 1881–1890 | 655,482 |
| 1882 | 14.6% | 20.6% | | | 84,000 | | |
| 1883 | | | 22.9% | 7.6% | 106,000 | | |
| 1884 | | | | | 73,000 | | |
| 1885 | 13.8% | 17.4% | | | 60,000 | | |
| 1886 | | | | | 61,000 | | |
| 1887 | | | | | 79,000 | | |
| 1888 | 13.2% | 15.6% | 19.7% | 7.8% | 73,000 | | |
| 1889 | | | | | 65,000 | | |
| 1890 | | | | | 57,000 | | |
| 1891 | 12.6% | 13.9% | | | 58,000 | 1891–1900 | 390,179 |
| 1892 | | | | | 53,000 | | |
| 1893 | | | 17.9% | 7.3% | 52,000 | | |
| 1894 | 12.0% | 12.6% | | | 42,000 | | |
| 1895 | | | | | 54,000 | | |
| 1896 | | | | | 42,000 | | |
| 1897 | 11.5% | 12.4% | | | 36,000 | | |
| 1898 | | | 17.5% | 7.2% | 34,000 | | |
| 1899 | | | | | 43,000 | | |
| 1900 | 11.0% | N.A. | | | 46,000 | | |
| 1901 | | | | | 39,000 | 1901–1910 | 339,065 |
| 1902 | | | | | 42,000 | | |
| 1903 | 10.7% | 11.8% | 16.5% | 7.5% | 46,000 | | |
| 1904 | | | | | 58,000 | | |
| 1905 | | | | | 50,000 | | |
| 1906 | 10.4% | 10.3% | | | 52,000 | | |
| 1907 | | | | | 64,000 | | |
| 1908 | | | 14.7% | 7.4% | 38,000 | | |
| 1909 | 10.1% | 9.7% | | | 44,000 | | |
| 1910 | | | | | 51,000 | | |
| 1911 | | | | | 49,000 | | |
| 1912 | 9.9% | 9.1% | | | 43,000 | | |
| 1913 | | | 14.7% | 7.0% | 44,000 | | |

* Rounded to the thousands.[55]

55 B. R. Mitchell, British Historical Statistics (Cambridge: Cambridge University Press, 1988), p.85.

† Holmes, *Sahib*, p.233.
‡ These numbers include only those who embarked from ports in Ireland for the United States. Many people went first to Britain and then shipped out to the United States. Others went to Canada and then moved to the United States.[56]

**Table 20 England and Wales, Scotland, and Others' Share of the British Army[57]**

| | England and Wales | | Scotland | | Others and Those Not Reported* |
|---|---|---|---|---|---|
| | Percent of UK Population | Percent of Army | Percent of UK Population | Percent of Army | Percent of Army |
| 1795–1810 | | 37.0% | | 21.0%† | |
| 1830 | 58.2% | 43.7% | 9.5% | 13.6% | – |
| 1840 | 59.4% | 46.5% | 9.5% | 13.7% | 2.6% |
| 1870 | 72.1% | 60.3% | 10.5% | 9.6% | 2.2% |
| 1873 | 72.9% | 67.0% | 10.5% | 8.5% | 0.9% |
| 1876 | 73.5% | 68.3% | 10.6% | 7.9% | 1.1% |
| 1879 | 74.0% | 66.8% | 10.6% | 7.7% | 5.2% |
| 1882 | 74.8% | 69.3% | 10.6% | 7.6% | 2.5% |
| 1885 | 75.5% | 71.6% | 10.6% | 7.7% | 3.3% |
| 1888 | 76.2% | 74.3% | 10.6% | 8.5% | 1.6% |
| 1891 | 76.8% | 76.2% | 10.6% | 8.3% | 1.6% |
| 1894 | 77.3% | 77.5% | 10.7% | 8.1% | 1.8% |
| 1897 | 77.7% | 77.0% | 10.7% | 7.8% | 2.8% |
| 1900 | 78.1% | N.A. | 10.8% | N.A. | N.A. |
| 1903 | 78.6% | 75.8% | 10.8% | 8.4% | 4.0% |
| 1906 | 78.9% | 77.8% | 10.7% | 8.0% | 3.8% |
| 1909 | 79.2% | 78.8% | 10.6% | 7.8% | 3.7% |
| 1912 | 79.6% | 79.6% | 10.4% | 7.8% | 3.5% |

* The 'others' category includes British subjects who were born abroad, those born in the Empire, and foreigners.
† Holmes, *Sahib*, p.233.

The Irish were not spread evenly across all branches of the army. The Irish served in all branches but tended to congregate in the infantry and artillery. In 1874, the former was 28 percent Irish, and the latter 18.5 percent Irish. These percentages fell to 14.2 and 14.7 percent, respectively, by 1899. Few served in the Foot Guards or Household Cavalry.[58]

56 Marjorie R. Fallows, Irish Americans: Identity and Assimilation (Hoboken, NJ: Prentice Hall, 1979), p.48.
57 Spiers, *Army Society*, p.50.
58 Spiers, 'Army Organisation', p.336.

The cavalry regiments held few Irish, even the so-called 'Irish' cavalry regiments. In 1872, the 5th Irish Lancers, with its 42 percent Irish, was the only cavalry regiment whose Irish component was over 30 percent. The 6th Inniskilling Dragoons had only 17 percent Irish in its ranks. Then, by 1878, the percentages fell in the 5th Lancers, and no cavalry regiment had more than 30 percent Irish in its ranks.[59]

The proportion of men who could neither read nor write fell from about 19 percent in 1861 to under two percent in 1889. Plus, the proportion of those who could read but not write dropped from 20 percent to a little over two percent.[60]

Line infantry – other rank.

The Scottish Highland Regiments, by the last half of the nineteenth century, were considered completely loyal and no longer the wild clansmen that had erupted out of the mists in the '45. As such, they were allowed to wear their special dress. They were even allowed to play 'Johnnie Cope' as part of 'Reveille', a satirical little tune. Its chorus begins, 'Hey, Johnnie Cope, are ye wauken yet?' It celebrates the Battle of Prestonpans in 1745, where a dawn attack by a Jacobite army under Prince Charles Stuart surprised and routed a government army under General Sir John Cope (this is the uprising that is known as the '45). This tune was played by most of the Highland regiments.

The Irish regiments, on the other hand, had nothing besides their badges to indicate they were Irish for most of their existence. This is likely because of the long history of simmering rebellion in Ireland. Why do anything to build up a sense of separate nationalism among the troops?

Between 1845 and 1881, Ireland's population, rather than growing, fell from 9,000,000 to 5,000,000.[61] The Irish population fell by about 32 percent between 1851 and 1901.[62] When the

59 Spiers, 'Army Organisation', p.337.

60 H. J. Hanham, 'Religion and Nationality in the Mid-Victorian Army', in J. R. Weston and M. R. D. Foot (eds), *War and Society: Historical Essays in Honour and Memory of J. R. Western 1928-1971* (London: Elek, 1973), p.170.

61 Julius N. Hook, *Family Names: The Origins, Meanings, Mutations, and History of More Than 2,800 American Names* (London: Collier Books, 1983), p.106.

62 Jeffery, 'Irish Military', p.103.

potato blight hit Ireland in 1845–1852, it was especially devastating, as, by the end of the eighteenth century, nearly 50 percent of the Irish ate no solid food other than potatoes.[63]

The Irish regiments in the early dismal months of the Boer War stood out as loyal and brave fighters. This level of performance continued throughout the war. Rewards followed. The Dublin Fusiliers was allowed to lead the relief column into Ladysmith as a special recognition of its devoted valour.[64] The Irish Guards regiment was also formed, and Irish soldiers were allowed to wear shamrocks on St Patrick's Day. This was a personal grant to them by the Queen, according to General Wolseley.[65]

While they were fusilier regiments that were not Irish based, a good many of them were. It is thought that granting plumes to be worn on the fusiliers' headdress was another way to reward the Irish regiments.

One of the abiding mysteries is why so many Irish men joined the army and served loyally while, at the same time, there was a constant low level of rebellion in Ireland. The troops stationed in Ireland were in part stationed 'at home' and in part an occupying force charged with putting down rebellious activities. The answer lies in the different socioeconomic backgrounds of the two groups.

The men who joined early on were the very poor, peasantry, and agricultural labourers. Later, the agricultural labourers were replaced by urban labourers or those with uncertain job prospects. In 1851, some 75 percent of Irishmen serving in regiments stationed in Scotland had been born in rural areas, compared to 35 percent of English troops and 26 percent of Scottish troops. These types of numbers generally held true in 1890.[66] The men in the Irish Guards, formed in 1900, were of the same class: farm labourers, navvies, and unskilled workers from towns, some of them illiterate, most of them semi-illiterate.[67]

On the other hand, the people doing the rebelling (called 'patriots' or 'nationalists' since their side eventually formed a country) were more middle class or lower middle class, such as farmer's sons, commercial assistants, and teachers.[68] There is also a smattering of what we would call 'intellectuals' today.

The main motivation for joining the army was economic hardship, as it was for the other volunteers of the British army. There is a rough relationship between recruitment in Ireland and emigration from Ireland. As emigration went up, the percentage of Irish in the army went down. What is not shown in the numbers giving emigration figures by decades is the relation between economic depressions and the number of Irish men volunteering. Many of the men who enlisted could not afford to emigrate, but many could. If times were hard in Ireland, they would look to England, America, Australia, Canada, and, later, South Africa. If the economies were depressed in all those countries, he might have no place to go and volunteer. On the other hand, if times were booming in one or more of those countries, he may elect to emigrate there in lieu of joining the army.[69]

63 Joel Mokyr, 'Great Famine', *Encyclopaedia Britannica* (2024), <https://www.britannica.com/event/Great-Famine-Irish-history>, accessed 26 Oct. 2023.
64 Terence Denman, '"Ethnic Soldiers Pure and Simple"? The Irish in the Late Victorian British Army', *War in History*, 3:3 (1996), p.267, DOI 10.1177/096834459600300301.
65 Denman, 'Ethnic Soldiers', pp.268, 271.
66 Karsten, 'Irish Soldiers', p.53.
67 Karsten, 'Irish Soldiers', p.53.
68 Karsten, 'Irish Soldiers', p.53.
69 Karsten, 'Irish Soldiers', p.55.

Line infantry – other rank.

The British authorities felt that there was no doubt about the loyalty of Irish soldiers serving outside Ireland but that it was not wise to station them in Ireland, where they would be subject to nationalist influences.[70]

The men who joined the army were, like many of the poor, uninterested in politics or social or literary matters, the things that were like breath itself to many of the nationalists.[71] Therefore, in spite of the authorities' fears, they were less likely to be talked out of joining or to be talked into rebelling or deserting once in their regiment than the authorities feared. Proof of this can be seen in the recruiting numbers during the Time of Troubles in Ireland, 1919–1921. With an active rebellion taking place in Ireland and the British army and the Black and Tans fighting, one would have expected this to have affected recruiting. However, the period, as far as recruiting went, was business as usual for both northern and southern Ireland.[72] There was a post-war economic slump, and army pay looked good to apolitical men.

Besides economic factors, there seem to have been other common causes that led men to join. A family history of military service, a wish to see the world, a spirit of adventure, the glamour of the military, and so on. But, for the Irish, there was another factor in play: the call of their fighting history, the past valour of its soldiers,[73] and a pugnacious temperament. One soldier described the mission of the Irish as 'to win their way through the world, like true Irishmen by fighting those whom they never saw before'.[74]

A good description of the Irish soldier is given by a John Company soldier who served with them:

> The Irish! who shall describe their protean nature of their phases of character… They were 'everything by turns and nothing long.' The first in mischief, merriment, and devilment of all descriptions; brave to temerity, never at a loss for an answer or an excuse, no matter how difficult the question, or how grave the subject to be discussed. With a 'half-laugh, whole earnest' expression of countenance, backed by speech of a similar description; invariably respectful, and perpetually 'jolly.'[75]

70 Denman, 'Ethnic Soldiers', p.260.
71 Karsten, 'Irish Soldiers', p.57.
72 Jeffery, 'Irish Military', p.101.
73 Karsten, 'Irish Soldiers', pp.55–56.
74 Karsten, 'Irish Soldiers', p.56.
75 N. W. Bancroft, *From Recruit to Staff Sergeant* (Essex: Ian Henry Publications, 1979), p.29.

What the description leaves out is the Irish well-known affinity for drink. Kipling wrote about this often, and his character Mulvaney was what many believed to be the archetypal Irish soldier: resourceful humour, courage at its highest, and an unconquerable lure for drink. The best soldier in the regiment – when sober – and when drunk – should be passed over at parade if it is humanly possible to do so.[76]

Line infantry – other rank.

Kipling felt that there was no better way of getting an Irish regiment in a fighting mood than by making sure they got no drink until they had successfully completed their fighting mission.[77]

On a more modern note, I was told a story about a man's father, who, in the late 1920s, was posted to the 8th Irish Hussars. It had a heavy Irish component. He would volunteer for stable duty at night on each St Patrick's Day to get himself out of the barracks. Otherwise, when the Irish troops came back drunk, they would beat him up on general principles. The next morning, when sober, they reverted to being their normal pleasant messmates.[78]

There was some disagreement about the nature of the Irish. Kipling said an Irish regiment was 'the choicest collection of unmitigated blackguards, dog stealers, robbers of hen-roosts, assaulters of innocent citizens, and recklessly daring heroes in the army list'.[79]

Others held the view that 'there is no better fighting material in the world than an Irish regiment well led and in a high state of discipline'.[80] The Irish were the perfect fighting material: brave but childlike.[81]

### *Lowland Scots*

These are the men from the traditional Kingdom of Scotland. They have a fighting history against the English and as mercenaries on the continent. Gustavus Adolphus is believed to

76 Denman, 'Ethnic Soldiers', p.265.
77 Denman, 'Ethnic Soldiers', p.264.
78 Robert Marrion, personal interview.
79 Denman, 'Ethnic Soldiers', p.264.
80 Denman, 'Ethnic Soldiers', p.257.
81 Denman, 'Ethnic Soldiers', p.257.

have had 20,000 Scots in his army, while France at one point had 10,000.[82] The First Royal Scots traces its origins back to a regiment that served under Gustavus Adolphus in the Thirty Years' War and then for the kings of France. They obtained their nickname 'Pontius Pilates Bodyguard' while in French service.[83] The kings of France had a Scots bodyguard from 1421 on (others say from 1440 on).[84] They were formed when a large Scottish army came to the aid of France. The Scottish Archers (later Scottish Company) were the senior company of the French *Garde du Corps*. The military history of the Scottish Kingdom is one of victories and disasters against the English. But they always managed to keep the English at bay. This led to the saying 'Scotland was born fighting.'

Scotland kept her independence until Joshua swallowed the whale when James I took the English crown in 1603 and the two kingdoms were joined. In 1608, James offered land confiscated from the Irish in Ulster to Lowland Scots and Englishmen. The bulk of the new settlers were Scots. Their descendants, in turn, migrated to America, where they have historically been one of the best ethnic fighting groups in the country.

The Lowland regiments were treated as just another British regiment for most of their histories. The exception may be the Cameronians. The Cameronians had a background as a religious group, and the regiment, and later the 1st Battalion of the Scottish Rifles, was allowed to follow certain regimental customs that recalled their days as an outlawed religion.

Other than that, the authorities treated the regiments that were heavy with Lowland soldiers just as they did any line regiment. Officially, there was no tie to a local area or group for most regiments, with exceptions such as the Connaught Rangers, some other Irish regiments, and, of course, the Highland regiments. Thus, there was no need to recognise the ethnic makeup of a regiment in any manner. This started to change when Cardwell and Childers moved to localise the regiments during the reforms of 1872 and 1881. As part of the reform of 1881, the regiments tied to Lowland recruiting areas were dressed in trews, doublets, and, where appropriate, 'Scottish' headdresses.

In being given trews and doublets, the Lowland soldiers were being forced to ape a group of society that their ancestors had despised and, to a certain degree, feared. At first, they wore the government tartan (Black Watch tartan), which was given the mocking name 'MacChilders' tartan.

Obtaining Lowland men for the Lowland regiments had been an ongoing problem. The Scottish Lowland regiments drew less than 15 percent of their NCOs and men from Scotland in the 1870s.[85] The Lowland regiments ranked in the bottom categories of regiments that had men serving in them who were born in that regiment's recruiting district. Four out of five of them were under 25 percent for the period 1883–1900. The exception was the Cameronians, at 38 percent.

In the mid-1880s, the King's Own Scottish Borderers (KOSB), whose recruiting district was in southern Scotland, had to fill up its numbers with Irish immigrants living in Glasgow.[86]

82 Stephen Wood, *The Scottish Soldier* (Manchester: Archive Publications, 1987), p.13.
83 Carew, *Regiments*, p.40.
84 Carew, *Regiments*, p.40.
85 Hanham, 'Religion', p.166.
86 French, *Military*, p.45.

Lowland Scots – officer and men.

***Highland Scots***

The Highlands of Scotland were an area often outside the civil and political life of the Kingdom of Scotland in the early 1700s. The people of Scotland feared and looked down on the Highlanders as wild, criminal, and, as James I said, utterly barbarous. The Lowlanders called them Irish because of the many similarities between their customs and Irish customs.[87] Many were followers of the Stuart cause and had taken part in revolutions in 1689 and 1715. For this, they had been subject to the Glencoe Massacre of 1692, and the government had built a fort to control them at Inverlochy. Highlanders had been used in the Lowlands in 1678 to subdue the Covenanters.[88]

Many of the Highland clans rose to follow the Young Pretender in the '45. After being crushed at Culloden, the government set out to wipe out the Highland way of life and destroy the clan system. First, they marched through the Highlands with swords and fire. Then, a programme of clearing the land of its small farmers was undertaken in order to raise cattle and sheep. Forts were built at key points in the Highlands, and military roads were built throughout the Highlands. The wearing of kilts and pipe music was outlawed. The carrying of weapons was also banned. Efforts were made to civilise Highlanders through education and religion. Education meant teaching English, and religion meant the presence of the Church of Scotland (Presbyterian) to the exclusion of all others.[89]

87 Robert McCrum, William Cran, and Robert MacNeil, *The Story of English* (New York: Viking Press, 1986), p.138.

88 Robert Clyde, *From Rebel to Hero: The Image of the Highlander, 1745-1830* (East Linton: Tuckwell Press, 1995), p.1.

89 Clyde, *Rebel*, p.57.

Other ranks – Gordon Highlanders.

NCO Argil and Southerland Highlanders.

As is well known, the first Highland regiment to have a continuous existence was the Black Watch. The government had earlier raised two regiments from the Whig clans, and one was used against the MacDonalds in 1692.[90] But they were later disbanded.

The start of the permanent recruitment of Highlanders for government goes back to before the '45. In 1725, six independent companies of more or less police (Watch) were raised. In 1739, four more companies were raised, and all of them were joined into one regiment, the Earl of Crawford's Regiment of Foot in the Highlands (later the Black Watch). The regiment marched south into England in 1742 and, in 1743, mutinied at the thought of being sent to Flanders, or, worse yet, the Caribbean.[91] The end result was approximately 100 mutineers imprisoned and three shot. The regiment then went to Flanders.[92] The regiment performed well at Fontenoy and was singled out for praise by the French commander, Saxe.[93] The regiment was stationed in the

90 Clyde, *Rebel*, p.150.
91 Wood, *Scottish*, pp.29–31.
92 Wood, *Scottish*, p.31.
93 Clyde, *Rebel*, pp.151–52.

south of England during the '45 probably to keep them away from the temptation of going over to the Jacobites. A number of men from three newly raised companies of the regiment turned their coats at the Battle of Prestonpans.[94]

During the Seven Years' War, 10 Highland regiments were raised.[95] These served in all theatres of war, including India. But they were thought to be especially useful in America, where their savagery was thought to be a match for the Native Americans fighting on the side of the French.[96] The Highlanders did so well that William Pitt congratulated himself in a speech to the Commons in 1766 for discovering the Highlanders as loyal British soldiers.[97]

Many believed the military nature of the Highlanders came from the nature of their homeland and its clan system. It was influenced by the harsh living conditions, which allowed him to sustain privations. He considered courage a high virtue and cowardice the most disgraceful failing. He venerated and obeyed his clan chief and devoted himself to his country and clan.[98]

During the Seven Years' War and the Napoleonic Wars, the performance of the Highlanders was such that a belief grew up that 'the Highland soldier was religious, sober, and well behaved in peace, fierce and utterly fearless in battle, and loyal to the end'.[99]

By 1820, a commission in a Highland regiment was a sought-after prize. This was a sea change from the old view of savages and rebels. In an 1891 advice book for prospective officers, the Highland regiments are ranked just below the Guards, the Rifle Brigade, and the 60th Rifles in status and absolutely ahead of all other infantry regiments.[100] Kipling said, 'A powerfully prayerful Highland regiment, officered by rank Presbyterians, is, perhaps, one degree more terrible in action than a hard-bitten thousand of irresponsible Irish ruffians.'[101]

The Highlanders were thought to share the Irish Celtic élan and impulsiveness in battle. In this, they were very unlike the dour Lowlander Scot, or the phlegmatic Yorkshireman, or many other men from the English shires.

Sometimes, this impulsiveness in battle could go too far. Thanks to Kipling, many people know that the Fuzzy-Wuzzies (Beja warriors supporting the Mahdi of Sudan during the Mahdist War) broke a British square. Fewer may know that this was done at the 1884 Battle of Tamai in the Sudan, because the 1st Battalion of the Black Watch left its position in the square and charged forwards against the enemy. This left a gaping hole, which the Fuzzy-Wuzzies used to get inside the square. Hand-to-hand fighting soon followed with the Fuzzy-Wuzzies, who were using swords and spears against bayonets, having an advantage. This went on until men from another square fired into the mass of fighting men, killing both friend and foe. Eventually, enough of the enemy were killed that the first square was saved.[102] The Black Watch later claimed it heard an order to charge. This seems unlikely, as sending part of the wall

94 Clyde, *Rebel*, p.152.
95 Wood, *Scottish*, p.36.
96 Wood, *Scottish*, p.36.
97 Clyde, *Rebel*, p.153.
98 Clyde, *Rebel*, p.175.
99 Clyde, *Rebel*, pp.176–77.
100 George J. Younghusband, *The Queen's Commission: How to Prepare for It, How to Obtain It, and How to Use It: With Practical Information on the Cost and Prospects of a Military Career* (John Murray, 2009, Google Books e-book), p.20.
101 Denman, 'Ethnic Soldiers', p.264.
102 Keown-Boyd, *Good Dusting*, pp.31–32.

of soldiers out of the square would defeat the whole point of the square. The attack can perhaps better be attributed to Highlander impulsiveness.

### *Cockneys*

The other really distinctive group to serve in the British army was the Cockneys. Since they were and still are front and centre in the capital, a number of stereotypes have been attached to them, some negative and some affectionate. Within the military, they were known as soldiers with buckets of guts who had a personality that was a mixture of cocky, cheeky, crafty, loquacious, and cheerful. The Cockney tendency to joke in stressful situations made an impression on soldiers from other parts of Britain during the First World War. As a result, a book of their wisecracks was brought out after the war.[103]

Living in London, a recruiting area for most of the regiments of the pre-war army, meant they could and did serve in many different regiments. They, overall, tended to do well in these regiments, first because they had the makings of good soldiers and second because their glib manner gave them a bit of an advantage when compared to their often dour, tongue-tied, and phlegmatic companions. If leadership is inducing people to do what they do not want to do and making them think it is a good plan, then the gift of the gab and the ability to make jokes are a real plus. Also, it helps reinforce instructions that are being given to subordinates. On the downside was the Cockney's tendency to get into scraps and crazy escapades and to skate close to what the rules and regulations allowed. In this area, they were more or less a match for Irish troops, who were led astray by drink and their mercurial natures.

Drink was the abiding problem of the British soldier down the years. Two spectacular examples show how the soldiers lost their heads in the presence of alcohol. During the retreat to Corunna, several divisions of the army spent the night in the village of Bembibre, which had a wine warehouse in it. Despite being closely followed by the French army, many hundreds of the British soldiers broke into wine vaults and cellars and began drinking. The next morning, nearly 1,000 were so drunk that they were passed out in the houses and streets. The following day, British troops tried all day to get these men to start marching, but there were still many who could not or would not march. At the end of the day, the French dragoons arrived and rode among the drunken men, slashing them with their swords. With this prodding, a few managed to overtake Moore's army with dreadful cuts to their heads and shoulders. But most were still so drunk that they just stood there, taking the cuts. They did not even try to get out of the way.[104]

During the Indian Mutiny, the British forces at the siege of Delhi at last had enough men to try to recapture the city. A gate was blown, and the British forces began fighting their way towards the Red Fort and the emperor. However, the route taken included the area of the Kashmir Gate occupied by liquor merchants. The British soldiers could not resist the alcohol, and discipline and forward movement were severely affected. This state of affairs went on until Lieutenant General Archdale Wilson ordered the destruction of all the captured alcohol.[105]

Closer to the First World War, Frank Richards, in his memoirs of life in the Royal Welch Fusiliers at the turn of the twentieth century, described a life with alcohol as a central part of it.

103 Bert Thomas, *The Best 500 Cockney War Stories: Reprinted from the London Evening News, Early 1920s* (Gloucestershire: Amberley Publishing, 2012).
104 Charles Oman, *A History of the Peninsular War* (Barnsley: Greenhill Books, 1995), vol. 1, pp.566–67.
105 John Harris, *The Indian Mutiny* (London: Hart-Davis MacGibbon, 1973), p.141.

Officers and men – Royal Fusiliers. Note how much shorter the middle other ranker is than the two officers. This may be due to poor nutrition in his childhood.

He admired an old soldier for his ability to put away large amounts of booze. Groups of soldiers would save their money so they could go on drinking binges together. Men would work out schemes to save up their daily ration of grog so they would have enough to get really drunk.[106]

## Rankers

It is often thought that the British class system meant that other ranks could never rise to an officer's rank. This is not true. Officer ranks were granted in wartime, and, while rarer, they were also given in peacetime. A few men were able to win their way from the ranks to the status of officer. Men who rose from the ranks to officer status are referred to as 'rankers' in the text below. The best known and most successful were William Robertson and Hector MacDonald. Robertson became a field marshal, and MacDonald, after winning an immediate battlefield commission for gallantry in Afghanistan, became a major general. However, MacDonald committed suicide after being called upon to meet a panel investigating charges of homosexuality that had been brought against him.

As the following tables show, many soldiers became officers by obtaining the largely honorary rank of quartermaster or riding master.

106 Richards, *Old Soldier*.

Table 21 shows two things. First, a small number of NCOs were able to obtain officer's rank. The tables that follow show that most of these men would have had the nebulous officer's rank while serving as quartermaster or riding master. But some must have obtained true officer's status. The other point shown is that the rankers were a sizeable percentage of the officers who did not purchase their commissions.

Table 22 is the most germane when dealing with rankers. It shows the number and percentage of rankers in the infantry and cavalry during the period 1871–1885. During this period, an average of 2.26 percent of the new line officers were rankers.

Then, for reasons known only to the mandarins in the Horse Guards, these statistics stopped being collected. Table 23 shows rankers in all arms for 1886–1910. However, this table, when read with Table 24, allows for some information about rankers to be teased out.

Table 24 clearly shows the number of cavalry troopers granted commissions during the period 1885–1906. As can be seen, the number of rankers decreased after 1894.

Unfortunately, the table combines the number of rankers who obtained officer status in the infantry and Army Service Corps. In looking at these numbers, it can be assumed that a large percentage of them went into the Army Service Corps like their financially stressed brother officers who had come through Sandhurst. It took a private income to live in almost every line infantry regiment. Montgomery chose one of the cheapest he could find, and he still needed monetary help from his family. The Army Service Corps, on the other hand, while it did not have much prestige, was paid better and had fewer expenses than line infantry regiments.[107]

**Table 21 Officers Commissioned from the Ranks, 1830–1859[108]**

| | Promoted NCOs including Quartermaster and Riding Masters | All Officers Who Did Not Purchase Their Rank | Percentage of the Rankers to the Total Who Did Not Purchase Their Rank |
|---|---|---|---|
| 1830–1839 | 182 | 795 | 22.9% |
| 1840–1847 | 264 | 1,390 | 18.99% |
| 1850–1859 | 570 | 4,001 | 14.2% |

**Table 22 Officers Commissioned from the Ranks, in the Cavalry and Infantry excluding Quartermasters and Riding Masters, 1871–1910[109]**

| | Promoted NCOs in the Cavalry and Infantry, excluding Quartermasters and Riding Masters | All Commissions in Cavalry and Infantry | Percentage of Rankers |
|---|---|---|---|
| 1871–1875 | 25 | 1,257 | 1.98% |
| 1875–1880 | 35 | 2,026 | 1.7% |
| 1880–1885 | 63 | 2,052 | 3.1% |

107 French, *Military*, pp.53, 165.
108 Spiers, *Army Society*, p.4.
109 Spiers, *Army Society*, p.4.

**Table 23 Officers Commissioned from the Ranks, in All Arms excluding Quartermasters and Riding Masters, 1886–1910[110]**

| | Promoted NCOs in All Arms, excluding Quartermasters and Riding Masters | All Commissions in the Cavalry, Infantry, Artillery, Engineers, and Army Service Corps | Percentage of Rankers |
|---|---|---|---|
| 1886–1890 | 154 | 3,222 | 4.8% |
| 1891–1895 | 118 | 3,593 | 3.3% |
| 1896–1900 | 111 | 5,427 | 2.0% |
| 1901–1905 | 117 | 3,664 | 3.2% |
| 1906–1910 | 64 | 2,944 | 2.2% |

**Table 24 Commissions Granted from the Ranks, 1885–1906[111]**

| Year | Second Lieutenants | | | | | Quartermasters | | | | | Riding Masters | | | | Grand Total |
|---|---|---|---|---|---|---|---|---|---|---|---|---|---|---|---|
| | Cavalry | Infantry and Army Service Corps | Royal Artillery (District Officers) | Royal Engineers (Coast Battalion) | Total | Cavalry | Infantry | Army Service Corps | Other Branches[*] | Total | Cavalry | Army Service Corps | Other Branches† | Total | |
| 1885 | 7 | 15 | 6 | 4 | 32 | 5 | 27 | 11 | 20 | 63 | 4 | – | 2 | 6 | 101 |
| 1886 | 7 | 17 | 6 | 1 | 31 | 2 | 25 | – | 5 | 32 | 1 | – | – | 1 | 64 |
| 1887 | 7 | 23 | 1 | 2 | 33 | 2 | 17 | – | 9 | 28 | 2 | – | – | 2 | 63 |
| 1888 | 6 | 29 | 2 | 4 | 41 | 2 | 9 | 4 | 5 | 20 | 3 | – | 2 | 5 | 66 |
| 1889 | 2 | 12 | 7 | 1 | 22 | 1 | 17 | 3 | 12 | 33 | 1 | – | 2 | 3 | 58 |
| 1890 | 3 | 15 | 7 | 2 | 27 | 1 | 16 | – | 15 | 32 | 2 | – | – | 2 | 61 |
| 1891 | 6 | 6 | 8[‡] | 1 | 21 | 1 | 24 | 3 | 18 | 46 | 2 | – | – | 2 | 69 |
| 1892 | 3 | 9 | 7[§] | 1 | 20 | 5 | 29 | 1 | 16 | 51 | 4 | 1 | 1 | 6 | 77 |
| 1893 | 4 | 13 | 8[**] | – | 25 | 3 | 22 | 1 | 8 | 34 | 1 | – | 1 | 2 | 61 |
| 1894 | 6 | 19 | 3 | – | 28 | 3 | 30 | 6 | 10 | 49 | 1 | 1 | 3 | 5 | 82 |
| 1895 | 1 | 23 | – | – | 24 | 5 | 28 | 11 | 22 | 66 | 7 | – | 2 | 9 | 99 |
| 1896 | – | 14 | – | 2 | 16 | 1 | 24 | 2 | 22 | 49 | 2 | 1 | – | 3 | 68 |
| 1897 | – | 8 | – | 1 | 9 | – | 25 | 1 | 15 | 41 | 2 | – | 5 | 7 | 57 |
| 1898 | 1 | 12 | 1 | – | 14 | 1 | 24 | 6 | 22 | 53 | 2 | – | 1 | 3 | 70 |
| 1899 | 1 | 11 | 12 | – | 24 | 3 | 24 | 21 | 34 | 82 | 1 | 1 | 1 | 3 | 109 |
| 1900 | – | 27 | 21 | – | 48 | 9 | 49 | 17 | 66 | 141 | 1 | 1 | 5 | 7 | 196 |
| 1901 | 1 | 19 | 13 | 3 | 36 | 8 | 29 | 9 | 27 | 73 | 4 | – | 3 | 7 | 116 |

110 Spiers, *Army Society*, p.4.

111 'British Army Soldiers up to 1913', *The National Archives*, <https://www.nationalarchives.gov.uk/help-with-your-research/research-guides/british-army-soldiers-up-to-1913/>, accessed 14 Sept. 2022.

| | | | | | | | | | | | | | | | |
|---|---|---|---|---|---|---|---|---|---|---|---|---|---|---|---|
| 1902 | 1 | 26 | 6 | 1 | 34 | 2 | 32 | 4 | 23 | 61 | 3 | – | 1 | 4 | 99 |
| 1903 | – | 14 | 2 | – | 16 | 3 | 26 | 4 | 8 | 41 | 5 | – | 3 | 8 | 65 |
| 1904 | – | 8 | 8 | – | 16 | 3 | 18 | 2 | 15 | 38 | 3 | – | 1 | 4 | 58 |
| 1905 | – | 6 | 9 | – | 15 | 3 | 10 | – | 13 | 26 | – | 1 | – | 1 | 42 |
| 1906 | – | 10 | 7 | – | 17 | 4 | 12 | 7 | 15 | 38 | 2 | – | – | 2 | 57 |
| **Grand Total** | **56** | **336** | **134** | **23** | **549** | **67** | **517** | **113** | **400** | **1,097** | **53** | **6** | **33** | **92** | **1,738** |

* Includes Royal Artillery, Royal Engineers, and Army Ordinance Department.
† Includes Royal Artillery and Royal Engineers.
‡ Includes six inspectors of ordinance machinery.
§ Includes two inspectors of ordinance machinery.
** Includes six inspectors of ordinance machinery.

Life was not easy for rankers. They did not have a family giving them the all-important extra income, so it was unlikely they could survive in any of the regiments stationed on the home islands. That meant that they would need to transfer to a regiment or battalion in India or another overseas station and hope they could scrape by there.

Service in India, even with its extra pay, was not a panacea. Depending on the regiment, life for an officer could still be very expensive. Frank Richards told of talking to an officer of the Royal Welch Fusiliers who was having money problems because his family could only give him an allowance of £200 a year (£20,594 or $24,265 in current value). He went on to add that the officer must have been hard-pressed to have told his troubles to a private.[112] How much worse would it be for a ranker with no extra income?

Line infantry – other rank.

After 1882, an option to the Army Service Corps was service in the Egyptian army if they could get accepted. However, based on the bibliography listed in *Soldiers of the Nile* by Henry Keown-Boyd (1996), relatively few rankers were accepted. Towards the turn of the twentieth century, service in East and West Africa with its higher pay would have been attractive in spite of the higher chance of death and disability from disease.

112 Richards, *Old Soldier*, pp.274–75.

Given these hard financial facts of life, men were known to turn down the chance to become officers. William Robertson did so once, before he put aside his fears and took the risk of failure owing to a lack of funds two years later.[113]

Line infantry – other rank.

Once among the officers, the ranker often did not really fit in. Those from infantry regiments did not know how to ride in a horse-centric officers' society. His lack of funds kept him from taking a full part in mess and other regiment social life. His accent, relationships, tastes, and habits were all different.

A major point was the ranker's habits and bearing. He had risen through the NCO ranks by closely supervising the men under him, as one never knew when they would go off the rails. NCOs were also required to be expert keepers of the regiments' books, with everything in apple-pie order. The ideal sergeant was ramrod straight with his uniform immaculate and pressed with creases with a knife's edge. This contrasted with the junior officer's cheerful, larky amateurishness, where the ethos was to be seen as not trying too hard at anything. They wore their spotless uniforms with a casual elegance. When officers wished to describe and slightly disparage an officer from the ranks, they would say he was an officer of the sergeant major type.

William Robertson found a way to make the habits of attention to detail and hard work help him as a junior officer, in spite of the officer corps' ethos of not trying too hard at anything. He became an officer in 1888 and was placed in a regiment in India, where he had a better chance of living on his pay. First, he started learning Indian languages, as this brought an increase in pay. He learned a lower level of Hindustani after three months of study and received the increase in pay that went with it.[114] By 1892, he had learned five languages, and he was able to move away from the regiment to staff service,[115] where attention to details would be valued rather than disparaged.

The officer corps did not object by and large to men from the ranks being promoted to the officer corps. In fact, the CO of the regiment or battalion had to give his permission for this to happen. There were some cases where they refused to do so, but, in most cases, they did. In addition, often the officers encouraged good NCOs to try for the rank of officer and bought gifts for the man when he attained officer rank.[116] The new officer would need to change regiments so he could have a fresh start unhindered by anyone remembering his old status. The receiving regiment was normally welcoming to the new officer. They, however, did not make any special allowances for his lack of funds.

113 William Robertson, *From Private to Field-Marshall* (Forest Grove, OR: University Press of the Pacific, 2005), pp.30–32.
114 Robertson, *Private*, p.36.
115 Robertson, *Private*, p.49.
116 Robertson, *Private*, p.33.

3

# British Indian Officers

The Indian army was commanded by British and native personnel. The Indian officers were promoted from the ranks. British officers in the infantry and cavalry during the period 1880–1914 were, for the most part, graduates of the military academy at Sandhurst, England.

British officer – 106th Haraz Pioneers.

By the 1880s, the British had an almost mystical belief in the ability of British men to lead native troops. Comments made during this period contain self-congratulatory statements about the ability of British officers to lead and command Kipling's Lesser Breeds. This was often attributed to the social moulding of officers in public school. In its most exaggerated form, it did not matter what the British white man's background, education, or training were. All that mattered was that the British man had the all-important lack of melanin.

In one notable example, at the siege of Kut in 1915–1916, the trapped Indian regiments suffered heavy casualties among the regiment's British officers. To make up for these losses, offers were made to the other ranks of the garrison's British regiments to move to Indian regiments as officers. Apparently, even the type of British soldiers that Wellington called 'the scum of the earth' could become officers in native regiments.

In 1906, additional routes to becoming an Indian army officer were developed, and old routes were made easier. Because of Kitchener's 1902 reforms of the Indian army, more British officers were needed. An inter-department committee suggested several changes to produce the 900-odd officers needed. Not all their suggestions were adopted. In the end, it was agreed that

Above: British officer – 5th Gurkha Rifles.

Left: British officer – 62nd Punjab Regiment.

the Indian army would take more university candidates and applicants from battalions outside of India. They would continue to accept transfers from battalions in India, as this would help smooth out the intake of new officers. Entrants from England only came out two times a year. If an Indian regiment needed an officer between these times, there were problems finding one. They also noted that some of the best officers in the Indian army came from the Royal Artillery in India. It was made easier for artillery officers outside of India to apply to become officers in the Indian army to tap this resource.[1]

The British officers were of a largely middle-class background, and, often, their family had a tradition of serving in India. One officer, Lieutenant Colonel Charles Stack, wounded near Nukhaila, Mesopotamia, in 1915, was the third man in his family to command the 33rd Light Cavalry. His father and grandfather had commanded it when it was the 3rd Bombay Light Cavalry.[2] John Masters, in his *Bugles and a Tiger*, noted his great-grandfather had come out to India in 1805. His family had served in India since then in the army, schools, the police, and the

1 T. A. Heathcote, *The Military in British India: The Development of British Land Forces in South Asia, 1600–1947* (Manchester: Manchester University Press, 1995), pp.200–01.

2 Marquess of Anglesey, *A History of the British Cavalry, 1816–1919* (Barnsley: Leo Cooper, 1986), vol. 6, p.15, footnote.

opium department.[3] When Vere Ogilvie married Christopher Birdwood (1931), the son of the Indian commander-in-chief, it was a union of the fifth and sixth generations of British families who had lived in India.[4] One could go on and on.

Many were as pushed by a lack of an acceptable alternative way to earn a living as they were pulled by the attractions of Indian army life and family traditions of service. Trade was an avenue that was unlikely to attract many, given the social attitudes of the time and the fact that most professions were out of reach because of a lack of money. Lack of money barred service in the British army for many, where an independent income was necessary in almost every regiment.[5] On the other hand, in the Indian army, one was paid enough to live a pleasant upper-class type of life – with servants, polo, and so on – and engage in other activities that had high social status.

However, there was a catch. Because it was such an attractive life, the competition to join the Indian officer corps was quite stiff. Typically, one had to rank in the top 35 of his Sandhurst class to join the Indian army. (Montgomery wanted to join but did not rank high enough.) It would be hard to find a more effective way to hamstring the empire. Year after year, the intellectual cream of each Sandhurst class was skimmed off, sent to India, and then left there to largely stagnate. They were far from the court, the centre of army of command, and were looked down upon by regular army officers. After all, they were not really of Britain's high social class. In India, the regiments that the young officers joined had different levels of social desirability. The cavalry generally had the highest social status. Among the infantry, social status seemed to follow the martial-race propensities of the men. The Gurkhas, Sikhs, and Punjab frontier regiments were probably the most desirable. Next came the pure-class regiments, with those of the Bengal army having the edge. The Madras and Bombay regiments had lower social status. But, as always, it is almost impossible to give a specific ranking that everyone would agree with. Family connections, faith and knowledge in the men, differences in perceptions, and acquaintances would all affect an individual's views.

No matter what regiment the officer joined, he was expected to learn the language spoken by his men. This often required him to learn two new languages. Normally, this meant learning Urdu and, if his men spoke another language, that language as well. A new officer had three years to pass examinations in Hindustani Urdu. Urdu later broke into two languages, which were used in Pakistan and in India. Urdu was a Pidgin trade language of Northern India.

**Table 25 Social Background of Sandhurst Cadets Going to the Indian Army, 1890–1895**[6]

| | **Number of Cadets** | **Percentage** |
|---|---|---|
| *Fathers Employed in India* | | |
| Indian Army Officers | 29 | 24.1% |
| Indian Civil Service | 9 | 6.9% |
| Others Connected with India | 2 | 1.5% |
| **Total India Connected** | **40** | **32.5%** |

3 Masters, *Bugles*, p.28.
4 Charles Allen, *Plain Tales from the Raj* (London: Futura Publications, 1978), p.37.
5 Masters, *Bugles*, pp.28–29.
6 Heathcote, *Indian*, p.141.

| | Number of Cadets | Percentage |
|---|---|---|
| *Father a Resident in the UK* | | |
| Army Officers | 57 | 44.1% |
| Naval Officers | 5 | 3.8% |
| **Total British Service Related** | **62** | **47.9%** |
| *Father in Other Professions* | | |
| Surgeons | 5 | 3.8% |
| Private gentlemen | 4 | 3.1% |
| Clergy | 4 | 3.1% |
| Civil Engineers | 2 | 1.5% |
| Gentlemen Farmers | 2 | 1.5% |
| Doctors | 2 | 1.5% |
| Others | 8 | 6.2% |
| **Total Other Professions** | **27** | **20.7%** |
| ***Grand Total*** | ***129**** | ***101.1%*** |

* No member of the nobility sent his son to the Indian army staff corps during this period, and only one knight did so. During this period, the term 'Indian staff corps' meant general Indian army. The British army, by contrast, recruited four sons of earls, four sons of viscounts, six sons of barons, and eight sons of baronets. A further five fathers have their occupation listed as 'lord', but, as this includes among them Lord Randolph Churchill, father of Gentleman Cadet Winston Churchill, this term clearly includes the younger sons of nobles, who were not really peers of the realm.[7]

## Jewish Officers

The British *Jewish Year Book* shows seven Jewish British officers serving in the Indian army in 1914. Most of them had several years of experience in the army and had risen to the rank of captain by 1914. Table 26 below gives their names, regiments, and years of experience.

**Table 26 Regiment, Rank, and Experience of Jewish Officers[8]**

| Name | Regiment | Rank in 1914 | Years Experience in India |
|---|---|---|---|
| B. I. H. Adler | 113th Infantry (Bombay) | Captain | 13 years |
| C. E. Montefiore | 110th Maratha Light Infantry* | Captain | 10 years |
| E. H. Lewin | 46th Punjabis | Captain | 8 years |
| C. M. Gabriel† | | – | – |
| E. Enriquez | 21st Punjabis* | Captain | 8 years |
| H. M. Liepmann | 13th Rajputs | Captain | 4 years |
| F. A. de Pass | 34th Poona Horse (Bombay) | Lieutenant | 2 years |

* These officers were on supernumerary or seconded lists.
† There were several officers named Gabriel, but none of them had these initials.

7 Heathcote, Indian, pp.140–41.
8 The British *Jewish Year Book* is not an official publication. Therefore, while generally correct, it can fail to list some people. Table compiled using Harris, *Jewish #5661*, *Jewish #5666*, *Jewish #5668-9*, and *Jewish #5674-75*, vol. 18.

Frank Alexander 'F. A.' de Pass was an interesting officer, and we know more about him than the other officers because he won a VC. He won his VC in November 1914 in the trenches of France. This was early enough in the First World War that each VC was given special attention. Later, the fighting involved such large numbers that individual acts tended to be overlooked.

He was educated at Rugby and Woolwich. In 1906, he went into the Royal Field Artillery as a second lieutenant. In 1910, while stationed in India, he was exchanged into the 34th Poona Horse, Indian army. The exchange was likely helped by the opening of the 'side door' created in 1908, making it easier for artillery officers to move into the Indian army.

He must have done well and had good contacts, because, from November 1913 until the start of the First World War, he was an orderly officer, with the local rank of captain, to Sir Percy Lake, Chief of the Staff in India. He shipped out with his regiment as part of the Secunderabad Cavalry Brigade (part of the 1st Indian Cavalry Division), which reached France in October 1914.[9]

He lost his life and earned his VC in the trenches near Festubert on 25 November 1914.[10] He is said to be the first Indian army officer and the first man of the Jewish faith to win a VC in the First World War.

None of the Jewish officers listed in Table 26 served in the high-status, high-demand regiments, such as the Gurkhas, Sikhs, or Guides. Two of them, Adler and Montefiore, were in regiments, the 110th and 11th, that had been part of the old Bombay army. This old association, close to the First World War, still lowered a regiment's status. On top of that, the personnel of the 110th consisted, for the most part, of Marathas, a class that was out of favour in 1914. The 113th drew its men mostly from Rajputana, so its drawback was being a mixed-class regiment and its connection with the Bombay army.

Lewin and Enriquez were in the 46th and 21st. Both regiments consisted of companies of different fighting classes: Pathans, Sikhs, Punjabi Muslims, and so on. While being made up of the most favoured fighting classes, a mixed-class regiment was a cut below a single-class regiment because it was a bit harder for an officer to handle. He had to learn more languages, there were more internal disputes to deal with, and the regiment never developed quite as high *esprit de corps* as the single-class regiments.

Liepmann was in the 13th Rajputs, a single-class regiment composed of Rajputs from Rajputana. As such, his regiment was fairly high on the status ladder, falling only below the Gurkha and Sikh regiments and the Guides. The Rajputs were the premier Hindu fighting class. Dogras were normally Rajputs who lived in a specific area.

Looking at the regiments these Jewish officers went into, it is hard to tell if anti-Semitism played a part in where they ended up. Generally, to join a regiment, one had to be approved by the officers already in the regiment. But it is likely that the further down the pecking order, the less demanding the officers will be. As a group, these officers skewed towards lower-status regiments, but it is not so marked that one can say there was a strong anti-Semitic feeling in play.

In addition to the above Jewish officers serving in the cavalry and infantry in 1914, there were two Jewish officers in the Indian Medical Service and one in the Indian Commissariat.

9 F. W. Perry, *Order of Battle of Divisions, Part 5B: Indian Army Divisions* (Newport, VA: Ray Westlake Military Books, 1993), p.13.

10 L. A. Clutterbuck, W. T. Dooner, and C. A. Denison (eds), *The Bond of Sacrifice: A Biographical Record of All British Officers Who Fell in the Great War* (London: Anglo-African Publishing Contractors, 1917), pp.109–10.

For those who were able to become British officers in the British Indian army, an upper-class lifestyle awaited since pay in the Indian army was higher than that given to the same rank in the British army. Most of the British officers in the Indian army could live a life largely devoted to polo and pig-sticking wild boars. There was almost always no fox hunting. In India, boar hunting on horseback with spears took its place. It was a hard, dangerous sport. Falls off the horse were common, and, if a boar gored a man with its tusks, death was not unknown in the pre-antibiotic days. There was a saying about the British officers in both the British and Indian armies: they pretend to pay us, and we pretend to work.

British officers – polo team.

## Servants

The officer and his wife were cared for by a number of servants. The number of servants grew as rank and pay went up. A typical household staff is given in a household management book:[11]

1. Bearer (head of household servants)
2. Cook

11 Flora A. Steel and Grace Gardiner, *The Complete Indian Housekeeper and Cook* (Oxford: Oxford University Press, 2011), pp.64–65.

3. Table waiter
4. Housekeepers
5. Scullery man
6. Sweeper
7. Water carrier
8. Lady's maid/nurses for children
9. Tailor
10. Washerman
11. Groom for horses
12. Grasscutter
13. Gardener
14. Cow keeper.

Depending on the amount of money available, there could be more than one of each type of servant. For those with money, it was possible to have several cooks and one waiter for each diner at a meal. Each child often had a nurse of their own.

The traditional rule was for a groom and grasscutter for each horse in the stable.[12] Often, there were several housekeepers, scullery men, sweepers, water carriers, washermen, and even tailors.[13] In the days before pasteurisation, many households kept their own cows, if possible, to try to avoid tuberculosis (TB) and other diseases.[14] This was far beyond the dream of a middle-class family in Britain.

There was a darker side never considered by the young men who clamoured to become officers in the Indian army. Heat and disease were constant companions. In addition, when children came, it was customary to send them back to England at the age of eight or so to attend boarding school. Because of the distance, this meant that father and child basically never saw each other again. The child was often left to the tender mercies of a boarding school or a distant relative.

## Officers' Wives

A word should also be said about the officers' wives. They faced the same heat and diseases as their husbands without the compensation of sport or regimental fellowship.

During the period under study, the only real option available to a young girl was to marry well. Most married young men who were home from India on several months of leave. Some improved their chances by sailing out to India to 'visit' friends and relatives. This option was so common that the boats carrying them to India were known as the 'fishing fleet'.

Regardless of the route taken to marriage, the result was that the young girl was married to an older man (young officers could not afford to marry, and the authorities frowned on them getting married), whom she hardly knew and who was distracted by his duties and the joys of army life. In addition, she was left to run a household of several servants. A job for which she had no real training. This was harder than it might sound. Almost always, the Indian idea of

12 Steel and Gardiner, *Complete*, p.96.
13 Steel and Gardiner, *Complete*, pp.64–96.
14 Steel and Gardiner, *Complete*, pp.109–11.

Memsahib, husband, children, and close household servants.

healthful cleanliness was far lower than British standards. In addition, the Indian servants were notorious for trying to avoid work.

There is a well-known story of a British wife who found a dead animal – a bird or dog, stories vary – in her yard. She tried different servants to get the dead body removed. All turned the work down, citing caste and religions reasons. She had at least 10 people who worked as household help, but none would deal with the dead body. There were castes that dealt with dead bodies. However, they ranked low in the social pecking order, and none of the servants were willing to deal with them. In addition, in India, dead animals were normally just left alone to be eaten by the many vultures that were everywhere. Finally, in desperation, the wife snuck out in the dead of night and removed it herself. All the servants knew what she did, but, outwardly, social order and face were saved by everyone.

Another problem was that her new world was composed of just other army wives, and she lived in a closed world separated from other women and the general population.

As is the case with any small group, not everyone got along with each other. The result was that the wives, who had little real work to do, often fell into feuds with each other.

All too often, the sensible British girl who married metamorphosised into the fearsome *memsahib.* Memsahibs were a group that was commonly criticised and even went so far as to blame the enactment of the Hindu Widows' Remarriage Act in 1856 on them. The thinking is that, before there were British women in India, the officers often took local women as concubines. They, in turn, provided the officer with knowledge of local ways and an introduction into the local language. These women were known as 'sleeping dictionaries'. When the British women came to India, they put pressure on the officer class to marry and stop consorting with the sleeping dictionaries. This, in turn, caused the officers to lose understanding of the native rank and file.

The hardest part for the officer's wife came when it came time to send their young child back to Britain for school. Would she stay to be with her husband in India or go with the child to Britain? Most felt that the child had to go back to Britain to keep them from being spoiled rotten by the Indian servants and to remove the child from the deadly dangers of the Indian environment.

## Native Officers

The Indian army of the period had a large number of native officers. These men were known as 'viceroy's commissioned officers' (VCOs). The VCOs were men who had been promoted from the ranks. This meant that a young Indian recruit had a much better chance of becoming an officer than a young recruit in the regular British army.

They were normally men who had long service with good records and had strong personalities. They had a good command of English. However, there were limits on the authority of the VCO. They were subordinate to all regular British and Indian officers. Despite this, many new British lieutenants were afraid of them.

As a group, they had the strong and weak points of their regiment's rank and file. They sometimes lacked initiative and sometimes carried over village politics into the regiment.

There was a limit to how high they could rise. Most topped out at the equivalent of lieutenant. A few rose to the rank of captain, and one attained the rank of regimental major. But, again, they were junior in status to white British officers and, in most cases, could not give orders to white troops. In addition to commanding native troops, they served as a bridge between the native troops and the British officers.

Mixed group of viceroy's commissioned officers (VCOs). The men in this photo were King's Orderly Officers.

Mixed group of VCOs. The men in this photo were King's Orderly Officers.

Mixed group of VCOs. The men in this photo were King's Orderly Officers.

Gurkha VCO.

4

# Indian Men

The Indian army was the largest and most successful of all the colonial armies because of the men that chose to serve in its ranks. 'Chose' is the correct word because it was an all-volunteer army, the largest in the world at the time. The Indians volunteered because of personal acquaintance, desirability of life, and military tradition in their class. The men joining the cavalry came typically from a higher economic stratum, as, under the Silladar system, they had to contribute a set fee, that is, buy their way into their regiment. Ostensibly, this was to cover the value of their horse and equipment. The infantry was largely made up of yeoman stock – fairly prosperous agricultural men.

The steady employment and social desirability of a warrior's life were attractive to many classes in India. The British played on this by periodically threatening to recruit other lower-class groups if class leadership did not produce enough young men. Certain classes made determined efforts to be accepted for military service.

When the EIC first came to India, they were able to secure three toeholds in widely different parts of the subcontinent: Bombay, Madras, and Bengal. In turn, each had its own history as it struggled to survive and fought local enemies. Having command of the sea allowed the different presidencies, to some extent, to aid each other. For example, there were troops from Madras at the decisive Battle of Plassey in Bengal in 1757.

Under the company, all three presidencies used essentially the same recruiting system that was used back home. The ranks were open to anyone who was physically fit and willing to serve. There were no restrictions as to caste. That having been said, it should be noted that, in the Bengal army, there was a strong tendency to crowd out the lower-status castes in favour of high-caste Brahmins and Jats. When the Mutiny of the (mostly) Bengal army occurred, almost all the army's regiments mutinied.

After the Mutiny, two things happened. The trust the British heretofore had in their men was gone, and greater attention was paid to their nature and background. Since the ostensible reason for the revolt was religion, more attention and deference were paid to their religion.

In time, this meant that the men of a given class were joined together in class companies and, in some cases, class regiments. It also meant that the men were allowed – actually encouraged – to tie their turbans in a way that showed their class. In doing this, the army was only reflecting civilian practice, albeit with some tightening up of the ways the turbans were tied.

Only certain classes were allowed in the army, and, within those classes, often only men from the right locality. Military service was popular among the Indians, as it brought status

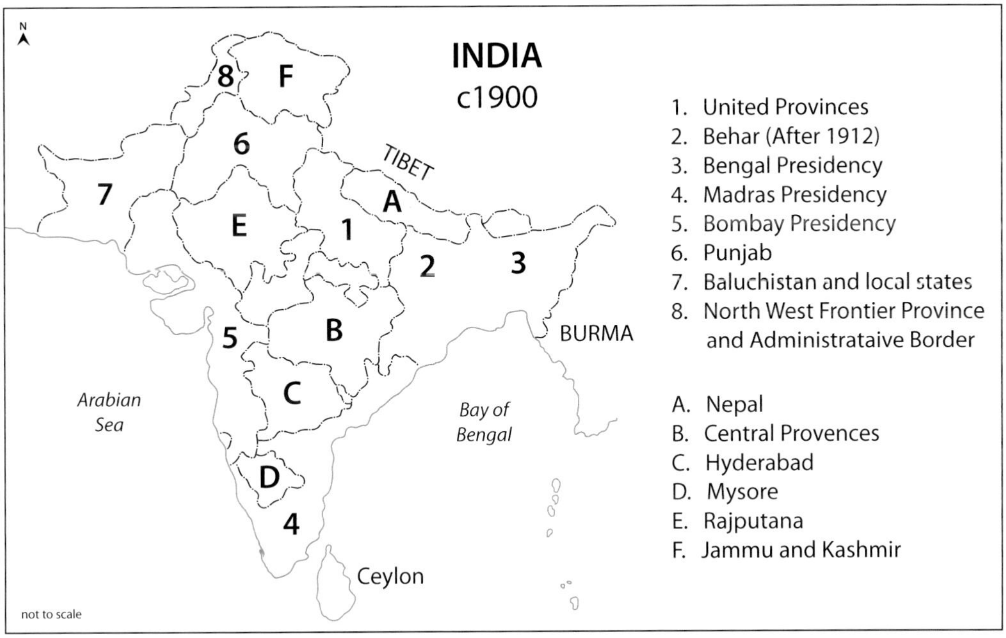


British Provinces and Princely States.

and a good income. Since only certain groups were accepted, it was natural for less-favoured individuals to try to pass themselves off as members of one of the selected groups. There were two ways to combat this. The army command printed handbooks for each class in the army. These handbooks gave general information on the history and customs of the class. In addition, part of each handbook prior to the Great War included a section of questions to ask to expose someone trying to claim he was a member of the favoured class. These handbooks were made for the use of regimental officers, and the question part was necessary when they did the recruiting. During the war and afterwards, recruiting was moved to centralised specialists, and the potted questions were no longer needed by regimental officers.

The other method of recruiting men into the regiment was to have men talk to friends, family, and others in the village when home on leave. This was a good way to produce men, but it had a major drawback that the officers having drinks in the officers' mess were only hardly aware of. When friends and family were brought back to the regiment, it was only a matter of time before village politics were reproduced in the regiment. This could all too often mean that promotions were rigged so that they went not to the best qualified but to the person whose family was most powerful back in the village, or perhaps to pay off a family or personal monetary debt.[1]

As time passed, the authorities came more and more to favour the Gurkhas, the men from the Punjab, and the Northwest Frontier. Groups from these areas are often called the 'martial-races' or the 'martial classes'. At the same time, the loyal sepoys of Madras fell out of favour, and

1 See Kaushik Roy, *Brown Warriors of the Raj: Recruitment and the Mechanics of Command in the Sepoy Army* (New Delhi: Manohar Publishers, 2008), and David Omissi, *The Sepoy and the Raj: The Indian Army, 1860–1940* (Houndmills: Macmillan Press, 1994), for discussions regarding recruitment.

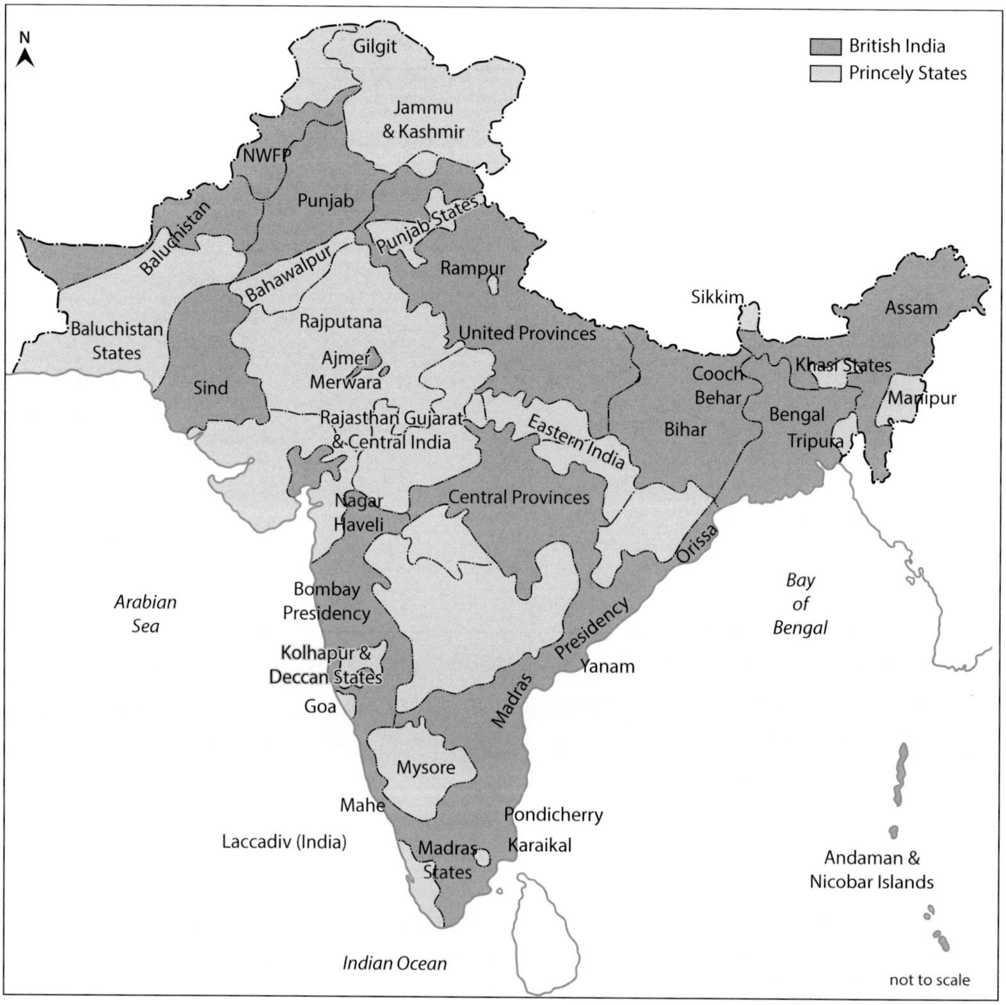


British Provinces and Princely State.

the Madras regiments were either disbanded or the regiments retained, with the Madras sepoys replaced by men from the Punjab. Several of the Madras regiments that remained were reduced in strength. In 1824, the Madras army had 52 regiments. Forty were disbanded, mostly in the 1860s and 1880s. Sixteen converted to men from the Punjab. The other five were disbanded or converted to Punjabi personnel in the 1890s and early years of the twentieth century. By 1914, they had 12 left. Of those, three were pioneer regiments, and the rest were understrength garrison regiments. This made the Indian army rely further on sepoys from the Punjab.[2] In time, this meant a majority of the armies' fighting men came from a narrow base.

2 F. W. Perry, *Order of Battle of Divisions, Part 1* (Newport, VA: Ray Westlake Military Books, 1988), pp.134–37.

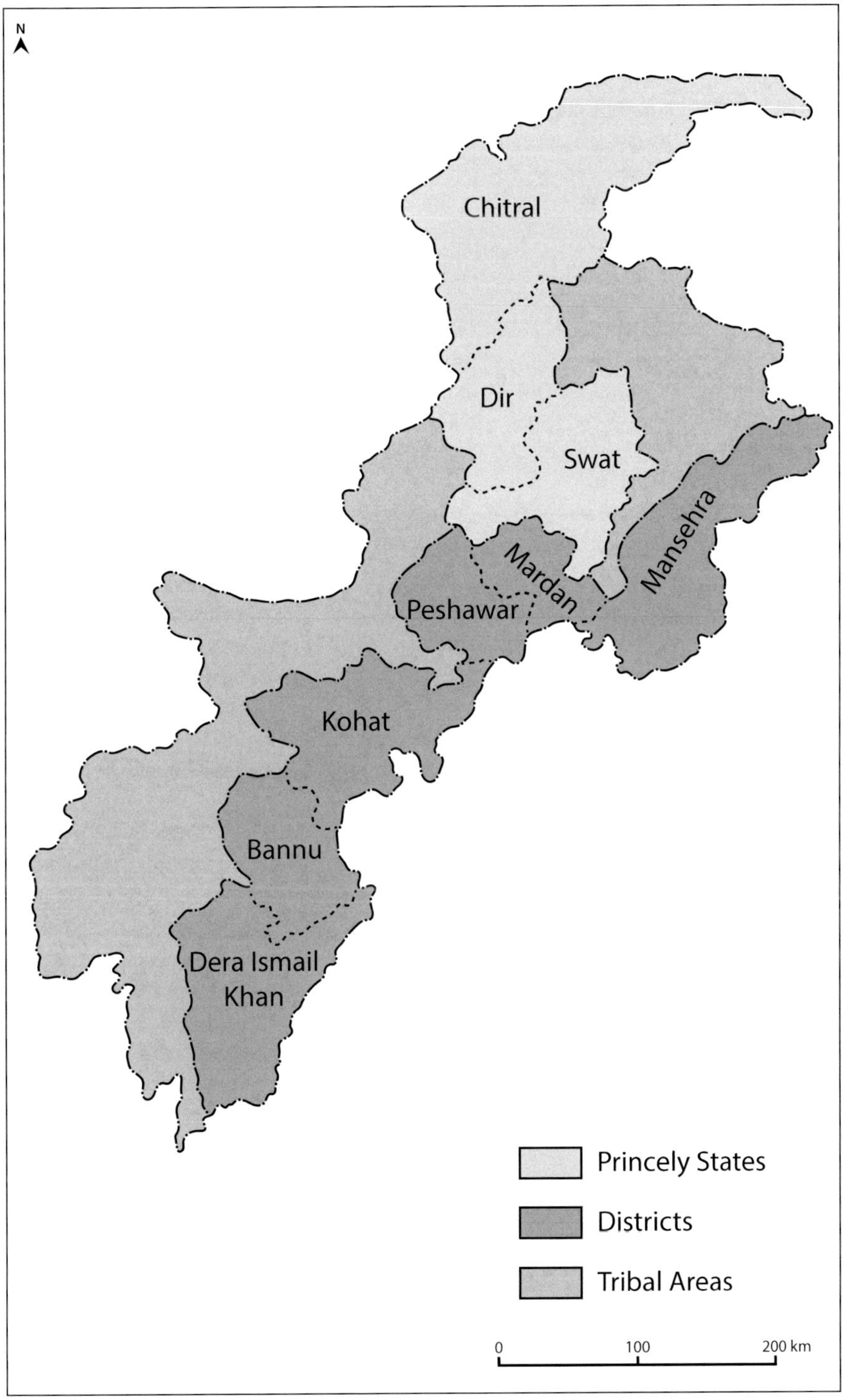


The North West Frontier of British India.

## Martial Classes

Who were the groups that the British came to favour in recruiting? As noted above, by the 1890s, the British had adopted a 'martial-races' or 'martial classes' theory. These were groups of men who were felt to have a natural bent towards combat but, at the same time, would remain loyal to the British. This latter element ruled out most of the high-class men from Hindustan – Oudh, Agra, and Behar (also referred to as 'Eastern Purbiya') – who had mutinied in 1857. In addition, as a practical matter, the class had to be large enough to be worth recruiting and be willing to come forwards in large enough numbers to make enlisting them worthwhile.

The British did not limit themselves to just a few castes but also recruited from certain locales and ethnic groups. These different groups were called 'classes'.

The invading Aryans are thought to have brought with them a four-fold class division of social classes when they came into India. This general division later hardened into religious law. They were (1) Brahmin (priests), (2) Ksatriya (warriors), (3) Vaisya (farmers and merchants), and (4) Sudra (servants) for the other three classes. The first three classes are 'twice-born', born once when they are born and again when they are initiated into the holy rites.[3] The first three groups wore a cord of three threads twisted together. The cord was made of cotton, hemp, or wool for Brahmins, Ksatriyas, and Vaisyas, respectively. The cords hung over the right shoulder and under the left arm, and they were worn continuously from the initiation forwards. Its removal rendered the wearer impure and forced the person to undergo rigorous and expensive penance.[4] The Rajputs wore the Ksatriyas' cord. The cord worn by Rajputs was shorter than a Brahmin's cord, and the Brahmins and Rajputs had different knots in their cords.[5]

Over time, these four groupings divided into the thousands of castes and subcastes found in modern India.[6] To these Hindu castes should be added the Muslim castes and groups that live all over India. These are made up of converts among the local inhabitants and descendants of invaders.[7]

Below the four main Hindu castes and the many subcastes they had evolved into were the untouchables. The untouchables were, in general, made up of three groups. First were people who did work that Hindu society found abhorrent or unpleasant. These were often descendants of the original conquered peoples of India who lived on the outskirts of Indian villages. Second were the remnants of the original inhabitants of India who were living in some type of tribal organisation, often in the jungles. The third group were individuals who, for some reason, had lost their standing in one of the higher castes.

In the first group of outcastes, those doing dirty and abhorrent work, are people who cremated corpses, executed criminals, scavenged and removed night soil, made and sold alcohol, worked in leather, and were washer men.[8] The second group is the aboriginal tribes that held on when

3 Arthur L. Basham, *The Wonder that Was India: A Survey of the History and Culture of the Indian Sub-Continent before the Coming of the Muslims* (London: Sidgwick and Jackson, 1967), p.139.

4 Basham, *Wonder*, p.163.

5 A. H. Bingley and A. Nicholls, *Caste Handbooks for the Indian Army: Brahmans* (Simla: Government Central Printing Office, 1897), p.53.

6 Basham, *Wonder*, p.149, says 3,000 or more.

7 E. A. H. Blunt, *The Caste System of Northern India: With Special Reference to the United Provinces of Agra and Qudh* (New Delhi: S. Chand and Co., 1969), pp.177–91.

8 Basham, *Wonder*, pp.145–46.

India was being ruled by its invaders. They lived in the jungles and kept a tribal system. The third group of untouchables consisted of people who broke the rules of class purity and found themselves punished by being declared an untouchable. Some breaches could be resolved by acts of penance. Others required acts so rigorous that they would likely result in the death of the penitent. Foreigners (such as the British) would also be untouchables.[9] These individuals tended to remain in untouchable status.

Over time, the untouchables developed their own caste hierarchy, and, eventually, every group had another group they felt was lower than them.[10]

The discussion of the classes below will reflect the British view of these men. In some cases, information will be drawn from government documents published in the 1920s and 1930s, but these merely carry over the pre-First World War views. These views are stereotypes of the groups, but they do give a good insight into the nature of the men and how their British officers interacted with them.

The British considered the following to be martial classes at the turn of the twentieth century:

- Jats
- Pathans
- Baluchis
- Punjabi Muslims
- Hindustani and Eastern Punjabi Muslims
- Sikhs
- Gurkhas
- Rajputs
- Dogras
- Aboriginal Tribes
    * Meenas (or Minas)
    * Mhers (or Mers)
- Garhwalis
- Madras Classes
- Marathas and Dekhani Muslims
- Brahmins
- Other Classes
    * Christians
    * Ahirs
    * Gujars
    * Jews and Parsis.

Table 27 gives a picture of the Indian army after the martial-races strategy had taken firm hold. It includes the new favoured classes and the remains of classes, such as Jews, that were being eliminated from the army.

9 Basham, *Wonder*, p.147.
10 Basham, *Wonder*, p.146.

**Table 27 Number of Sepoys from Different Classes as of 1 January 1904[11]**

| Class | Number* |
|---|---|
| ***Muslims*** | |
| Cis-Frontier | 6,835 |
| Trans-Frontier | 1,612 |
| Afridis | 2,758 |
| Punjab proper including Hazara | 21,773 |
| Hindustan and Cis-Sutlej Punjab | 10,661 |
| Rajputana and Central India | 1,486 |
| Bombay | 162 |
| Madras | 5,588 |
| Dekhan | 2,647 |
| Others | 446 |
| *Subtotal* | *53,968* |
| ***Sikhs*** | |
| Jat Sikhs | 23,108 |
| Other Sikhs | 7,867 |
| *Subtotal* | *30,975* |
| Gurkhas | 14,224 |
| Garhwalis | 1,901 |
| *Subtotal* | *16,125* |
| ***Hindus*** | |
| Dogras and Punjabi Hindus | 8,669 |
| Rajputs | 10,813 |
| Jats | 8,407 |
| Brahmins | 2,880 |
| Marathas | 5,735 |
| Gujars | 1,210 |
| Mers | 869 |
| Minas | 503 |
| Bhil | 1,085 |
| Tamils | 3,024 |
| Pariahs | 1,073 |
| Other Hindus | 5,446 |
| *Subtotal* | *49,714* |
| ***Others*** | |
| Christians | 1,867 |
| Jews (including one Parsi)† | 37 |
| Burmans, Karens, Assamese‡ | 161 |
| *Subtotal* | *2,065* |
| ***Total*** | ***152,847*** |

* Includes Indian officers, NCOs, other ranks, and musicians.
† Parsis seldom served in the army.
‡ Karens were an ethnic group that lived in the interior of Burma along the border with Thailand. They normally served in the local Burma military police.[12] 'Assamese' is a term that covers several tribes of hillmen that live in Assam. In the past, some served in the Gurkhas, but now they normally serve only in the Burma and Assam military police.[13]

11 Omissi, *Sepoy*, p.20, Table 1.4.
12 P. D. Bonarjee, A Handbook of the Fighting Races of India (Calcutta: Thacker, Spink, and Company, 1899), pp.208–09.
13 Bonarjee, Handbook, pp.207–08.

### *Jats*

The Jats are found all over Punjab and in parts of Rajputana, Central India, and in Hindustan.[14] The name 'Jat' is almost synonymous with cultivator. They were described by MacMunn as a 'race of cultivators who till the land while the Rajput looks on'.[15]

The Jats practiced widow remarriage, which moved them down the social scale below the Rajputs.

The Jats were felt to be independent, doing what they thought was best at all times and not willing to be told no by any man. They were brave, industrious, and orderly. They were conscientious and painstaking workers with great endurance. For the most part, they were free from troublesome caste rules about the preparation of food. However, those from Eastern Rajputana and Hindustan were pickier about how their food was prepared.[16] They were peculiarly sensitive to perceived abuse or injustice and, unless treated fairly and well, were likely to leave the army. They enlisted for money, not for the love of soldiering. On the other hand, they were more straightforward and less given to intrigue than most other classes in the army.[17] As soldiers, they were considered stolid and have more dogged courage than dash.[18]

The Jats were considered to not be very bright.[19] However, this was considered to vary by the district they lived in.[20]

The Hindu Jats tended to be disliked by other classes, perhaps because of the prosperity their hard work had brought. This resulted in negative feelings about them and a number of negative proverbs.[21] For example, 'A Jat is such a fool that only God can take care of him', and 'Three things are improved by beating: women, wheat and a Jat.'[22]

One unusual custom of the Jats was that they bore a hole in their upper front teeth and placed a small plug of gold in the cavities. The object was to be sure they had gold in their mouths to pay for passage to the next world. Having gold in the mouth also encouraged truthfulness, as it was considered a great sin to lie with gold in one's teeth.[23]

### *Pathans*

The British used the term 'Pathan' to describe the tribes living along the border with Afghanistan. Most, though not all, spoke Pastun. Pastun is spoken by about 40 percent of Afghanistan's people, and these live along the Indian border.[24] All shared a similar lifestyle.

The frontier with Afghanistan was approximately 1,000 miles (1,609km) long, and inside the Indian side, running next to the Punjab, was an area that the British did not try to settle and govern. This strip of land, the Administrative Border, also called the Federally Unadministered Tribal Areas, was a belt of wild and mountainous land, some 400 miles long and about 100

14 Bonarjee, *Handbook*, p.134.
15 G. F. MacMunn, *The Armies of India* (London: Adam and Charles Black, 1911), pp.160–61.
16 R. C. Christie, *Handbooks for the Indian Army: Jats, Gujars, and Ahirs* (Calcutta: Office of the Superintendent, Government Printing, India, 1924), p.52.
17 Christie, *Jats*, p.51.
18 Omissi, *Sepoy*, p.31.
19 MacMunn, *Armies*, p.136.
20 Christie, *Jats*, pp.30, 33.
21 Christie, *Jats*, p.51.
22 Omissi, *Sepoy*, p.26.
23 Christie, *Jats*, p.54.
24 Olaf Caroe, *The Pathans, 550 B.C.–A.D. 1957* (New York: St. Martin's Press, 1959).

miles wide (644km by 161km). This was British territory, but, inside it, British law was not administered.[25]

A great deal has been written about the Pathans and their way. Not only did the army recruit from them, but they were also the people the army fought most often between 1861 and 1947.

The tribes can be divided into the following groups, based on those who live:

A. Along the routes from Khaiber to Kabul
B. Along the routes from Ghuzni to Kabul
C. Along the routes from Kandahar through Baluchistan
D.Within the Administrative Border.

### *A. Khaiber to Kabul Routes*

The main tribes along this route were the Afridi, Orakzai, Bangash, Mullagori, Zaimukt, Chamkani, and Shiah.

### *B. Ghuzni to Kabul Routes*

The main tribes along the Ghuzni route were the Waziris and their two great divisions, the Mahsuds and the Darwesh Khel.

### *C. Kandahar through Baluchistan Routes*

The tribes along this route were the Kakars, Duranis, Sheranis, Khetrans, and Baluchs.

### *D. Administrative Border Area*

The tribes that live within the Administrative Border were the Yusafzais, the Khattaks, and tribes in Hazara.[26]

Each of these tribes were broken down into innumerable subdivisions. Most of the tribes were Sunni Muslims ('of a bigoted sort').[27]

Most of the Pathans who entered the Indian army lived within the British border or in the unadministered belt of land between the Administrated Border and the Afghan frontier. A few men, however, such as those in the Guides and the 124th and 126th Baluchistan Regiments, came from Afghanistan.[28]

The two main characteristics of the Pathans were that they were constantly engaged in blood feuds and were unwilling to recognise the authority of any person or government over them. This made for strong individualism, as every man was on his own and, among those who survived, self-confident.[29]

His personality was one of grim moroseness and sourness of disposition. This, when coupled with his odd code of honour and strong individualism, made him a not very lovable type of human:

25 Philip Mason, *A Matter of Honour* (Austin: Holt, Rinehart and Winston, 1974), p.336.
26 George F. MacMunn, *The Martial Races of India* (London: Low, Marston and Company, 1933), pp.238–39.
27 Bonarjee, *Handbook*, Appendix and p.17.
28 MacMunn, *Armies*, pp.149–50.
29 Bonarjee, *Handbook*, pp.8–9.

The fidelity of the Pathan as a soldier has often been doubted, but in the British service he has usually been a loyal and devoted soldier. It would be absurd to expect a high code of honour among a wild and savage people unaccustomed from time immemorial to loyal adhesion to anything in particular. Treachery, often of a cowardly sort, is therefore a common characteristic among them. The Pathan has no sentimental regard and respect for an ideal standard of right, and although he has a code of conduct known as Pakhtunwali, his actions are generally guided by self-interest without any ethical notions of right entering into them. Robbery and murder are as the breath of his nostrils, and his thieving achievements often display an ingenuity worthy of a better cause.

The true Pathan is perhaps the most barbaric of all the races with which we are brought into contact in the Punjab ... But he is bloodthirsty, cruel, and vindictive in the highest degree; he does not know what truth or faith is ... and though he is not without courage of a sort and is often curiously reckless of his life, he would scorn to face an enemy whom he could stab from behind, or to meet him on equal terms if it were possible to take advantage of him, however meanly ... At the same time he has a code of honour which he strictly observes, and which he quotes with pride under the name of Pakhtunwali. It imposes on him three chief obligations, *Nanawatai*, or the right of asylum, which compels him to shelter and protect even an enemy who comes as a suppliant; *badal*, or the necessity of revenge by retaliation; and *melmastia*, or open-handed hospitality to all who may demand it. And of these three perhaps the last is the greatest. And there is a charm about him, especially about the leading men, which almost makes one forget his treacherous nature. As the proverb says – 'The Pathan is one moment a saint, and the next a devil.' For centuries he has been, on our frontier at least, subject to no man. He leads a wild, free, active life in the rugged fastnesses of his mountains; and there is an air of masculine independence about him which is refreshing in a country like India. He is a bigot of the most fanatical type, exceedingly proud and extraordinarily superstitious.

Such is a Pathan in his home among the fastnesses of the frontier ranges. But the Pathans of our territory have been much softened by our rule and by the agricultural life of the plains, so that they look down upon the Pathans of the hills. The nearer he is to the frontier, the more closely he assimilates to the original type; while on this side of the Indus there is little or nothing, not even language, to distinguish him from his neighbours of the same religion as himself. The Pathans are extraordinarily jealous of female honour, and most of the blood feuds for which they are so famous originate in quarrels about women.[30]

Winston Churchill described their ethics:

Their system of ethics, which regards treachery and violence as virtues rather than vices, had produced a code of honour so strange and inconsistent, that is incomprehensible to a logical mind. I have been told that if a white man could grasp it fully, and were to understand their mental impulses – if he knew, when it was their honour to stand by him, and when it was their honour to betray him; when they were bound to protect and when to kill him – he might, by judging his times and opportunities, pass safely from one end of the mountains to the other.[31]

30 Bonarjee, *Handbook*, pp.9–12.
31 Winston L. S. Churchill, *The Story of the Malakand Field Force: An Episode of Frontier War* (London: Longmans, Green and Co., 1898), p.8.

He went on to say that a civilised European could not accomplish this feat.

Among the Pathans, a truce was called while crops were planted and being harvested, likewise while in British military service. But, when the men who were feuding went on leave, the feud could begin again.

In such a society, a modern rifle was a prized item. The Pathans tried to make copies of the British army rifle by hand, but of course these were not as good as the original item. To obtain them, the Pathans would take all of their clothes and cover themselves with cheetah grease. The grease made it hard to hold onto them if they were discovered. Dogs are afraid of cheetahs, so they would not bark and would stay away from anything that had a cheetah smell. Thus prepared, they would sneak into British camps to steal rifles. If they obtained one, they had a powerful weapon to use in their fights. Or they could sell it. Frank Richards, a British private who served in India, estimated the sale would bring enough to buy a plot of land, build a house, obtain three or four wives, and be comfortably well off.[32]

Richards also described the different steps the British soldiers took to protect their rifles on the march. They would take the bolt out, put it in their kit bag, and then use the bag as a pillow. They would also either (A) sleep with a leg thrust through the sling of the rifle, (B) attach the rifle to the tent poles by lock and chains if they had them, or (C) dig a pit and put their rifles in it with bags on top and have a soldier sleep on top of the filled-in hole. In addition, there were the normal sentries.[33] In permanent stations, the rifles were placed in strong, heavy rifle racks. The lids would hold the rifles in place, and chains would be run through the trigger guards. Yet, on occasion, even these rifles could be stolen.[34]

The fighting against the Pathans was hard, with no quarter being asked for or given.

When the British took the Punjab from the Sikhs, there was no border to say where the Punjab ended and Afghanistan began. The Amir in Kabul had never exercised control over the border tribes. It was only in 1894, with the drawing of the Durand Line, that a border between Afghanistan and India was established. This, in turn, created the official Unadministered Tribal Area. But, long before this, a de facto border had been set by the British, beyond which they did not try to govern the tribes.[35]

The Pathan, for all his many faults, had several redeeming characteristics. He had an air of masculine independence about him, which was refreshing in India,[36] where so many people are sycophantic and servile. They were hardy and strong, inured to fatigue and exposure.[37] Frank Richards, in *Old Soldier Sahib*, noted how the Pathans were tall, strong, and muscular men. This contrasted with the Indians of the plains, who were extremely skinny.[38] They were proud, resolute, and self-reliant. Fearless, they were ready to meet death as well as inflict it. They had dash and élan when they fought.[39] Their passionate nature, which, in the wild, they had never been taught to control, often carried them away, and they were very apt to lose their heads in the excitement of battle. This left them at a disadvantage as compared with

32 Richards, *Old Soldier*, p.97.
33 Richards, *Old Soldier*, pp.97–107.
34 Richards, *Old Soldier*, pp.105–06.
35 Mason, *Honour*, pp.335–36.
36 Bonarjee, *Handbook*, p.12.
37 Bonarjee, *Handbook*, p.31.
38 Richards, *Old Soldier*, p.96.
39 Bonarjee, *Handbook*, p.23.

cooler-headed soldiers, who, though inferior in physique, fought with greater deliberation and cooler courage.[40] Much of this problem was solved by discipline when the Pathans served in the British regiments.

Once they undertook service in the British regiments, there were almost no desertions, despite the fact that the Pathan soldiers were often closely related to the tribesmen being fought.[41] However, there were exceptions. A young Afridi of the Guides, through an unusual series of circumstances, found himself on a dark night near his village with two rifles. He deserted with them. The CO of the Guides summoned 17 men, who were all the men in the regiment who belonged to that subgroup of the Afridis. They were told what happened and to take off their uniforms. They were then sent out to recover the rifles and told not to come back until they had them. It was thought that this mission would take two days. But it was two years before they returned with the rifles. They would not say why it had taken so long or what they had needed to do to take back the rifles.[42]

This record of not deserting was badly broken during the First World War by the Pathans, especially the Afridi, far too freely. This turned the Indian army against these groups, and enlistment from them was rigorously curtailed.[43] George MacMunn offered a possible explanation for this change in desertion rates. Different tribal groups and subgroups, for ease of management, were concentrated into certain companies within a regiment. In the First World War, it was common for whole companies to be almost totally wiped out in heavy fighting. This would leave the subgroup at a disadvantage in intertribal wars back home. With fewer men, the tribal group could lose their grazing grounds and water rights.[44] The logical answer was to leave the army so that they could maintain their tribal numbers.

Most of the Pathans had a sly sense of humour, which has been called their saving grace.[45] Humour was unusual for India. The only other group that seemed to have it was the Gurkhas. There were occasions when Pathans who had served in the British army while fighting the British would signal back that the British they were now fighting were firing too low and needed to raise their sights. It was just like he was back on an army rifle range.[46] It is said that the same thing happened when artillery fire was off target.[47] Pathans would often wear their British medals to peace talks.[48] At night, British troops could hear British army bugle calls being blown from Pathan territory, doubtlessly being done by Pathan ex-servicemen. While both sides tried their best to kill each other when the fighting was on, when it ended, there was no malice on either side.[49] It was almost like a game of cricket.

In 1908, the British sent out the Bazar Valley Field Force on a typical frontier field operation. There is a story that, after the fighting was over, the men of the Zakka Khel, a clan of the Afridis, crowded around their political agent and asked, 'Did we fight well?' The agent said, 'I

40 Bonarjee, *Handbook*, p.9.
41 Mason, *Honour*, p.338.
42 Mason, *Honour*, pp.338–39.
43 MacMunn, *Martial*, pp.245–46.
44 MacMunn, *Martial*, p.245, footnote 1.
45 MacMunn, *Martial*, p.242.
46 Mason, *Honour*, p.338.
47 MacMunn, *Martial*, pp.240–42.
48 MacMunn, *Martial*, p.242.
49 Mason, *Honour*, p.337.

wouldn't have shaken hands with you if you hadn't.'[50] Both sides admired the same things: most of all, courage; loyalty to the side you happened to be on; and personal honour.[51]

The Pathans delighted in exercise and sport, which appealed to the British.[52] On the other hand, if a British or Indian soldier fell into the hands of the Pathans, their women would torture him to death. Kipling had advice here, as he so often did. Rather than be tortured by the women, it was best for the man to kill himself and go to his God like a soldier.[53] Given these hard facts, the British made every effort to never leave a wounded man behind. If necessary, counterattacks were mounted to get the wounded man back.[54]

It took a special type of officer to lead the Pathans with their mix of reckless courage, strong individualism, theft, stab-in-the-back treachery, and general disrespect for right and wrong. Their leaders needed to be the Pathan's ideal man – strong, resolute, fearless, inflexible, just, brave, and endowed with a stern integrity of purpose.[55] No by-the-book, spit-shine officer could do it. It is no wonder that the British officers, who led and fought the Pathans, thought themselves to be the *elite* of the army.

### *Baluchis*

Baluchistan was the frontier area of the Bombay Presidency. It was located in the bottom south-east corner of India, bounded by Afghanistan on the north, Persia on the west, the Arabian Sea on the south, and Sind and Punjab on the east. It was generally hilly with some mountains, but the mountains were nowhere near as high as those in the Pathan homeland. In general, the area was rugged and lacked water.[56]

There were two main groups of people that lived in the area: the Baluchis and the Brahuis. The Baluchis were in control of most of the area, but the Brahuis had dominance over the province of Khelat. Both were mainly nomad pastoralists.[57] The Baluchs were tall and had oval features, while the Brahuis were thickset, were muscular, had flat features, and were comparatively short in stature.[58]

The Baluchis spoke a Persian dialect, the Brahuis one that had either an Indian or Persian affinity.[59] Some of the men had an Asian slant to their eyes. This was likely inherited from Mongol troops that were stationed for a long time in Persia in the late Middle Ages following the Mamluk defeat of a large Mongol advance party in 1260.

The Baluchs and the Pathans lived in similar conditions next to each other, so it is natural when describing the Baluchs to refer to the better-known Pathans. The Baluchs were manly, frank, brave, strong, and inured to hardship and exposure. They were not as brutal or treacherous as the Pathans, and they had a better reputation for truth and fidelity. They were independent

50 Mason, *Honour*, p.338.
51 Mason, *Honour*, p.337.
52 MacMunn, *Armies*, p.148.
53 Rudyard Kipling, 'The Young British Soldier', in *Rudyard Kipling's Verse* (London: Hodder and Stoughton, 1921), p.474.
54 Allen, *Plain Tales*, p.207.
55 Bonarjee, *Handbook*, p.10.
56 Bonarjee, *Handbook*, pp.39–40.
57 Bonarjee, *Handbook*, pp.41, 46.
58 Bonarjee, *Handbook*, pp.41–42.
59 Bonarjee, *Handbook*, pp.41–42.

but respectful and had contempt for the sycophancy often found among the people of India. They were fairly faithful to their word. As a whole, they were expert horse and camel breeders.

On the other hand, the Baluchs had their faults. They had a cruel and bloodthirsty nature. The Baluchs had a strong tendency to engage in quarrels. They were thieves and took pride in it. At the same time, they were greatly averse to manual labour and were lazy and lacking in industry. They had dirty personal habits and a fondness for gambling, opium, and hemp.[60]

The issue of the nature of the Baluchs was a bit academic, as few of them enlisted. To see this in action, one needs to merely examine the class makeup of the Bombay frontier regiments: the 36th Jacob's Horse and the 37th Lancers (Baluch Horse). Both have maybe one squadron of Baluchis.

The same is true of the so-called 'Baluch and Baluchistan' infantry regiments. Of the five Baluchistan and Brahuis regiments, the 124th, 126th, 127th, 129th, and 130th, only one, the 126th, had companies of Baluchis and Brahuis. And there were only two out of the eight.

### *Punjabi Muslims*

The Punjabi Muslims (or 'PMs' as the army referred to them) were divided into four main groups: Sheikh, Sayad, Mogul, and Pathan. Sheikh, which means 'lord', was a euphemism for the Hindus, mostly low-caste and untouchables, who became Muslims. Sayad were the descendants of the original Arab invaders. Many more claimed this descent than actually had it because of the status it had within the Muslim community. Mogul was the name of the different Turks, Tartars, and Mongol peoples who invaded India at one time or another and then settled down.[61] Pathans were the speakers of Pastun who had come into India as part of different invading armies and had been given land for their services. Once on the land, they lost the wild ways of the Pathans in the mountains. Each of these groups was broken down into many different tribes and clans.

Under the martial-races system, the PM was one of the mainstays of the army. Army service was a prestigious, well-paying profession, and there was generally a strong interest in serving.[62] Each class regiment and class company, by army regulations or regimental rules and customs, had certain tribes and clans it could enlist. This could be very detailed. Consider the example of the 20th Punjabis in 1912. Despite its name, half of it – four companies, B, C, F, and G – consisted of Pathans. The companies were divided into four sections of at least 16 men. The sections were each staffed by men from a different clan and never mixed. This took advantage of clan spirit. Companies B and G had Afridis. Company B had four sections staffed by Adam Khel, Malikdin Khel, Kuki Khel, and Zakka Khel Afridis in their own exclusive sections. Pathans were in Company F. As noted above, the Khattak tribe lived within the tribal Administrative Border. Two sections consisted of Sagri Khattaks, a clan of that tribe. The other two sections had Bangi Khel and Barak Khel Pathans.[63] This was an example of a system that was followed with PMs and throughout the Indian army.

60 Bonarjee, *Handbook*, pp.47–49.
61 MacMunn, *Martial*, pp.16–17.
62 MacMunn, *Armies*, p.142.
63 Roy, *Brown Warriors*, p.214.

The Indian army handbook for Punjab Muslims (1915 edition) lists 93 different PM tribes and classes.[64] Some were small, under 500 males; a few were in the 100,000 range. Within these groups, men from some districts or locales would be taken, and men from other locales would not.

**Table 28 Punjab Muslim Tribes Supplying Soldiers to the British Indian Army, c. 1911[65]**

| Male Population | Number of Tribes | Percentage of Tribes |
|---|---|---|
| Unknown | 9 | 9.68% |
| Under 500 | 5 | 5.38% |
| 501–1,500 | 8 | 8.60% |
| 1,501–2,500 | 10 | 10.75% |
| 2,501–5,000 | 16 | 17.20% |
| 5,001–7,500 | 5 | 5.38% |
| 7,501–10,000 | 7 | 7.53% |
| Over 10,000 | 33 | 35.48% |
| **Total** | **93** | **100.00%** |

**Table 29 Punjab Muslim Tribes with a Male Population Over 10,000**

| Tribe | Male Population |
|---|---|
| Awan | 227,000 |
| Bhatti | 180,650 (Rajput – 159,900; Jat – 20,750) |
| Baluch | 500,000 |
| Chauhan | 35,500 |
| Chaddar | 10,300 (Rajput – 1,800; Jat – 8,500) |
| Chib | 10,800 |
| Dhund | 36,800 (in British territory – 29,000; in Kashmir – 7,800) |
| Dogar | 30,000 |
| Gakkhar | 23,900 (in British territory – 17,200; in Jammu and Kashmir – 6,700) |
| Gondal | 19,000 |
| Ghorewaha | 16,230 |
| Gujars | 310,300 (in Punjab – 242,600; in Northwest Frontier Province – 67,700) |
| Janjua | 12,000 |
| Joiya | 18,595 |
| Kahlon | 13,000 |
| Karral | 11,300 |
| Kharral | 18,650 |
| Khokhar | 32,600 (Jats – 12,000) |
| Koreshi | 50,000+ |
| Kambohs | 98,480 (Muslims – 39,280; Hindus – 19,900; Sikhs – 39,300) |
| Malik | 29,000 |

64 J. M. Wikeley, *Handbooks for the Indian Army: Punjabi Musalmans* (Calcutta: Office of the Superintendent, Government Printing, India, 1915), pp.49–110.
65 Wikeley, *Punjabi*, pp.49–110.

| Tribe | Male Population |
|---|---|
| Moghal | 100,000+ |
| Naru | 12,000 |
| Panwar | 30,000 |
| Sayad | 250,000+ |
| Salehria | 12,000–14,000 |
| Sheikh | 187,370 |
| Sial | 50,000 |
| Sudhan | 28,200 |
| Tanaoli | 33,350 (in Feudal Tanawal – 19,000) |
| Varaich | 40,000 |
| Virk | 10,650 (Sikh – 8,145) |
| Wattu | 12,250 |

**Table 30 Size of Contingents from Punjab Muslim Tribes**

| Size of Contingent | Number of Tribes | Percentage of Tribes |
|---|---|---|
| Unknown | 24 | 25.81% |
| 0 | 10 | 10.75% |
| 1–100 | 19 | 20.43% |
| 101–200 | 12 | 12.90% |
| 201–300 | 9 | 9.68% |
| 301–400 | 2 | 2.15% |
| 401–500 | 2 | 2.15% |
| 501–600 | 2 | 2.15% |
| 601–700 | 2 | 2.15% |
| Over 700 | 11 | 11.83% |
| **Total** | **93** | **100.00%** |

**Table 31 Punjab Muslim Tribes with a Contingent Over 700**

| Tribe | Contingent Number |
|---|---|
| Awan | 8,146 |
| Bhatti | 2,000 |
| Baluch | 2,400 (half of which are in the Camel Corps) |
| Dhund | 787 |
| Gakkhar | 2,255 |
| Gujars | 1,600 |
| Janjua | 1,100 or more |
| Moghal | 1,743 |
| Sayad | 896 |
| Satti | 1,689 |
| Sudhan | 1,280 |

**Table 32 Foreign Tribes**

| Foreign Tribe | **Size of Foreign Tribe** | **Number of Men Supplied to Army by Tribe** |
|---|---|---|
| Gakkhar*† | 23,900 (in British territory –17,200; in Jammut and Kashmir – 6,700) | 2,255 |
| Awan* | 227,000 | 8,146 |
| Turk‡ | 1,750 | 50 |
| Moghal‡ | 100,000+ | 1,743 |
| Sayad§ | 250,000+ | 896 |
| Koreshi§ | 50,000+ | 280 |
| Sheikh** | 187,370 | 490 |

* Claim to have come with Mahmud of Ghazni.
† Claim Persian origin.
‡ Timur and Babar brought the Turks and Moghuls with them.
§ Of Arabic origin.
** Includes miscellaneous converts. Originally, 'Sheikh' was a title of respect originally applied to the Arab spiritual guides.

With so many different tribes and subgroups and only certain clans being accepted, it was hard for the men of a recruiting party to know what type of man they were dealing with. Army service had sufficient pay and high enough prestige that, to get in, people would try to pass themselves off as belonging to groups and clans that they did not belong to. Great care was taken to ensure that volunteers were really what they claimed to be. The early handbooks had questions the recruiter could ask on the spot to weed out imposters. In addition, should the guarantee of Indian officers in the regiment or other reliable evidence as to the inductee's tribal status not be available, inquiries were sent to the proper civil authorities.[66]

When dealing with the characteristics of PMs, perhaps because they were closer or more familiar, writers normally described them tribe by tribe. However, these did not vary much from group to group. Some were thought to be more quarrelsome than others. Almost all were described as having either a good physique or as being big and strong, or words like that. Most were said to have soldiering instincts, pride in their race and its history, or both. Most were said to be well-behaved and law-abiding. Many were viewed as industrious and hardworking (Gujars, depending on locale; Ahirs, Khokars, and so on). Others were troublemakers (Gujars, Gondals, and Kharrals – cattle thieves). Some were just idle and lazy (Gujars – depending on locale).[67]

All the PM groups had two things in common: illiteracy and a rural background. The male literacy rate among Muslims in the Punjab was low. In 1891, it was 53 per 1,000. The rate for all of India was 87 per 1,000. But it was worse than that. Among the rural Muslims of Eastern Punjab and Hindustan, scarcely one in 1,000 could sign his own name.[68] There is no reason to think the rate would be any different among the PMs who were cultivators.

66 MacMunn, *Armies*, p.142.
67 Bonarjee, *Handbook*, pp.51–62.
68 W. F. G. Bourne, *Handbooks for the Indian Army: Hindustani Musalmans and Musalmans of the Eastern Punjab* (Calcutta: Office of the Superintendent, Government Printing, India, 1914), p.25.

The recruiters took almost no one from the larger population centres, where education was more common. Roberts felt that the education of the Indians was a danger to the Raj. The educated middle class was seen as corrupted by city life's many temptations and softened by the long period of peace under British rule.[69] In general, this was a repeat of British feelings about British recruits in the home islands. The army would prefer to have recruits from rural areas than worldly wise men from the cities. The problem was that, in the home islands, the rural men had mostly disappeared.

### *Hindustani and Eastern Punjabi Muslims*

When the different Muslim conquerors were invading and settling India and the native people were converting to the Prophet's faith, these men had no idea of the administrative borders that the Sikhs and the Honourable EIC would later establish. Because of this, the Muslims found themselves living in two different recruitment areas and having two different histories, in spite of being essentially the same people. The Muslims of the Eastern Punjab and Hindustan (Oudh, Agra, and Behar) were part of the old Bengal army that mutinied. Most of the regiments, Hindu and Muslim soldiers alike, were disbanded. But a few loyal regiments survived, and, by 1914, the army was using Hindustani and Eastern Punjabi Muslims (abbreviated as 'H&EPM' in documents) in some class regiments and in some class squadrons and companies. Examples of regiments that, in theory, drew on H&EPM men were the 1st (Skinner's) Lancers and class squadrons in some cavalry regiments, which included the 1st through 8th Cavalry.[70] In 1900, the following Frontier Force and Central India regiments were allowed to start recruiting H&EPM personnel: the 21st, 22nd (1/2 squadron), 23rd, 25th, 38th, and 39th. The 30th Lancers (HM) of the old Hyderabad Contingent added this recruiting area in 1896. The last four cavalry regiments drew from Hindustani Muslims (HM) and not Muslims of the Eastern Punjab.[71]

In the infantry, examples of class regiments made up of H&EPM personnel in 1914 were the 5th, 17th, and 18th Regiments. In addition, the following infantry regiments had class companies drawn from the HM only: the 91st (Madras), 95th, 96th, 98th, and 99th (the last four of the old Hyderabad Contingent). Of the regiments of the old Bombay, the following regiments had HM class companies: the 119th, 120th, and 122nd.[72] These HM companies were added as the martial-races theory took a stronger hold. In regiments with high numbers that originally drew their personnel from the south, southern soldiers were replaced with more martial northerners. The H&EPM men did not, by definition, live in the Punjab, which was becoming the Mecca for recruiting. However, in their case, just being from the colder northern climates was qualification enough.

The handbook for H&EPM shows the type of men the army was looking for. 'The Musalmans of this district are all city-dwellers and unfit for enlistment.'[73] 'These [divisions] being all in the hills, there are Muslims in this division fit for enlistment.'[74] To repeat, the British wanted men who owned and worked the land. 'The Muslims of this district are mostly city-dwellers and

69 Omissi, *Sepoy*, p.28.
70 Bourne, *Hindustani*, p.105.
71 Bourne, *Hindustani*, p.105.
72 Bourne, *Hindustani*, pp.105–06; War Office [WO], *The Quarterly Indian Army List, July 1914* (Calcutta: Superintendent Government Printing, 1914).
73 Bourne, *Hindustani*, p.81.
74 Bourne, *Hindustani*, p.81.

Hindu converts. There are none fit for enlistment.'[75] 'City-dwellers should be avoided as they are an undesirable class and generally of bad character.'[76]

Being an early handbook, the handbook on H&EPM gave British recruiters stock questions to weed out men trying to pass themselves off as members of a class the army or regiment in question was willing to take.[77] As the army came to rely on a group of specialised recruiters for each class, these field tests became unnecessary and were removed from the handbooks.

Having somewhat less ground to cover, the H&EPM handbook could be more detailed about the Muslim classes and clans in these areas. But, by and large, the information given was the same as that set out in the handbook for Punjab Muslims.[78]

### *Sikhs*

The Sikhs were the mainstay of the British Indian army. In 1914, they consisted of 16.6 percent of the companies of the army, the largest of the Indian native groups. The Sikhs were mostly found in the Punjab. In the 1920s, Muslims were about one-half of the Punjab's population, Hindus were 36 percent, and the Sikhs about 12 percent.[79] More than two-thirds were Jats.[80] The army took most of its Sikh soldiers from among the Sikh Jats. The other main groups were Mazbhis and Ramdasia Sikhs, who went into pioneer battalions.[81] But there were also Brahmin Sikhs from the Mujhal, a clan that were cultivators,[82] and Sikhs from the Khatris from the business classes who had been enlisted because of their brains.[83] The Jhinwar class of carriers, watermen, and household servants served in hospitals since all the other classes would take food and other items from them.[84] Both the Brahmins and the Khatris were presumably needed to perform regimental bookkeeping.

The Khatris were the class that supplied almost all Sikh priests. Two of its clans supplied the Guru Nanak, the founder of Sikhism (a Bedi), and the remaining Gurus from Ram Das onwards were of the Khatris' Sodhis clan.[85] But their main occupation was commerce, though many farmed their own land. The Khatris monopolised the trade between Afghanistan and Punjab. In addition, in the Punjab, civil administrators and village clerical work of keeping accounts, banking, and dealing in gains were largely in their hands.[86] The great majority of the Khatris class were staunch Hindus.[87] With this clerical background, was it any wonder that the Sikh regiments would seek Sikh Khatris to keep regimental records, especially since the Jats, who supplied most of the men to the regiments, were considered blockheaded and were mostly illiterate? In 1901, in the Punjab (including the Northwest Frontier), 64 out of every 1,000

75 Bourne, *Hindustani*, p.81.
76 Bourne, *Hindustani*, p.103, footnote.
77 Bourne, *Hindustani*, pp.34–35.
78 Wikeley, *Punjabi*.
79 A. E. Barstow, *Handbooks for the Indian Army: Sikhs* (Calcutta: Office of the Superintendent, Government Printing, India, 1928), p.3.
80 Barstow, *Sikhs*, p.62.
81 Barstow, *Sikhs*, p.72; WO, *July 1914*, pp.491, 500, 502.
82 Barstow, *Sikhs*, p.73.
83 MacMunn, *Armies*, p.136.
84 Barstow, *Sikhs*, p.81.
85 Barstow, *Sikhs*, p.75.
86 Barstow, *Sikhs*, pp.73–74.
87 Barstow, *Sikhs*, p.74.

people could read and write.[88] This number included people living in the cities who were never recruited. The rural rate would be lower. One report states that most Jats, the main group that made up the Sikh intake, were quite illiterate.[89]

The Sikh soldier displayed cool, quiet, resolute courage and was able to keep himself unexcited in times of difficulty and danger. His religion had freed him from 'the religious prejudices of the Hindu... and the fanaticism of the Mohomedan... He is far less blinded by religious intolerance than either, and in most things is a level-headed, sober minded man with keen practical instincts'. He was much less liable to sudden panic than the Pathan. But he may not have had the dash and élan of the Pathan in the latter's most warlike mood.[90] The Sikh could be very vain about his appearance. With his splendid physique and full, tied-up beard, he was a good-looking soldier, and he knew it. He would often walk around showing off his good looks, and, sometimes, he would get into fights with others whose public preening was felt to be a challenge.[91] MacMunn felt the Sikhs had the slow and dogged courage of the English and Jats, whereas the Pathans were more irresponsible.[92]

The Sikhs are not a caste or tribe. Rather, they are a religious group. The Sikh religion was founded by a man named Nanak (1469–1538 or 1539) in the Lahore District. His new religion was a blend of the Hindu and Muslim faiths. He held that there was only one God, not the many found in Hinduism. He taught the spiritual and religious equality of all men and that Hindus and Muslims were alike in the eyes of the one God. Therefore, they should live in peace. In many ways, it was a reformed Hinduism. This peaceful religion ran its course until the fifth Guru, Arjan, assumed office in 1581. He made many beneficial improvements, but he also got involved in Mogul politics by helping a prince in his rebellion against his ruling father. For this, he was imprisoned after the rebellion failed, and there he died. The following Gurus also involved the Sikhs in court politics, and this brought brutal retaliations against them.[93] The ninth Guru, Tegh (or Teg) Bahadur (Guru 1664–1675), was captured by the Moguls, and he and many of his followers were put to a cruel death.[94]

During the period from Arjan (Guru 1581–1606) to Tegh Bahadur (Guru 1664–1675), the Sikh doctrine of equality of all men caused men of the lower Hindu castes to convert. However, a large number of Jats, Khattris, and some Rajputs also converted, drawn by the merits of the new religion.[95]

The tenth Guru was Govind Rai (Guru 1675–1708). He was the son of Tegh Bahadur and the last, and, most say, the greatest, Guru. He was the person who changed the Sikhs into a military religion. He was 15 years old at the time of his father's death, and, for several years, Govind Rai was inactive.

When he did begin to act, he preached that war, especially against the Muslims, was the first duty of a Sikh. He gave the title 'Khalsa' (pure or elect) to those who elected to follow his new doctrines.[96]

88 Omissi, *Sepoy*, p.27.
89 Omissi, *Sepoy*, p.27.
90 Bonarjee, *Handbook*, p.78.
91 Allen, *Plain Tales*, p.242.
92 Roy, *Brown Warriors*, p.85.
93 Bonarjee, *Handbook*, pp.63–70.
94 Bonarjee, *Handbook*, p.70.
95 Bonarjee, *Handbook*, pp.70–71.
96 Bonarjee, *Handbook*, pp.71–73; Barstow, *Sikhs*, pp.8–9.

Admission to the Khalsa was gained by a ceremony called the 'pahul' (gate or way of entrance). Part of the pahul consisted of drinking, in the presence of five believers, a mixture of sugar and water, which was stirred together by a steel dagger. The new member would also agree to the wearing of five 'K's: (1) Kes: uncut hair; (2) Kachh: shorts; (3) Kara: iron bangle (usually worn on the right wrist); (4) Xirpan: steel dagger or sword; and (5) Kanga: comb in hair. The members of the Khalsa were to add the title 'Singh' (lion) to their names. Thus, Govind Rai became Govind Singh, and this is the name he carries in history.[97]

Govind Singh also issued a prohibition against the use of tobacco, but the Sikhs freely drank liquor, and some took opium.[98]

Opium was extensively grown in upper India for years. So obtaining opium was not a problem despite British efforts to keep the Indian population from using it.

### *Low-Caste Sikhs*

As noted above, within Sikhism, there are several recognised groups. One is the Mazbhi. The word means 'faithful'. This group was formed when three outcaste sweepers went to rescue the broken body of Guru Tegh Bahadur, who had been killed in Delhi. When the three returned the body to his son, Guru Govind Singh, he baptised them into the Sikh faith. Later, when Muslims were forced to become Sikhs, they were given the Mazbhi classification. They served in the Sikhs' Khalsa army. When the British conquered the Punjab, the Mazbhis degenerated into a criminal class of robbers and dacoits. During the Mutiny, to get them out of the Punjab and because, when the British marched back into Hindustan, they likely could not employ local men, the British raised pioneer regiments from among the Mazbhis. The Mazbhis did so well that Mazbhi pioneer regiments were retained in the reformed Bengal army. They continued to be enlisted until 1914. The Mazbhi population was 21,500 in 1911.[99] The retrained regiments in 1861 were the 27th and 36th Bengal Native Infantry (in 1914, the 23rd and 32nd Sikh Pioneers, respectively).[100] After being disbanded in 1933, they were re-raised during the Second World War. The modern Indian army has a Mazbhi and Ramdassia regiment called the 'Sikh Light Infantry'.[101]

The old Sikh pioneer regiments also contained men from the Ramdasia class of Sikhs. These men were the descendants of a low-status outcaste group. Most of them, under the sway of religious leaders of low-caste origin, gave up their old occupations and cut ties to their old groups on conversion. Most of the Ramdasias became weavers. But the ones taken into the army were mostly field labourers in a few districts.[102] The Sikh handbook says, 'They have proved good soldiers in spite of their lowly origin, but are seldom of robust physique.'[103]

97 Heather Streets, *Martial Races: The Military, Race and Masculinity in British Imperial Culture, 1857–1914* (Manchester: Manchester University Press, 2004), pp.63–64; Barstow, *Sikhs*, p.8.
98 Barstow, *Sikhs*, p.174.
99 Barstow, *Sikhs*, pp.82–83.
100 Perry, *Order Part 1*, pp.130–31.
101 John Gaylor, *Sons of John Company: The Indian and Pakistan Armies, 1903–91* (Gloucestershire: Spellmount, 1992), pp.128, 278.
102 Barstow, *Sikhs*, p.81.
103 Barstow, *Sikhs*, pp.81–82.

The Sikhs were considered by many to be the best soldiers in Asia.[104] He was independent without being insolent, resolute, and firm in character, and he was free of the petty bias so often found in India. He had a splendid physique.[105] As a soldier, the Sikh had a cool, quiet, and resolute courage. As noted above, he was less likely to lose his head and panic in battle, but he did not have the dash and élan of the Pathans.[106] He was slow to feel beaten. He was hardy and not bound by the caste rules, which made so many Hindu classes difficult to control and feed in the field. It was part of his creed to never turn his back on his enemy, and he was more faithful and trustworthy than the Pathan. A Sikh was said to be at his best in the infantry. He could, with training, become an excellent cavalryman, but he did not have the natural touch for cavalry found in other classes. He knew his value and had a high opinion of his own military worth.[107]

There were good areas for recruiting Jat Sikhs and some bad ones. For example, the Sikh handbooks within the Ferozepore District of the Eastern Punjab ranked two subdistricts very differently. The Ferozepore subdistrict was rated 'very good', while the Faziika was 'bad' as of 1911. The Rawalpindi District in the Punjab was rated as 'Nix', that is, not worth bothering with. The reason given was that the Khatri class predominated in this area ('Tehsil'),[108] where Sikhs were found.

### *Gurkhas*

While the Sikhs had their aficionados who felt they were the best soldiers in Asia, there were just as many, if not more, who would award this title to the Gurkhas. The Gurkhas come from the small mountain Kingdom of Nepal. Nepal is slightly larger than England, about 520 miles long and roughly 100 miles wide (837km by 161km),[109] although this width can vary anywhere from 90 to 140 miles (145 to 225km) at some points.[110] In addition, the Gurkhas seem to have been the British soldiers' favourite Indian soldier because of his cheerful and outgoing disposition. The Gurkhas seemed to be one of the few Indian soldiers to deal with the British man to man and joke with them even though they could not speak each other's language. They would even joke with their regimental officers. They were also the bravest of the brave.

The term 'Gurkha' comes from the name of the family that ruled Nepal. They were first the rulers of the minor city state of Gurkha, which was about 25 miles (40.23km) northwest of Katmandu.[111] The city was captured in 1559 by a *coup de main* against the old ruler while he was in Durbar.[112]

In 1749, Prithwi Narayan, who had become king in 1742 at age 12, began his conquest of the central Katmandu (also called Nepal) Valley. The conquest was marked by defeats as well as victories. Treachery helped the Gurkhas capture many towns, and the Gurkhas exhibited great brutality following all of their triumphs.

104 Barstow, *Sikhs*, p.169.
105 Bonarjee, *Handbook*, p.79.
106 Bonarjee, *Handbook*, p.78.
107 Barstow, *Sikhs*, p.170.
108 Barstow, *Sikhs*, pp.215, 220. The handbook at pp.215–21 rates every subdistrict.
109 Byron Farwell, *The Gurkhas* (New York: W. W. Norton and Company, 1984), p.23.
110 E. Vansittart, *Handbooks for the Indian Army: Gurkhas* (revised by B. V. Nicolay, Calcutta: Office of the Superintendent, Government Printing, India, 1915), p.1.
111 Farwell, *Gurkhas*, p.12.
112 Vansittart, *Gurkhas*, p.26.

In 1768, Prithwi Narayan and his Gurkhas entered Katmandu by treachery. The last valley town, Bhatgaon, was taken via treachery in 1769.[113] The conquest of the Valley of Nepal from the first siege, Kirtipur, in 1765 to the taking of Bhatgaon in 1769 took four years.[114]

Prithwi Narayan made Katmandu the new capital. He died in 1775 after spending the remainder of his life after the fall of Bhatgaon waging war to expand his kingdom.[115] His heirs continued the same expansionist policy. During the period 1775–1794, through a series of wars, the Gurkhas expanded their kingdom to the east and west. In 1793, they conquered Kumaon and, then in 1794, Garhwal. At this point, the kingdom extended from Bhutan to Kashmir and from Tibet to British India.[116] Bhutan is a small eastern Himalayan kingdom, one-third the size of Nepal,[117] located below Tibet and above the Indian states of West Bengal and Assam.

In 1792, a commercial treaty between the Gurkhas and the EIC was signed, and a mission was sent to Nepal. The mission was withdrawn in 1793 when it became clear that the Gurkhas were not interested in a closer alliance. In 1801, another treaty was signed, and a British resident was sent to the Gurkha court. Because of the Gurkhas' political conduct and their failure to meet their treaty duties, the resident was pulled out in 1803, and the treaty dissolved in 1804.[118]

The Gurkhas, after their conquest of Garhwal, did not lose their expansionist spirit. Between 1804 and 1814, they began encroachments on company territories in Northern India. This led to the British declaring war on them in 1814.[119]

The EIC army sent troops into Nepal in 1814, 1815, and 1816. It was only the last effort that experienced success and overcame the Gurkha army. The resulting peace treaty forced the Gurkhas to take back a company resident, gave the company the right to recruit Nepalese, and Nepal gave up large blocks of land, chief among them the provinces of Kumaon and Garhwal.[120] All in all, Nepal lost about one-third of its territory, mostly in the lowlands next to British India.[121] They also gave up some hill districts, one of which would become Silma in later years. The peace treaty was silent on recruiting. This right seems to have come from a local treaty with a Nepalese army commander.[122]

The Anglo-Nepal War was said to be one of the few wars that left each side with an increased respect for the other. Recruitment of Gurkhas to company service began even before a peace treaty was signed.[123] This was an irregular battalion and consisted mostly of men from Garhwal, Kumaon, and other men from India who looked like Gurkhas.[124] They deserted as soon as they encountered their former brothers-in-arms, a pucka Gurkha regiment. This left a young officer, Frederick Young, to be captured. When asked why he had not run away with his men, Young

113 Vansittart, *Gurkhas*, pp.27–29.
114 Vansittart, *Gurkhas*, p.30.
115 Vansittart, *Gurkhas*, p.30.
116 Vansittart, *Gurkhas*, pp.30–32.
117 Gladys D. Clewell and Holland Thompson (eds), *Lands and People: The World in Color* (New York: Grolier Society, 1947), vol. 4, p.148.
118 Vansittart, *Gurkhas*, p.32.
119 Vansittart, *Gurkhas*, pp.32–33.
120 Farwell, *Gurkhas*, pp.29–31.
121 Lionel Caplan, *Warrior Gentlemen: 'Gurkhas' in the Western Imagination* (Oxford: Berghahn Books, 1995), p.17.
122 Caplan, *Warrior*, p.19.
123 Mason, *Honour*, p.137.
124 Farwell, *Gurkhas*, p.32.

claimed that he had not come so far in to run away. This bit of bravado pleased the Gurkhas, who are reported to have said, 'We could serve under men like you.' Soon, Young was going among Gurkha POWs looking for recruits for a new unit the company had authorised in 1815. Young gleefully wrote, 'I went there one man and came out 3,000.' From these volunteers, he raised what would be two battalions (later merged into one) at Sirmoor. He became their first commandant. These units lived on in 1914 as the 2nd King Edward's Own Gurkha Rifles (the Sirmoor Regiment).[125]

Two additional battalions, called the 'Nasiri' (friendly), were raised from prisoners captured after the fall of the Nepalese fortress of Malaun at Subathu in the Simla Hills. These were merged into one battalion called the 'Nasiri Battalion' in 1826. In 1850, they went into the Bengal line as the 66th Infantry. In 1861, the battalion was made part of a separate Gurkha force. In 1914, its name was the 1st King George's Own Gurkha Rifles (the Malaun Regiments).

A third battalion was raised at Almora in Kumaon in 1815, mostly from men of the Gorakhpur Hill Regiment. It had the name 'Kumaon Battalion'. In 1864, it became part of the separate Gurkha force. By 1914, it had the name '3rd Queen Alexandra's Own Gurkha Rifles'.[126]

The Gurkha soldiers did not lack self-confidence. The Sirmoor Battalion and the Nasir Battalions (later the 2nd and 1st Gurkha Regiments) took part in the 1826 siege of Bhurtpore. After the siege, the Gurkhas said the English soldiers were good fighters and very brave. They were 'very nearly the equal to us'.[127]

### *Gurkha Ethnic Groups*

The Indian army lists, which are so careful to list the exact ethnic composition of each Indian regiment, merely list 'Gurkha' for the 20 different battalions that served in the Indian army. However, in reality, Nepal contains a large number of different ethnic groups. The British recruited only some of them. The British were not allowed to recruit from the central Kathmandu Valley. That was reserved for the Nepalese army, and, to be sure, the central valley had a proper labour pool.[128]

### *Gurkha: Magars and Gurungs*

These two ethnic groups were, by common consent, recognised as the ideal of what a Gurkha soldier should be. They lived just to the west of the central Kathmandu Valley.[129]

The Gurungs were of the Tartar (Mongol) race and were farmers on a small scale. They were square-built, muscular, short men with large chests and limbs. The Gurkha handbook states they were merry-hearted, ate animal food (meat), and drank any type of liquor. They were intensely fond of soldiering. (Recruits would drill each other in their free hours to improve faster.) They were quite hardy and very simple-minded, as well as kind-hearted and generous. As recruits, they were absolutely truthful.

125 Farwell, *Gurkhas*, pp.32–33.
126 Farwell, *Gurkhas*, p.33; R. J. Marrion and D. S. V. Fosten, *The Tradition Book of the Gurkhas* (London: Belmont-Maitland, 1973), pp.5, 11, 16.
127 Farwell, *Gurkhas*, p.35.
128 Caplan, *Warrior*, pp.95–96.
129 E. D. Smith, *Valour: A History of the Gurkhas* (Gloucestershire: Spellmount, 1997), p.13, map of the location of different ethnic groups.

The Gurungs were said to be very obstinate and independent. They were very vain but, out of uniform, tended to be dirty. They were intensely loyal to their friends and officers.[130]

The other Gurkha class that was considered 'ideal' was the Magars. They also lived in central Nepal, generally farther to the west and south from the central Kathmandu Valley than the Gurungs.[131] However, the Magars and Gurungs could be found all over Nepal and thus in eastern Nepal. The Gurkha handbook opines that the eastern Magar and Gurung were less desirable as recruits, and it was the eastern classes that were being recruited.[132]

The Gurungs were so similar in build and character that the Gurkha handbook sees no need to cover these elements when dealing with the Gurkhas. On the other hand, the handbook is careful to point out which of the six Magar tribes and clans should be enlisted.[133]

### *Gurkha: Newars*[134]

The Newars made their home in the central Kathmandu Valley, and they were not a military race. For these reasons, few Newars were ever found in the Gurkha regiments. Newars were seldomly listed separately in counts of Nepalese serving in the Indian army. They were lumped with other groups under 'Other'. But they occasionally produced good soldiers.

A Subadar Newar of the 5th Gurkhas won three Order of Merits during the Kabul War (1842). He was given a clasp to the medal in 1888 for gallantry in the Black Mountains. This medal was the highest award for bravery an Indian soldier could win during these periods. As of 1899, one author stated that Newars were no longer taken into the Gurkha regiments.[135]

### *Gurkha: Line Boys*[136]

The sons of Gurkha soldiers who were brought up in the regiment were called 'line boys'. As was done with many Indian regiments when these boys were grown, they were taken as line soldiers. The British were only willing to take the offspring of purely Gurkha parents, and, among those, they took only a small percent. They were selected for the regiments because it was felt that growing up away from the Nepalese countryside led them to pick up bad habits and ways of thinking. But, to compensate for this, the first generation of line boys was physically almost as good as a man from the hills of Nepal, and he was almost invariably extremely intelligent and full of military ardour. He had played at being a soldier as soon as he could walk. They were good soldiers, having learned the ropes in their childhood, and often very brave. Of the seven men who earned the Indian Order of Merit (IOM) at the Battles of Aliwal and Sobraon (1846) against the Sikhs, five were line boys. And out of 25 IOMs given at the siege of Delhi, 12 went to Gurkha line boys.

### *Gurkha: Dhotials*[137]

Western Nepal was the home of the Dhotials, who the Gurkha handbook states were not Gurkhas at all and should never be enlisted.

130 Vansittart, *Gurkhas*, p.77.
131 Smith, *Valour*, p.13, map; Vansittart, *Gurkhas*, p.84.
132 Vansittart, *Gurkhas*, pp.81, 89.
133 Vansittart, *Gurkhas*, pp.86–91.
134 Vansittart, *Gurkhas*, pp.92–94.
135 Bonarjee, *Handbook*, p.112.
136 Vansittart, *Gurkhas*, pp.94–95; Farwell, *Gurkhas*, pp.81–82.
137 Vansittart, *Gurkhas*, p.95.

### *Gurkha: Thakurs and Khas*

The Thakurs were said to have the highest social standing in Nepal. The king of Nepal was a member of one of their clans, the Sabi. They, as a group, along with the Khas, were said to be the product of the fusion of Brahmins and Rajputs moving into central Nepal with the native Magar and Gurung (M&G) women.[138] They enlisted in only small numbers.

Their builds, caste rules, and characters were similar to those of the Khas.

Magars and Gurungs predominated in the 1st through 5th and the 8th Gurkha Rifles (GR). The 9th GR was manned by Khas and Thakuris from the middle hills.[139] The 6th, 7th, and 10th contained the eastern classes, the Limbus, Rais, and Kirantis.

### *Gurkha: Khas*

The British and most everyone else believed that, in the past, and particularly in the twelfth century (the time of the Muslim conquests), large numbers of Brahmins and Rajputs sought refuge in Nepal. Once there, they gained positions of influence because of their superior intelligence and civilisation. Once there, through unions with the local women, they created the class called 'Khas'. 'Khas' means 'fallen' and comes from the verb 'Khasna', to fall.[140]

The Brahmins ruled that the Khas class was entitled to wear a cord of three threads twisted together as members of the Ksatriya (warrior) class division. This gave them a higher social standing than the M&Gs.

There was a slightly different group within the general class called the 'Ekthariahs', who are the descendants of Rajputs on both the father's and mother's sides rather than the Khas mixture of Brahmin and a local woman. Because of this, the Ekthariahs claimed superiority over the Khas.

The Indians brought their language with them, and a type of Hindi patois grew up as the two sides tried to communicate with each other. This became the language of the Khas (called 'Khas-Khura'), and it became the lingua franca of Nepal.[141]

The Khas build was slighter and less sturdy than that of the M&Gs, but they were felt to be more intelligent and just as warlike. They were usually taller than the M&Gs.[142] They were felt to have a bit more facial and body hair than the M&Gs ('as hirsute as other races').[143]

The 9th Gurkhas, which was manned by Khas and Thakurs, was somewhat looked down upon as inferior fighters because of its class makeup.[144]

Because the name 'Khas' means 'fallen', the class started to adopt the name 'Chettris' towards the end of the nineteenth century.[145]

### *Gurkha: Kiranti*

The main tribes that lived east of the Kathmandu Valley are known collectively by the term 'Kiranti'. The tribes covered by this term are the Limbus (they call themselves 'Yakthumbas'),

138 Bonarjee, *Handbook*, pp.105–06.
139 Caplan, *Warrior*, p.122, endnote 13.
140 Vansittart, *Gurkhas*, p.69.
141 Vansittart, *Gurkhas*, pp.68, 70–71; Bonarjee, *Handbook*, p.107.
142 Bonarjee, *Handbook*, p.106.
143 Farwell, *Gurkhas*, p.303.
144 Caplan, *Warrior*, p.76.
145 Bonarjee, *Handbook*, p.106.

the Khambus, and the Yakkas. The latter two are often referred to jointly as the 'Rais'. The term 'Rai' was an honorific title given to the heads of the Khambus and Yakkas by the Gurkha Kingdom after they swore allegiance to the Gurkhas.[146]

The eastern Kiranti tribes were felt to be inferior to the Khas, Magar, and Gurung tribes. They were able to somewhat overcome their poor Gurkha reputation through their performance on the Northwest Frontier.[147] Others put it that the eastern regiments were different in character and performance than the regiments that recruited mostly from the west of the central Kathmandu Valley.[148]

For a period, the people of eastern Nepal, Limbus and Rais, were used only in paramilitary units such as the Burma Military Police and the Assam Rifles. They were felt to be too headstrong and quarrelsome and thus too undisciplined to be a martial class.[149] Of the two, the Limbus was felt to be more quarrelsome and less amenable to discipline than the Rais.[150]

After they were recruited, the easterners, perhaps because of their unruly nature, were thought to be better at the attack. The M&Gs were thought to be better when things were going wrong and in a retreat.[151]

Up to 1887, every Gurkha regiment had its own proportion of Kirantis. The 2/1st and 2/4th, on being raised, took a good many of them. The 6th, 7th, and 8th, because they took their recruits mostly from a recruiting station near eastern Nepal, had a very high percentage of their men from eastern Nepal.

In 1889, a battalion of Limbus and Rais was raised as the 10th Gurkha Rifles. Its actions won general approval. In 1902, a 2/10th was raised. It was also all eastern men, except for some 100 men from other Gurkha regiments who were transferred in at the time of its organisation.[152]

The relative importance of the different groups to the British Gurkha regiments can be seen from Table 33. One authority, Ragsdale, estimated that the different groups provided the following percentages to the Gurkha regiments at the turn of the twentieth century:

**Table 33 Percentages of Groups Enlisted, 1894–1913[153]**

| Ethnic Groups | Estimated Percentage |
|---|---|
| Magars and Gurungs (M&G) | 60.0% |
| Rais and Limbus | 27.5% |
| Other – including Khas and Thakurs | 12.5% |

146 Bonarjee, *Handbook*, pp.113–15.
147 Vansittart, *Gurkhas*, p.118.
148 Caplan, *Warrior*, p.76.
149 Caplan, *Warrior*, p.95.
150 Farwell, *Gurkhas*, p.302.
151 Gaylor, *Sons*, p.220.
152 Vansittart, *Gurkhas*, pp.101–02.
153 Caplan, *Warrior*, p.96.

***Gurkha Nature***

The Gurkhas are said to be the most written-about unit of the British Indian army, or, for that matter, the British army, since the Second World War.[154] So there is a wealth of stereotypes about the Gurkhas.

The Gurkhas were described as an 'ignorant, stupid, roving race of men... possessing very small aptitude for intellectual employments, which they invariably regard with the greatest dislike'.[155] This was often linked with stories of Gurkhas' thick skulls. One chestnut often told is about a mule that kicked a Gurkha in the head. The Gurkha complained of a headache, and the mule went lame.[156] Another story is about how Lieutenant Swinton of the 8th Gurkhas was killed in 1890 on the Northeast Frontier. A bullet ricocheted off the head of his Gurkha orderly and killed him. The orderly was only slightly injured.[157]

The Gurkhas were said by some to be unemotional and cool in battle, much like the English. He had dogged tenacity.[158] Others described him as crazed and bloodthirsty in battle.[159]

The bravery of Gurkhas was recognised during the Anglo-Nepal War and was a constant theme in British writing on the Gurkhas from there forwards. They were often called the 'bravest of the brave'.[160] It is said that there is no printed work on the Gurkhas that does not refer to their tenacity, strength, and courage. Their saying 'better to die than be a coward' is often quoted with approval. In fact, many writers went so far as to claim that Gurkhas knew no fear. Others said Gurkhas knew what fear was but were more frightened of showing their fear than of fear itself.[161]

But not all the Gurkhas are paragons of courage. The First and Second World Wars showed another side of them. Gurkha units suffered defeat in battle, were taken prisoners, and retreated without orders.[162]

Besides their courage, another theme that appears in most accounts about the Gurkhas is their sense of humour and unfailing cheerfulness. It has been said that their humour, more than any other single factor, helped to distinguish them from the peoples of India proper, where this trait was not found.[163] Different authors have described their sense of humour as banana-skin, earthy, and macabre.[164]

The Gurkhas were said to have contempt for the Indians of the plains ('Madhesias'). They, on the other hand, fraternised with and were said to look up to the Europeans (British).[165] The British encouraged this view and differentiated the Gurkhas in several ways. They wore a special uniform of rifle green, a Kilmarnock cap, and had a separate numbering system for their regiments. They were the only Indian army soldiers allowed into British soldiers' canteens and

154 Caplan, *Warrior*, p.1.
155 Caplan, *Warrior*, p.108.
156 Omissi, *Sepoy*, p.26.
157 Farwell, *Gurkhas*, p.52.
158 Bonarjee, *Handbook*, pp.103–04.
159 Omissi, *Sepoy*, p.31.
160 Caplan, *Warrior*, p.135.
161 Caplan, *Warrior*, pp.132–33.
162 Caplan, *Warrior*, p.135.
163 Caplan, *Warrior*, pp.144–45.
164 Caplan, *Warrior*, p.144; Farwell, *Gurkhas*, p.49.
165 Caplan, *Warrior*, p.146.

messes.[166] To further differentiate the Gurkhas, they were given the privilege of using British army canteens, a right normally denied to Indian soldiers.[167]

The disdain for Indians and their supposed unwillingness to serve under Indian officers were used as reasons to exempt the Gurkha regiments from the programme of Indianisation of the Indian army that began after the First World War.[168]

The views about the Gurkha soldiers did not carry over to the officers and affect their status. The 5th Gurkhas with the Frontier Force benefitted from the lustre attached to those regiments and was considered a cut above the rest. However, the 2nd Gurkhas had the reputation of being the most prestigious Gurkha regiment. One officer said, 'There are the 2nd Gurkhas and the rest.' As with most reputations, the reason for this was hard to pin down. The 2nd's officers tended to come from better public schools, and the regiment could take pride in its age and strong traditions. One officer said, 'You can tell a 2GR officer a mile off; he is a bit more pleased with himself.' Most officers looked down on the officers in the Ordnance and Army Service Corps.[169]

The events of 1948, therefore, came as a rude shock to the British. As part of Indian independence, the British and Indians negotiated the future of the Gurkha regiments. The British were to retain four: the 2nd, 6th, 7th, and 10th. This was said to be because most of the battalions of these regiments were stationed outside of India at the time of the decision. The men in these four regiments were allowed to choose to go with the British, join the Indian army, or take a discharge. To the great surprise of the British, many chose to join the Indian army and serve under Indian officers. On average, the eight battalions of the four regiments lost two-thirds of their men and had a strength of only 300 men each.[170]

So many men were from the 7th and 10th Gurkhas, the eastern Nepalese regiments, that the Indians formed a new regiment in 1948, the 11th Gurkhas. It used the badge of a Gurkha regiment that had been formed during the First World War in Palestine and Mesopotamia but did not get its battle honours.[171] The British authorities have proffered many different reasons for these totally unexpected results. While this is beyond the scope of this work, a list of these reasons can be found in Caplan's *Warrior Gentlemen*.[172]

The Gurkha, for all his many military virtues, was still a human being and had his failings. He had a short temper, which sometimes led him into trouble. But his anger went as fast as it came, and he seldom bore a grudge.

His other faults, in addition to being slow to learn, were a love of rum and gambling, often to excess.[173] Without strong control over them, they very soon became slovenly. The M&Gs were

166 Caplan, *Warrior*, p.146.
167 Gaylor, *Sons*, p.219.
168 Caplan, *Warrior*, p.146. Indianisation was a programme that granted King's Commissions to some Indians after they had successfully passed through Sandhurst. This gave them the power to command both Indian and British soldiers of a rank lower than them. Prior to Indianisation, the best an Indian could hope to do was work his way up through the ranks and obtain a warrant of rank from the viceroy. This did not allow him to command British soldiers. See Omissi, *Sepoy*, pp.163–78, for a good discussion of the programme and its problems.
169 Caplan, *Warrior*, p.76.
170 Gaylor, *Sons*, p.290.
171 Gaylor, *Sons*, p.297.
172 Caplan, *Warrior*, p.117; Gaylor, *Sons*, p.218.
173 Farwell, *Gurkhas*, p.52.

very superstitious.[174] They have at various times been described as dirty, lazy, and stupid with little aptitude for intellectual employment, which they invariably greatly disliked.[175]

### *Gurkha: Recruiting*

In the early years, it was not easy to enlist Gurkhas. The Nepal Durbar (ruling body) was unwilling to allow Europeans (British) into the country. They feared that was the first step towards the loss of independence. They had seen it happen too often with the Indian princely states. They had a saying to the effect, 'With the merchant comes the musket, and with the Bible comes the bayonet.'[176] This same fear was behind Nepal not building or repairing proper roads in the country.[177]

Furthermore, the Durbar issued orders that no one could enter British service without the prime minister's permission. This was almost never given. This left the British with only one option to obtain recruits. They sent secret agents or disguised sepoys to visit fairs in Nepal and collect volunteers. These were then taken, almost smuggled, into India to the headquarters at Gorukpore, set up for recruiting. In the middle of the nineteenth century, the prime minister caused the Durbar to become stricter. They would not help return the belongings to the heirs of dead Gurkha soldiers. If a man was detected trying to leave the company to serve the British, he would be imprisoned, and all his goods, including his house and lands, would be confiscated. Recruiters were to be cut in two.[178]

In order to understand why the Durbar's stance changed, a glance at Nepalese court politics must be examined at this point.

In 1816, just after the peace treaty between the company and the Gurkhas was signed, the young king, age 18, died, and he was succeeded by his two-year-old son. The son held the throne until 1847, when he was deposed as being insane. During most of his reign, the prime minister was in complete power. This set off a period of murders, expulsions, forced abdications, and battles.

Reading about these events presents many incidents that conform to one's stereotype of an old oriental court, or the Julio-Claudian dynasty.[179] One cannot help feeling that the Nepalese rulers were not worthy of the stalwart soldiers in the British Gurkha regiments.

Throughout these years, the prime ministers held the ruling power, not the king or queen.[180] After years of this low-level chaos, in 1846, a prime minister named Jung Bahadur was able to make the office of prime minister hereditary in his family by creating a roll of succession.[181] The office would pass from brother to brother rather than to the sons. He completely neutralised the king's power and gave Nepal an uninterrupted peaceful administration during his term in office (1847–1877) in place of the murders, *coup d'états*, and battles that had gone on before.[182]

174 Vansittart, *Gurkhas*, pp.54, 61.
175 Asad Husain, *British India's Relations with the Kingdom of Nepal, 1857–1947: A Diplomatic History of Nepal* (London: George Allen and Unwin, 1970), p.237.
176 Vansittart, *Gurkhas*, p.45.
177 Husain, *British*, p.120.
178 Husain, *British*, pp.239–41.
179 The Julio-Claudians were heirs of Caesar Augustus, who graced history with Caligula, Agrippina, and Nero.
180 Vansittart, *Gurkhas*, pp.39–43.
181 Husain, *British*, p.129.
182 Husain, *British*, p.56.

Then, in 1885, a man named Bir Shamsher decided to act on his own behalf. He was the nephew of the prime minister and was seventh on the succession list. Most likely, he would have died of old age before his turn to be prime minister arrived. Instead of waiting, he led a very bloody *coup d'état*. The prime minister was murdered, and most of the remaining leaders who had a claim to being prime minister were murdered or fled to the British Residency. They also killed members of the collateral branches of the prime minister's family. When the killing was over, Bir Shamsher, through his widespread killing, had eliminated almost all possible contenders for the prime minister's office. The others were living in India.[183]

There followed a period in which the fugitive exiles living in India lobbied for British help in being restored to power. Bir Shamsher waited anxiously for British recognition of the murderous coup. Bir Shamsher made all sorts of promises to the British, as did the exiles. Finally, the Indian government chose to follow – perhaps with a bit of schadenfreude towards a family who had caused them many recruiting problems – their old policy of not interfering in the internal affairs of sovereign native states. Bir Shamsher was recognised as prime minister.[184]

The new prime minister tried to collect more recruits for the British. First, he tried signing bonuses and then a rough form of a draft. These pulled in a large number of men, but many were not acceptable to the British. But, through back and forth, a way to greatly increase the number of proper recruits was found.[185] This allowed the British to raise second battalions for the five Gurkha regiments. This almost doubled the number of Gurkhas the British had under arms. At the same time, permanent recruiting was established at Gorakhpur in the United Provinces (now Uttar Pradesh) as a base for recruiting G&Ms.[186]

In exchange, the British agreed to provide Nepal with modern rifles, something it had long coveted, and European luxury goods were coming into the country at a greater volume.[187]

This background is important because some authors give the impression that the increase in Gurkha battalions took place because the Indian army needed more Gurkhas for possible use against Russia because of Russian war scares. They treat the men for the extra battalions as being produced by a sort of *deus ex machina*.

### *Rajputs*

There was a tendency to think that Rajputs must come from Rajasthan (or Rajputana, as the area was known during the Raj). While many do come from Rajputana, the Rajputs were a minority in the area. Male Rajputs were only 20.9 percent of the male population in Rajputana in 1911.[188] Table 34 gives a breakdown of the number of males in each fighting class living in Rajputana in 1911.

183 Husain, *British*, pp.243–44.
184 Husain, *British*, p.244.
185 Husain, *British*, pp.244–50.
186 Farwell, *Gurkhas*, p.73.
187 Caplan, *Warrior*, p.21; Husain, *British*, pp.136, 242.
188 B. L. Cole, *Handbooks for the Indian Army: Rajputana Classes* (Calcutta: Office of the Superintendent, Government Printing, India, 1924), p.67.

**Table 34 The Fighting Classes of Rajputana and the Male Population of Each Class in 1911**[189]

| Fighting Class | Total Male Population | Percentage |
|---|---|---|
| Rajputs | 342,834 | 20.88% |
| Jats | 504,697 | 79.12% |
| Gujars | 273,323 | |
| Ahirs | 73,450 | |
| Minas | 258,421 | |
| Mers | 48,359 | |
| Muslim Rajputs | 27,853 | |
| Kaimkhanis | 13,750 | |
| Khanzadas | 3,975 | |
| Meos | 85,282 | |
| Merata | 9,651 | |
| **Total** | **1,641,595** | **100%** |

The Rajputs (literally 'Sons of Kings') were found all over India. They were considered to be part of the Kshatriyas (warrior) class and were entitled to wear the cord.[190] However, not everyone agrees that the Rajputs, or even a majority of them, are descendants of the Vedic Aryans. Others say they are the descendants of Scythians or any number of other groups.[191]

Both Singh and Asopa, cited above, wrote about the origins of the Rajputs in the 1970s, before the development of DNA tracing. Therefore, they could do little but cite old authorities. But the situation was a little better in 2008, when the problem of Rajput origins remained 'more or less unsolved' at that time.[192] Of late, a new theory, perhaps under the influence of Hindutva (roughly Hindu nationalism and chauvinism), has come to prominence. It is that the Rajputs are descendants of peasant or pastoral people who became soldiers. In time, the soldiers became a hereditary class and then a caste.

If the Rajputs in the Punjab converted to the Muslim religion, they lost the name 'Rajput' and became classed as 'Punjab Muslims'. Rajputs were found in the hills, which housed the Dogras, and in the Deccan, where they went by the name 'Marathas'. The term 'Rajput' was normally understood to mean Rajputs of the Rajputana and Delhi, usually called 'Western Rajputs', and Rajputs living in Oudh and Agra were often called 'Eastern Rajputs'.

The Eastern Rajputs took to agriculture and, for many years, served as mercenaries in the Muslim armies. Later, many of them served in the Bengal army that mutinied, and so they were largely cut out of the recruiting base. The Rajputs of Rajputana tended to only serve as cavalry, while Easterners served as mostly infantry. With the passage of time, some Eastern Rajputs were again recruited. The 2nd, 4th, 7th, 8th, 11th, and 16th Infantry were Indian army class regiments that enlisted Eastern Rajputs and Rajputs from the Delhi area. The 13th Infantry

189 Cole, *Rajputana*, p.37.
190 MacMunn, *Armies*, p.156.
191 R. B. Singh, *Origin of the Rajputs* (Oakland: University of California Press, 1975); Jai Narayan Asopa, *Origin of the Rajputs* (Delhi: Bharatiya Publishing House, 1976).
192 R. K. Gupta and S. R. Bakshi (eds), *Rajasthan through the Ages: Jaipur Rulers and Administration* (New Delhi: Sarup and Sons, 2008), vol. 4, p.137.

was a class regiment composed of Rajputs from Rajputana. Several other infantry and cavalry regiments enlisted class companies or squadrons of Eastern or Western Rajputs.[193] For example, the cavalry had eight regiments with Rajput-class squadrons. Most of these called for Rajputs only, namely, the 2nd, 3rd, 5th, and 8th. Two specified Rajputs of Rajputana. These were the 26th and 28th Regiments of the old Madras army. Finally, two regiments, the 27th (old Madras army) and 34th (old Bombay army),[194] went so far as to specify Rathore Rajputs. The southern armies of Bombay and Madras also pulled men from Rajputana.

The Rahtore Rajputs were a clan of the sun branch of the Rajputs, the highest rank among the Rajputs. The Maharaja (also spelled 'Maharajah') of Jodhpur was the paramount chief of the clan.[195] In addition to ruling Jodhpur (also known as Marwar), a member of the clan also ruled in Bikanir and Kisengarh. Like most of the superior Rajput clans, their preference was for the cavalry, and only necessity forced them to enlist in the infantry.[196]

In the Bengal army, other than the above class regiments, none of the infantry regiments enlisted Rajputs. Only one local force, the old Bhopal Levy, which was under the command of the Bengal army after it came into the army lists as the 9th Bhopal Infantry, had Rajput class companies. Two other irregular forces, later the 42nd Deoli and the Erinpura, had class companies of Rajputana Hindus.[197] This, of course, was a wider net than just Rajputs.

The Bombay army poached men from Rajputana for its infantry regiments. The 104th Rifles, 120th and 122nd Infantry, and the 123rd and 125th Rifles all had class companies of Rajputana Rajputs (as well as other classes from Rajputana).[198]

The Rajputs are traditionally divided into three branches. The two main ones are the Suryavanshis and the Chandravanshis, who trace their ancestry to the Sun and Moon gods. The third group, Agniculars (or Agrikuls), are said to descend from Fire.[199] The Fire or Fire-born Rajputs were said to be 'created by the god Mahadeo to destroy demons who desecrated sacrifices offered at his shrine in Ajmere'. There are only four fire clans created by the god.[200]

MacMunn stated that Agniculars are Scythian clans from central Asia admitted into the Rajput circle for political reasons. He went on to say, 'In fact, there is no doubt that many of the aboriginal chiefs were endowed with Rajput ancestors exactly on the same principle as the Herald's College will find ancestors of renown for parvenu families.' Some leaders of the Jats may have also been given the status of Rajputs as members of the fire clan when they converted to Hinduism. The three branches were subdivided into 36 Royal Houses, which were to be found in various parts of India.[201]

Rajputana was considered one of the backwaters of India. It consisted entirely of native states, except for small British holdings at Ajmer-Merwara.[202] Rajputana, except for the British hold-

193 MacMunn, *Armies*, pp.156–59.
194 Edward M. Nevins, *Forces of the British Empire, 1914* (St Petersburg, FL: Vandamere Press, 1992), pp.202–15.
195 Rosita Forbes, *India of the Princes* (Boston: E. P. Dutton and Company, 1941), p.110.
196 Bonarjee, *Handbook*, pp.197–99.
197 Nevins, *Forces*, generally and pp.220–21, 230.
198 Nevins, *Forces*, pp.245, 249–51.
199 V. K. Shrivastava, *The Rajputana Rifles* (New Delhi: Lancer Publishers, 2000), p.26.
200 Bonarjee, *Handbook*, p.202.
201 MacMunn, *Armies*, pp.158, 160.
202 Cole, *Rajputana*, p.3.

ings, was ruled by 18 native states and three chiefships. Of these, 15 states and all three chiefships were ruled by Rajputs. Of the others, two had a Jat ruler, and one had a Muslim ruler.[203]

Since recruiting had to be done in what were, in theory, independent states, Indian army recruiting depended on the goodwill of the ruling princes. Recruiters were warned about the necessity of having good relations with all levels of state officials and officeholders.[204]

The army recruited from a limited number of Rajput clans and their subdivisions. The Rajputana handbook goes into detail about these clans and subgroups and what states they should be recruited from.[205]

The handbooks of Rajputana classes make the following comments on the nature of Rajputana Rajputs:

> The Rajputs still exhibited many feudal characteristics, among which is a disdain for manual labour and commerce. If he can afford it, he would always pay for someone to cultivate his land rather than do it himself. The Rajputs look upon themselves, par excellence, as fighting men. As soldiers, they were said to be brave, obedient, and undemonstrative with great pride of race. They were free from intrigues. They were also free of caste religious guidelines or prejudices and did not subordinate military efficiency to religious requirements.[206]

Others were not so kind. Bonarjee stated in his *A Handbook of the Fighting Races of India*, 'The dominant characteristic of the Rajput is pride of blood. In fact, his pride of blood borders very close on the ridiculous. Time was when his one ambition was to wield a sword; in these peace-loving days he is generally content to toy with it.'[207] He went on to say that he did not mean to say that Rajputs had lost their soldierly qualities and their ability to make good soldiers, just that they were not the men they used to be. He also said that the worst characteristic of the Rajput soldier was his tendency to be easily depressed by failure and defeat. The Rajputs were brave, would go anywhere and do anything, and undertook any desperate mission in the heat of battle or when things were going well. But the slow, steady, depressing conditions of war left him spiritless and broken.[208]

The steps that Rajputs would take to defend their honour, standing, and independence were symbolised by the defence of the fortress of Chitoor (or Chitor). In addition to other attacks over the years by different parties, the fortress was under close siege three times by vast Mogul armies of different emperors. These occurred in 1303 (some authorities say 1275), 1533, and 1568. In each siege, the defenders held out as long as they could. Then, when it looked like the fortress was fated to fall, two things were done. The women burned themselves en masse, a rite called '*johur*'. This saved them from being raped and otherwise dishonoured after the attackers captured the fortress. It also prevented the men of their families from being dishonoured by what would happen to them. The badly outnumbered fighting men in Chitor put on saffron (yellow) robes that symbolised victory or death and rode out to die fighting.[209] This allowed the

203 Cole, *Rajputana*, pp.5–6.
204 Cole, *Rajputana*, p.66.
205 Cole, *Rajputana*, pp.24–28.
206 Cole, *Rajputana*, pp.28–29.
207 Bonarjee, *Handbook*, p.191.
208 Bonarjee, *Handbook*, pp.192–93.
209 MacMunn, *Martial*, pp.80–89; Forbes, *India*, pp.92–97.

state of Mewar – Udaipur of today – to claim that they were never conquered and were the only Rajput state never be subjected to the humiliation of sending a princess to the bed of an emperor in Delhi. It also allowed the rulers of Udaipur to claim that their rulers had never paid homage to the Moguls.[210] They all died first.

Forbes gave a popular folklore-type account of what led to the attacks and the sieges. They revolved largely around women as causes and actors.[211]

James Skinner, whose mother was a Rajput, knew about the story of Chitor and the victory-or-death attacks wearing saffron robes. It is said that this was what led him to dress his men in yellow coats.

After the last siege and sack of Chitor in 1568, the fortress was not rebuilt and is still in ruins. Instead, a new capital city, Udaipur, was founded on Lake Pichola. Udaipur and its rulers are considered the premier state in Rajputana.[212]

The best-known Indian prince of the Victorian and Edwardian eras was Sir Pratap Singh (also spelled 'Pertab'; 1845–1922), the third son of the ruler of Jodhpur. Jodhpur (also known by its ancient name of Marwar) was ruled by members of the Rahtor clan. He was Regent of Jodhpur three different times during the minorities of its Maharajas. The British, for years, gave him the honours due a head of state, although he was only briefly the Maharaja of Idar, a small state in the Bombay Presidency whose ruling house was of the same line as Jodhpur's.

He knew how to make gestures that pleased Victoria. He seemed to be without fear and had a thirst for battle. He was friends with Sir Frederick Roberts (later Lord Roberts). In 1897, a young English officer died while he was his guest. Sir Pratap helped carry his body to the grave. The Brahmins warned him this was a very serious breach of caste rules, and major purification rites would need to be carried out. Sir Pratap sent them away, saying that, between soldiers, there are no caste limitations.

He was the force behind Jodhpur being one of the first of the princely states to raise, in 1889, Imperial Service Troops. Sir Pratap took the regiment to China in 1899 to help put down the Boxer Rebellion. In 1914, the regiment sailed with orders to help defend the Suez Canal. Sir Pratap refused to land the regiment in Egypt because there were no Germans to fight. The regiment went on to France, where it served for several years. Like all First World War cavalry, it saw very little fighting on the Western Front, and, in early 1918, it was shipped out to Palestine.[213]

Sir Pratap was also responsible for introducing 'jodhpur breeches' to the world. The style of breeches he wore, called 'jodhpurs', was widely admired, but no one could figure out how to make them. When he went to Queen Victoria's Golden Jubilee, the ship carrying his clothes was lost in a shipwreck. This forced Sir Pratap to tell a London tailor how to make the jodhpurs.[214] Soon, the secret was out, and people around the world were wearing them.

The Rajputana state that is best known today is Jaipur because of the pink colouring of many of the buildings and the Hall of Winds. However, prior to the First World War, it received almost no attention. What changed the situation was Maharaja Man Singh, who ruled from

210 John Lord, *The Maharajas* (New Delhi: Vikas, 1971), p.195.

211 Forbes, *India*, pp.93–97.

212 Forbes, *India*, p.97.

213 Lord, *Maharajas*, pp.196–202; Byron Farwell, *Armies of the Raj: From the Great Indian Mutiny to Independence: 1858–1947* (New York: W. W. Norton and Company, 1989), p.230.

214 Lord, *Maharajas*, p.201.

1922 to India's independence in 1947–1948,[215] and a legend about treasure. In 1933, Man Singh took his polo team to England, and they won every tournament they played in. This fixed his reputation as an outstanding sportsman and celebrity for the rest of his life.[216]

The legend was the treasure of the princes of Jaipur. It was said to be hidden somewhere high up above the old palace–fortress of Amber in the Jaigarh Fort, about seven miles (11km) from the Pink City. The treasure was believed to be gold and jewels looted from Kabul by a past Maharaja who served in a Mogul army. It was thought to be guarded by an aboriginal tribe, the Minas. The Maharajas themselves did not know where the treasure was hidden, and a Maharaja was only allowed to see it once in his life. That was during his reign, when the guardians considered him mature enough. At that time, he was allowed to choose one item from the treasure hoard to take out with him. Man Singh's predecessor had selected a bird of solid gold studded with rubies (à la the Maltese Falcon). It was so heavy that a woman could not lift it.

Man Singh had ruled from 1922 until India gained its independence in 1947–1948, and he had still not been allowed to see the treasure and choose an item from it. At this point, some say he went to the guardian Minas and told them they could either let him, who had a family claim on it, have the entire treasure or they might have to be prepared to surrender to the new government of India. No one knows if this story is true or what was done with the treasure. But it has been noted that, when he died in 1970, Man Singh was the third richest man in England.[217]

There is one more act in the history of the Jaipur treasure. After independence, Man Singh's third wife, Gayatri Devi, or the Maharani of Jaipur, began a very successful political career in elective politics. In time, she came to oppose Indira Gandhi, who led the country for many years. During one period of her leadership, for 21 months in 1975–1977, Gandhi declared a state of emergency in India. During this period, elections were suspended, and she ruled by decree. Gandhi also had many of her political foes jailed. One of these was the Maharani of Jaipur, who was imprisoned in July 1975 without being charged with anything. Earlier, in February of 1975, tax officials came to look for hidden, unreported items of value.[218] There, they made a most thorough, and, in some cases, destructive, search for the treasure. It can be assumed that this involved looking for hidden chambers. No one, outside of a few top government officials, knows what, if anything, the search found. With that final search, the treasure legend has passed largely from the public's mind.

### *Rajputs: Doing Homage to Power*

When the British replaced the Moguls as the power in the land, the lords of Udaipur followed the same no-homage policy that they had with the Moguls and did not do homage before the British. The ruler of the state (Fateh Singh, ruler from 1885 to 1930) during the high tide of the empire for years used claims of bouts of fever and other devices to avoid having to bow before the viceroy. The British, with their own eye for honour and eccentricity, became as sensitive to his honour as he was and helped him maintain his streak.

215 Gayatri Devi, *A Princess Remembers: The Memoirs of the Maharani of Jaipur* (New Delhi: Rupa Publications, 1995), pp.94–98. He was adopted by the Maharaja of Jaipur to be the next Maharaja in 1921 at age 10. In 1922, the old Maharaja died, and Man Singh ascended the throne. But he was too young to rule, and a council ruled for him until he became an adult.

216 Lord, *Maharajas*, p.210.

217 Lord, *Maharajas*, p.212.

218 Lucy Moore, *Maharanis: The Lives and Times of Three Generations of Indian Princesses* (London: Penguin Books, 2004), pp.282–84.

Things came to a head at the 1911 Delhi Durbar, where George V, the King-Emperor, would be crowned Emperor of India in person. All the rulers of the Indian states were required to be there to bow to the emperor and pledge their loyalty. The British were dead serious about this, and there were to be no exceptions for eccentric rulers. However, someone on the British side came up with a way to keep Fateh Singh out of the line of bowing princes. He was appointed to the personal staff of George V; that way, he would be a part of the ceremony by appearing on the dais with the emperor but would not have to bow to him. In the end, Fateh Singh avoided even this by claiming illness. His motive seems to be the same thing that caused him to turn down the office of Grand Commander of the Order of the Star of India. As a member of the Order and George's staff, he could, in theory, be called upon to perform duties for the emperor. Fateh Singh said he would be at no man's beck and call.[219]

A hint of how serious the British were can be gathered from their reaction to a faux pas by the Maharaja Gaekwad of Baroda. He bowed to the King-Emperor only once instead of the proper three times and seemed to turn his back on the King-Emperor as he backed away. The British press went wild and called his actions treason, sedition, and disloyalty. The Indian nationalists also saw the events as a snub to the throne, and he became a hero to them.[220]

The granddaughter of the Gaekwadof Baroda said that he always claimed he had no intent to insult the King-Emperor and that his actions were the result of not knowing what to do. He had missed the dress rehearsal and did not watch what the prince in front of him did. So he did not know the proper number of bows to make. As he was backing away, he did not remember where the exit was, and, in looking for someone to tell him, he appeared to turn his back on George V.[221] He does seem to have been sailing very close to the wind in the years prior to the Durbar. He gave speeches saying discontent was normal among the educated and that subjects should have a share in the administration of their country.[222] These, in the context of the time, could be viewed as sedition. His talks before Indian and nationalist-leaning audiences were somewhat bolder.[223] Nationalists were found to have been operating a printing press in Baroda. They produced a book describing ways to overthrow the colonial power. The British wanted the Baroda officials in charge of the area fired and deported from Baroda. The Gaekwad ignored these suggestions. He ruled the officers innocent of significant wrongdoing and transferred them to less-prestigious positions. When one retired, rather than take a demotion, he was given a retirement gift of 10,000 rupees (current value: £64,240 or $74,490).[224]

By 1910, the Maharaja's speeches and activities had made him a popular and heroic figure to the fledging nationalist movement.[225]

The claims by the Gaekwad that he did not know protocol and what to do in front of the King-Emperor and Queen Mary are undercut by the fact that he had attended two previous Durbars, in 1877 and in 1902–1903.[226] At the 1902–1903 Durbar, he caused problems by not wanting to

219 Lord, *Maharajas*, pp.195–96.
220 Devi, *Princess*, pp.31–32. Gayatri Devi was a grandchild of the Maharaja Gaekwad of Baroda.
221 Devi, *Princess*, p.32.
222 Manu B. Bhagavan, *Sovereign Spheres: Princes, Education, and Empire in Colonial India* (Oxford: Oxford University Press, 2003), pp.56–57.
223 Bhagavan, *Sovereign*, p.57.
224 Bhagavan, *Sovereign*, pp.59–61.
225 Bhagavan, *Sovereign*, p.57.
226 Bhagavan, *Sovereign*, p.61.

take part in a parade of Indian rulers on elephants that the British wanted to make part of the Durbar ritual. At last, when the British put some pressure on him, he agreed to do so with ill grace. In the end, he found a way to avoid the elephant parade by claiming he was in mourning for his adoptive mother. In addition, he slightly breached protocol during a ceremony of paying respects to the viceroy in a ceremony where the viceroy was representing the King-Emperor.[227]

To get an idea of how the British press handled the incident, complete with photographs showing the Gaekwad turning his back, see *The Illustrated London News* of 20 January 1912.[228]

### *Dogras*

While not recruited in anywhere near the numbers of the Sikhs, Gurkhas, or Punjabi Muslims, the Dogras were an important element in the Indian army. In 1914, they provided three class infantry regiments, the 37th, 38th, and 41st, and men to 23 infantry regiments (56 companies) and 11 cavalry regiments (nine squadrons worth; several had only half squadrons). The Dogras also supplied men to the Guides, a half squadron to the cavalry, and a company to the infantry. In 1914, Dogras were 3.7 percent of the approximately 41 percent of the Indian army that came from the Punjab and frontier.

The term 'Dogra' was a slippery one, as it applied to people who lived in an area and not a caste or a religion. The area is in the hills between the Punjab and Kashmir. These hills are the foothills of the Himalayas.[229] In modern times, these hills are known as the Pir Panjal Range and the lower Shivalik and Dhauladhar Ranges. These are found in the state of Himachal Pradesh.[230] This area is about 150 miles (241km) long and averages about 80 miles (129km) across.[231]

There are a great many theories on where the term 'Dogra' came from.[232] The Dogra handbook states that the term comes from *Durgara*, which was an ancient name of the Jammu state.[233]

Since the term 'Dogra' is a geographical one and not a caste, racial, or religious one, then, in theory, anyone who lived between the Punjab and Kashmir and the Dogra Hills could be recruited under the title 'Dogra'. They are Brahmins, Rajputs, Jats, and so on who refused the prophet when others succumbed and who kept clear of the Sikh movement.[234] But, in practice, when the British used the term 'Dogra', they usually meant a Rajput from the hills. However, some Hill Brahmins and Jats were enlisted, as well as a few Rajputs from a few Punjab districts.[235] The term 'Dogra' came to be applied to Hindu fighting classes living in the Dogra Hills, in certain Rajput hill states in the state of Jammu, and a few districts of the Punjab.[236]

Since the Rajputs were the main element in the British idea of a Dogra, the Dogra handbook covers Rajputs in great detail. In contrast to the normal British preference for yeoman farmers, in recruiting Dogra Rajputs, the British wanted high-status Rajput classes and clans.

227 Bhagavan, *Sovereign*, pp.49–50.
228 *The Illustrated London News*, 50:1289 (20 January 1912), pp.65, 67.
229 MacMunn, *Armies*, p.143.
230 Shankar Prasad, *The Gallant Dogras: An Illustrated History of the Dogra Regiment* (New Delhi: Lancer Publishers, 2005), pp.1, 4, 5.
231 Bonarjee, *Handbook*, p.116.
232 Bonarjee, *Handbook*, p.116; W. B. Cunningham, *Handbooks for the Indian Army: Dogras* (Calcutta: Office of the Superintendent, Government Printing, India, 1932), p.34.
233 Cunningham, *Dogras*, p.34.
234 MacMunn, *Armies*, p.143.
235 Cunningham, *Dogras*, pp.34–36.
236 Prasad, *Gallant*, pp.9–10.

The Rajput classes with the highest status were those who never touched a plough or seemed to never plough.[237] It is said some high-class Rajputs, caught between their need to maintain status and to make a living, went out at night to sow and plough their land so as to avoid detection of this status-breaking action.[238] For this type, army service was heaven-sent, because it produced an income while doing work that was consistent with his status views that his purpose in life was to be a warrior. Their pride led them to want to serve in the cavalry rather than the infantry.[239] But their poverty would have often prevented them from doing so. Almost all cavalry regiments operated under the Silladar system, which required the applicant to pay a sum of money to cover the cost of his horse and equipment.

The Punjabi Rajputs enlisted before 1914 were felt to produce a lower-grade soldier than the Hill Rajputs. The Dogra handbook makes a point of noting that all of the Punjabi Rajputs had taken to agriculture.[240]

The army also took Brahmins who lived in the Dogra Hills. Generally speaking, there were two types: those who practiced their priestly profession and those who had been forced by a lack of religious employment to take to agriculture. The priestly Brahmins were not enlisted at all, but the agricultural Dogra Hills Brahmins were accepted after being carefully vetted.[241]

There were also Jats living in the Dogra Hills, although their distribution was said to be patchy. They were also found in the low hills of the Jammu state, where the British did some recruiting.[242] At one time, the 'Hill Jats' were freely enlisted in regiments taking Dogras. But then, it was decided that the Jats did not mix well with the Rajputs and Brahmins, and enlistment of Jats in the infantry practically ceased.[243]

Dogras have only been enlisted since the 1880s, and 'as a body, they have not had the opportunity for acquiring fame that has presented itself to some of the other races'.[244] But they had served in several frontier campaigns and done well. And almost everyone had a good opinion of them: 'Their good behaviour, courtly manners, high courage, and physical endurance make the Dogra a valued soldier.'[245] They are said to be shy and somewhat reserved, but they have an unflinching adherence to what they believe honour calls for.[246]

Dogras were said to have a quiet, resolute courage in battle, which made them very reliable soldiers. The Dogra has the reputation of being very loyal to his superiors, so much so that it has been called a sort of religion with them.[247] But one observer felt that the Dogras were more superstitious and priest-ridden than most Hindus.[248]

The army of the princely state of Jammu had several regiments that were mainly Dogras who served with distinction in the late frontier campaigns.[249]

237 Cunningham, *Dogras*, pp.39–40.
238 Bonarjee, *Handbook*, p.129.
239 Bonarjee, *Handbook*, p.129.
240 Bonarjee, *Handbook*, p.131; Cunningham, *Dogras*, p.50.
241 Bonarjee, *Handbook*, pp.125–26; Cunningham, *Dogras*, pp.57–58.
242 Cunningham, *Dogras*, p.58.
243 Cunningham, *Dogras*, p.59.
244 MacMunn, *Armies*, p.144.
245 MacMunn, *Armies*, p.144.
246 Bonarjee, *Handbook*, p.122.
247 Bonarjee, *Handbook*, pp.122–23.
248 Bonarjee, *Handbook*, p.132.
249 MacMunn, *Armies*, p.145.

### *Aboriginal Tribes*

When the Indo-Europeans and other conquering groups swept into India, they forced the original inhabitants ('aboriginals') into the margins of society. Some of these aboriginals became menials in the villages or in towns, and others lived in tribal societies in the forests. Usually, this latter group made at least part of their living by robbing travellers or collecting 'tolls' for safe passage.

To wean the tribes away from this activity and to maintain peace, the British formed at least four different local Bhil Corps: the Candeish (1825–1891, then they became the Khandesh Armed Police Bhil Corps), Malwa (1840–1907), Meywar (1840–1907), and Nimaur (1845 only?).[250]

### *Malwa Bhil Corps*

The 1901 dress regulations provide the following for native officers of the Malwa (or Malwah) Bhil Corps and, by implication, the other ranks: a rifle-green Kilmarnock cap with black silk trim and a badge. Because of the trim on the cap, officers did not wear a badge, but all the other ranks did. There was also an emblem of a French hunting horn as part of the uniform, and Carman stated that the letters 'MBC' were inside the strings.[251] But, in the mid-1890s, the regiment wore turbans.

All ranks wore a single-breasted rifle-green coat with five buttons. The collar and cuffs were scarlet. The trousers were of a 'Zouave pattern' and dark green. However, they were never as full as true Zouave trousers. The regulations state that puttees – a covering worn on the lower part of the legs, also known as legwraps – were to be worn and were of drab-coloured cloth.

The officers' leather pouch belt was black with a whistle and a chain. The pouch was also black leather with a 7.62cm (three-inch) wide bronze plate that showed the regimental badge.[252]

Under an 1818 treaty between John Company and Indore, the state was required to pay money towards the maintenance of the Malwa Bhil Corps.[253] This unit was transferred to the princely state of Indore in 1947.[254]

The British officers of the Malwa Bhil Corps wore tropical spiked helmets covered with rifle green in full dress. A regimental badge of a French hunting horn with the letters 'MBC' inside the strings was worn on the front of the pagri. The pagri worn around the helmet was dark green.

The hussar-style tunic was rifle green, rounded off in front. It had five rows of braid across the front. Carman stated that, in 1886, there were five drop loops, and this continued on into 1901.[255] The collar and cuffs were scarlet. The tunic had 2.54cm (one inch) of black mohair along all openings. Officers also had black braid at the collar and cuff. The size of the braid depended on their rank. Their overalls (trousers) and pantaloons were rifle green with black mohair stripes.

250 Perry, *Order Part 1*, p.164.
251 W. Y. Carman, *Indian Army Uniforms under the British from the 18th Century to 1947: Artillery, Engineers, and Infantry* (London: Morgan-Grampian Books, 1969), p.195.
252 Army Department [AD], *Army Regulations, India, 1901, Volume 1, Dress* (Calcutta: Superintendent Government Printing, 1901), pp.205–06.
253 Richard Head and Tony McClenaghan, *The Maharajas' Paltans: A History of the Indian State Forces, 1888–1948* (New Delhi: Manohar Publishers, 2013), part 1, p.363.
254 Head and McClenaghan, *Maharajas' Paltans*, part 1, p.375.
255 Carman, *Indian Army Uniforms*, p.194.

Mer and Merat.

Muslims of Eastern Punjab and Hindustan.

Rajputan and Hindustan Muslims.

Mazhabi Sikhs.

Punjabi Muslims.

Dogras.

Madras soldier. Traditionally in the Madras Presidency, different castes served in the same regiment.

Sikhs.

Bombay soldier. Traditionally in the Bombay Presidency, different castes served in the same regiment.

Brahmans.

The pouch belt was black patent leather, 7.30cm (2.88in) wide, with a regimental badge of silver, a French hunting horn, and 'MBC' between the strings and whistle and chain on it. The pouch was of black patent leather with the regimental badge on it.

### *Meywar (Mewar) Bhil Corps*

The 1901 dress regulations for native officers, which would also apply roughly to the enlisted men, provided for a dress similar to that worn by the Malwa Bhils. The coat was rifle green and had four buttons. The coat was cut away at the bottom. There was no collar, but the neck opening had scarlet trim 1.91cm (0.75in) wide around it. The pointed cuffs were scarlet.

The trousers were rifle green. The regulations stated they were pegtop. But some historical photographs show loose trouser bottoms. Black leather gaiters were worn. The regulations stated

Gurkhas.

Heavy artillery drawn by elephants. In British India, with rare exceptions, native personal did not man artillery guns.

that native officers had a black leather pouch and pouch belt without ornamentations. However, images exist that clearly show a plate, chains, and whistle on the native officers' pouch belt.[256]

British officers wore the same uniform as the Malwa Bhil Corps.[257]

256 AD, *Regulations 1901*, vol. 1, p.224.
257 Carman, *Indian Army Uniforms*, p.195.

The state of Udaipur paid 50,000 rupees (current value: £73,285,710 or $87,000,030) per year towards the cost of this regiment.[258] This corps was turned over to the Indian state of Udaipur in 1938.[259]

Two other local regiments composed of aboriginal tribesmen were in existence in 1914. They were the Mers, the Merats, and the Minas.

### *Mers and Merats*

The Mers and Merats are basically the same people. The difference is that the Mers are nominally Hindu and the Merats are nominally Muslim. For many years, the difference in religion made no difference to them, and they freely ate together and intermarried. Then, this changed as they started to come into more contact with the outside world through delegations of soldiers being sent to encampments, jubilees, and so on, among other things. One writer traced this change specifically to the men going to the coronation of King Edward VII in 1904.[260] Their fellow region's members put pressure on them to end the free and easy inter-religious mingling they were practicing. And, in time, they did.[261]

The Mers and Merats lived in a range of hills near the central area of Rajputana. From there, they tended to engage in dacoity.[262] The British, by forming a unit of this ethnic group, gave employment to a portion of the community, thus pulling them away from dacoity and setting thieves to guard thieves.

These men went into the 44th Mharwara Regiment. This was a local infantry regiment stationed in Rajputana. Military service was extremely popular among them,[263] doubtlessly because of the improvement in status it gave these untouchable people. During the First World War, their percentage of enlistment to population was higher than that of any other class in India.[264]

### *Minas (Meenas)*

The Minas (or Meenas) were found in the western part of Central India and Rajputana.[265] They were enlisted in what were, using 1914 titles, the 42nd Deoli Regiment and the 43rd Erinpura Regiment.[266] In fact, when the Deoli Regiment was formed in 1857, its title was the 'Meena Battalion'.

There was a dispute as to whether the Minas were an aboriginal people or the descendants of invaders who had come into India and reached Central India and Rajputana ahead of the Rajputs. They are listed here under aboriginal tribes because most people during the Raj period considered them to be aboriginal people.

258 Richard Head and Tony McClenaghan, *The Maharajas' Paltans: A History of the Indian State Forces, 1888–1948* (New Delhi: Manohar Publishers, 2013), part 2, p.553.
259 Head and McClenaghan, *Maharajas' Paltans*, part 2, pp.560–61.
260 Edmund Candler, *The Sepoy* (London: John Murray, 1919), p.176.
261 Cole, *Rajputana*, p.46.
262 Bonarjee, *Handbook*, pp.148–49.
263 Cole, *Rajputana*, p.46.
264 Cole, *Rajputana*, p.46.
265 Bonarjee, *Handbook*, p.147.
266 Bonarjee, *Handbook*, p.148.

It is claimed that Minas were the people that built the Amber Fortress, the place of the Maharajas of Jaipur. They were the guardians of the treasure of the Maharajas of Jaipur and were said to hold charge of the palace–fortress as well as filling many confidential posts in the Maharajas' household.[267]

The higher-status clans of Minas, those who claim to have Rajput blood, went into the Deoli Regiment.[268] It is one of these clans, the Ujlas, who are the guardians of the Jaipur treasure.[269] The aboriginal clans from Sirohi and Jodhpur – those with less Rajput blood – were enlisted by the 43rd Erinpura Regiment.[270]

### *Garhwalis*

The Garhwalis (or Garhwals) are another class that takes their name from a location. Thus, in theory, the term could apply to anyone who lives there. But what the British, and later the modern Indian army, meant by the term was Khasa. The Khasa claim to be Rajputs, and they speak a language akin to the Hindus of Rajputana.[271] To this element is added a Mongol strain. This strain is more pronounced in the north near the Tibet border and thins out as one moves south.[272]

The term 'Garhwal' comes from 'garh', a fort, and 'wal', the place of.[273] It is said the entire area is studded with forts, reminders of a war-like past.

Garhwal is a western district of the Kumaon (alternatively spelled 'Kumaun') Division.[274] Kumaon, in turn, is the most northern division of a province that confusingly went by two names. Up to 1902, it was the Lieutenant Governorship of the North-Western Provinces and Oudh.[275] Then, in 1902, it became the United Provinces. The Kumaon Division is against Tibet in the north and Nepal in the east. Its border on the west was against the princely state of Tehri (also known as Tehri-Garhwal) and Dehra Dun District.[276] The Garhwal District lies against Tibet on the north and the princely state of Tehri on the northwest. It consists for the most part of high, rugged mountains.[277] The literacy rate for males in the district in 1901 was 13 percent, which was fairly high among Indian populations.[278]

The typical Garhwali that went into the 39th Garhwal Rifles lived high up in the Himalaya Mountains, and this produced a short man with strong leg, back, neck, and chest muscles. Recruits in the pre-First World War days were on average 1.61m (five feet, 3.5in) tall with a 86cm (34in) chest.[279] The regiment preferred men who were 'wild highland agriculturist[s] from

267 Cole, *Rajputana*, p.41.
268 Candler, *Sepoy*, p.188.
269 Candler, *Sepoy*, p.197.
270 Candler, *Sepoy*, pp.188–89.
271 J. Evatt, *Historical Record of the 39th Royal Garhwal Rifles, 1887–1922* (Aldershot: Gale and Polden, 1922), vol. 1, p.6, footnote.
272 Bonarjee, *Handbook*, pp.169–71.
273 Evatt, *Royal Garhwal*, p.1.
274 Herbert Hope Risley, William Stevenson Meyer, Richard Burn, and James Sutherland Cotton (eds), 'Garhwāl District', in *The Imperial Gazetteer of India* (Oxford: Clarendon Press, 1908), vol. 12, p.163.
275 Bonarjee, *Handbook*, p.167.
276 Herbert Hope Risley, William Stevenson Meyer, Richard Burn, and James Sutherland Cotton (eds), 'Kumaun', in *The Imperial Gazetteer of India* (Oxford: Clarendon Press, 1908), vol. 16, p.18.
277 Hope Risley, Stevenson Meyer, Burn, and Sutherland Cotton (eds), 'Garhwāl', p.163.
278 Hope Risley, Stevenson Meyer, Burn, and Sutherland Cotton (eds), 'Garhwāl', p.171.
279 Evatt, *Royal Garhwal*, p.7.

the intermost recesses of the Himalayas'.[280] The result was a soldier that looked like a Gurkha, often like a Khas Gurkha, and other times like a Magar or Gurung. It is claimed that 90 percent of the people of Garhwal belong to what in Nepal would be called the Khas ethnic group.[281]

The Gurkhas invaded the state of Garhwal in 1791 but did not complete their conquest of the state because the Gurkha army was called back to deal with a Tibetan attack on Nepal. However, the Rajah of Garhwal did begin paying an annual tribute of 25,000 rupees (£31,920,000 or $37,890,000 in modern monies). In 1803, the Gurkhas came back in force and overran Garhwal. The Garhwal Rajah was killed in battle.[282]

The Gurkha subjected Garhwal to a harsh rule, destroying property, taking people as slaves, and killing members of the leading families.[283] The Nepalese government took the men of the Garhwal and Kumaon into its army. The Gazetteer of the United Provinces asserted that two-thirds of Nepalese forces in the western possessions in 1814 were men from the upper areas of Garhwal and Kumaon.[284]

At the end of the war with Nepal, the British, in 1815, received Garhwal and made it the present district. They, however, reduced its size by giving a portion, about half, to a descendant of the last Garhwal Rajah. This became the princely state of Tehri.[285] One of the first three Gurkha battalions raised by the British from among the remains of the old Gurkha army was the Kumaon Battalion (which was the 3rd Queen Alexandra's Own Gurkha Rifles in 1914). The original members of the battalion were men from the Garhwal and Kumaon areas.[286]

Men from Garhwal were subsequently enlisted by the British in the first five Gurkha regiments, particularly the 5th Gurkhas. They seem to have done well and were held in high regard as a fighting class.[287]

In 1880, it was proposed to raise a regiment of Garhwalis, but it went nowhere until 1886, when Lord Roberts was commander-in-chief of the Indian army and recommended the action.[288] With this support, in April 1887, the formation of an all-Garhwali 2nd Battalion of the 3rd (Kumaon) Gurkha Rifles was started. A nucleus was created by transferring Garhwalis from other regiments.[289] At first, recruits were to come only from the northern portion of the Garhwal District. But this did not yield enough men. After a short time, the entire district was opened to recruiting, and later the northern portion of the Kumaon border. This still did not produce sufficient recruits, so the makeup of the battalion was changed to have two Gurkha companies and six of Garhwalis.[290]

In 1891, the Garhwalis were given a new regimental number. The old 39th (Allyghur Levy) Regiment had been disbanded. The new 39th adopted a phoenix as its crest to reflect the 39th's

280 Evatt, *Royal Garhwal*, p.7.
281 MacMunn, *Martial*, p.285.
282 Bonarjee, *Handbook*, p.173.
283 Bonarjee, *Handbook*, pp.173–74.
284 Evatt, *Royal Garhwal*, p.8.
285 Bonarjee, *Handbook*, p.174; Herbert Hope Risley, William Stevenson Meyer, Richard Burn, and James Sutherland Cotton (eds), 'Tehri State', in *The Imperial Gazetteer of India* (Oxford: Clarendon Press, 1908), vol. 23, p.270.
286 Marrion and Fosten, *Tradition*, p.16.
287 Evatt, *Royal Garhwal*, p.9.
288 Evatt, *Royal Garhwal*, p.9.
289 Evatt, *Royal Garhwal*, pp.9–10.
290 Evatt, *Royal Garhwal*, pp.9–11.

rebirth.[291] In 1892, the 39th was given the title of Rifles.[292] Then, in March 1901, a second Garhwali regiment, the 49th, was raised. But, in November of 1901, it was changed into the 2nd Battalion of the 39th Garhwal Rifles.[293] This made it the only line regiment to have two battalions. With two battalions and wearing essentially the same uniform as the Gurkhas, they were outwardly very much like the Gurkhas.

Before 1914, opinions differed on the value and nature of the Garhwali. Their officers, as often happened with British officers with any class in which they served, were full of praise for them. The history of the Garhwal regiment, written by a British officer, says the Garhwali was bright, cheery, intelligent, and a thorough and willing worker. He was also very painstaking in learning and punctilious in regard to any trust given to him. Furthermore, he was generous and open-handed to a fault. They were so honest that, for a long time, there were no police in Garhwal. He had an independent, obstinate personality. This made him a splendid soldier to lead but a hard one to drive.[294]

Others were not so sure. One Indian author gave these assessments: he was agreed to be brave and had good endurance. He was more intelligent than the Gurkhas and not as caste ridden as the Rajputs of the plains. But he was not as free of caste prejudices as the Gurkhas. He did not have the soldier-fighting instinct of the Sikhs and the Gurkhas, but it could be brought out. They were quiet and orderly. When compared to the Gurkhas, he did not have the Gurkhas' cheerful and good-humoured nonchalance under stress. He was more likely to be depressed by failure, did not have as much grit and backbone, nor was he likeable as the Gurkha, whose jokes made him a favourite with the British.[295]

However, despite these nitpicking comparisons with the Gurkhas, the Garhwalis more than proved their worth as soldiers in the First World War. Both battalions were sent to Flanders, where they fought very well. They suffered such heavy casualties that, by the next year, when the Indian troops were pulled out, the two battalions were down to one combined battalion.[296] After being reformed into the two battalions again, both went to Mesopotamia. The 2nd Battalion later went to Salonika and to Turkey.[297]

The regiment's outstanding wartime performance was recognised by the expanded four-wartime battalion Garhwali regiment being carried over to the revised post-First World War Indian army. It was very unusual for war-raised units to be carried over to the post-First World War army. Even regular regiments were being disbanded after the war. Clearly, the army thought well of the Garhwalis. In addition, in 1921, the 39th was made a royal regiment for its outstanding record in the First World War.[298]

A battalion raised from the Kumaon District during the First World War was also carried over in 1922 as part of the 19th Hyderabad Regiment.[299] In recognition of the Kumaon battalion's services in the First World War, one of its officers was made a King's Orderly Officer in 1922.

291 Evatt, *Royal Garhwal*, pp.9, 13.
292 Gaylor, *Sons*, p.192.
293 Evatt, *Royal Garhwal*, p.29.
294 Evatt, *Royal Garhwal*, p.8.
295 Bonarjee, *Handbook*, pp.175–76.
296 Gaylor, *Sons*, p.192.
297 Gaylor, *Sons*, p.192.
298 Gaylor, *Sons*, p.192.
299 Gaylor, *Sons*, p.196.

### *Madras Classes*

The town of Madras (now called Chennai) was created in 1639, and a fort for it, Fort St George, was built in 1644. Knowing that war is bad for business, the EIC tried to avoid fighting whenever possible and to maintain the minimum number of soldiers possible.[300] The French also had a trading company in India, the French East India Company. For most of a century, the two trading companies had found it in their best interests not to fight one another, even when their home countries were at war.[301] This changed when the French attacked the city of Madras in 1746.[302] To defend the city, the EIC had a handful of soldiers. Only 200 British, who were invariably drunk, could be hurriedly raised. There were also a few ill-disciplined sepoys. Madras surrendered in a few hours.[303]

The city was restored to the company at the end of the War of Austrian Succession (1740–1748).[304] The creation of the Madras army dates to 1746,[305] which makes it the second oldest of the presidential armies. Bombay's dates to 1662, and Bengal's to 1754.[306] In 1758, the men were formed into regular battalions, which marked the formation of Madras regiments.[307]

The Madras regiments went on to break French interests and power in India and sent their European soldiers and sepoys to Bengal with Robert Clive.[308] They helped win the Battle of Plassey in 1757.[309] In fact, they were the majority of the British troops that took part in the battle.[310] Later, they defeated the forces of Mysore under Hyder Ali and his son, the better-known Tipu Sultan, the 'Tiger of Mysore'. The general British public may know Tipu best by 'Tipu's Tiger', one of the most popular exhibits at the Victoria and Albert Museum. It is a near-life-sized semi-automaton that shows a European man in a red coat, probably a British soldier or civilian, being savaged by a tiger.

General Wellesley, the future Duke of Wellington, while he was just a sepoy general, won the Battle of Assaye in 1803 using mostly Madras troops. He also had several regular British regiments.[311] This victory went far towards breaking Maratha's power. Wellington was later to say that Assaye had been his greatest victory.[312]

To accomplish these deeds, the Madras soldiers needed to beat in battle French sepoys given the same training by the French as the Madras soldiers had from the British. They had captured strong fortresses, such as Tipu's Seringapatam, and won battles against long odds. At Assaye, the British–Madras army was outnumbered five to one.[313] They, in contrast to the Purbiyas of

300 E. G. Phythian-Adams, *The Madras Regiment, 1758–1958* (Wellington: Defence Services Staff College Press, 1958), p.1, footnote.
301 Brian Gardner, *The East India Company: A History* (London: Hart-Davis, 1971), pp.53–54.
302 Phythian-Adams, *Madras*, p.1.
303 Gardner, *Company*, p.56.
304 Gardner, *Company*, p.59.
305 Gardner, *Company*, p.58, footnote.
306 Gardner, *Company*, p.58, footnote.
307 Phythian-Adams, *Madras*, p.3.
308 Gardner, *Company*, p.82.
309 Gardner, *Company*, p.87.
310 Phythian-Adams, *Madras*, p.22.
311 Phythian-Adams, *Madras*, pp.138–42; MacMunn, *Armies*, pp.44–47.
312 Bryan Perrett, *The Battle Book: Crucial Conflicts in History from 1469 BC to the Present* (London: Arms and Armour, 1992), p.33.
313 Phythian-Adams, *Madras*, p.138.

the Bengal army, had no problem with movement by sea. They had moved up to Bengal by sea in 1756 to help win the Battle of Plassey. In 1762, 650 Madras sepoys, as part of an ad hoc unit, took part in the largely forgotten expedition that captured Manila.[314]

The Madras sepoy was described as having an 'undeviating loyalty, devotion to his officers, and a remarkable power of endurance'. He had a steadiness that was almost unknown in Europe during this period. When treated well, they were the most loyal of soldiers. In the First Mysore War, their pay was 16 months in arrears, famine was present all over the countryside, the enemy was at the gates of Madras, and the foe offered large sums of money to the Madras sepoys to desert. Through all this, the men stayed loyal and fought several battles. Frederick the Great of Prussia, when he read an account of the Madras sepoys' actions during the war, is said to have remarked that, if he commanded troops that acted like the Madras sepoys, he could conquer all of Europe.[315]

The Madras army was almost totally loyal during the Indian Mutiny.[316] None of the infantry regiments mutinied, and six of the battalions (regiments) served in Central India, helping to put down the rebellion there.[317] In 1914, the two surviving Madras regiments with the Central India Horse Battle Honour were the 61st Pioneers and the 79th Carnatic Infantry.[318] Madras artillery served at Cawnpore and in the Oudh campaign.[319]

In the Madras army, in stark contrast to the company's Bengal army, there was no attention paid to caste. The army accepted whatever classes volunteered, and, once in the army, the different castes ate, slept, and stood in ranks together without regard to their caste or position in the world outside.[320] One soldier in the 1830s put it this way: 'we put our religion into our knapsacks whenever our colours are unfurled'.[321]

When a Madras soldier fell out of favour, the Madras population was subject to comment that they lacked backbone and moral hardihood and were too pliable, plastic, and soft. Furthermore, they were 'too prone to inertness and dependence to be capable of becoming a great people'.[322] A 1904 government security study states the Madrassi were being eliminated from the army because they lacked soldierly instincts.[323]

There were several different reasons and theories advanced to explain why the Madras soldier, in spite of his outstanding history, was no longer fit to fight. One was a crude Darwinism that the people of the north were simply superior to those of the south. Others said the cooler weather bred superior races. The Northern Indians were superior to the Southern Indians; the Europeans were superior to the Indians; and the northern Europeans were superior to the southern Europeans. Others claimed the long years of peace would drain the fighting spirit out

314 Mason, *Honour*, p.242.
315 G. E. D. Mouat, *Handbooks for the Indian Army: Madras Classes* (Calcutta: Office of the Superintendent, Government Printing, India, 1938), pp.8–9.
316 Perry, *Order Part 1*, p.119. The 8th Madras Cavalry, formed in 1808, was disbanded in 1857, so there may have been questions about its loyalty.
317 Mason, *Honour*, p.305.
318 N. B. Leslie, *Battle Honours of the British and Indian Armies, 1695–1914* (London: Leo Cooper, 1970), p.85.
319 Mason, *Honour*, p.305.
320 Mason, *Honour*, p.23.
321 Mason, *Honour*, p.23.
322 Bonarjee, *Handbook*, p.152.
323 Omissi, *Sepoy*, p.213.

of the Asian population, and this is what had happened to the Madras population. Several other theories were based on the fact that, for the last three-fourths of the nineteenth century, the Madras army saw almost no combat, while the Bengal army was frequently in action.

The first dealt with officers. It held that the fire-eating, go-getting officers would tend to go to the north, where there was a better chance of seeing combat and earning promotions. On the other hand, Madras would end up with sedate, less energetic, and plain bad officers. To the latter group, one might also add officers with fewer contacts with the powers in the army administration, which was in the north.

The second concerned the men. With little combat to expect in the future, all that the sepoys had to look forward to on volunteering was a life of garrison duty, doing the maintenance labour that garrison life involved. Over time, the men with real fighting spirit would avoid such a prospect and not join.

A third idea had to do with the rot that just naturally sets in to even the best troops when they pull garrison duty for too long. Corners tend to be cut, combat skills atrophy, and the men and officers lose their edge. How much worse must it be if a regiment pulls garrison duty for generations? They certainly would not perform well if thrown right from long garrison duty into combat or a combat theatre.

The last, it must be said, is that the Madras soldier is generally a short, dark, and slight man. In this, he compared himself unfavourably with the lighter, taller, and more muscular men in the Punjab who conformed more closely to the Victorian ideal. In India, as a rule of thumb, the lower castes tend to be shorter and darker, while the higher ones are taller and fairer. It is also generally the case that, as one moves from India's north to south and from her west to east, the inhabitants are more often small and dark.[324] The Victorians had prejudices against Negro and Mongolian races and, in some cases, against other Europeans ('the WOGs start at Calais'). This carried over into their evaluation of the fighting ability of different groups of people. But it was not all controlling. They gave high marks to the Gurkhas and favoured the Senegalese, a black group, over the lighter-skinned Egyptians. However, with the Madras soldier, his slight build and dark skin seemed to have worked against him.

In their glory days, the Madras regiments placed their men in their regiments with no attention paid to class. Furthermore, it was an army largely composed of men from the Madras Presidency or other Southern Indian areas. Table 35, which is a blending of the muster roles of 36 Madras regiments picked at random between 1808 and 1829, shows the percent of sepoys drawn from different areas.

Later, the Madras regiments began to poach men from Northern India. The Eden Commission of 1879 stressed that each of the presidential armies was to retain its geographical composition and recruit only from its own area. If an army could not recruit enough men to man its regiments, then the number of regiments needed to be reduced. The decline of the Madras army dates from this time.[325]

324 Mason, *Honour*, p.125.

325 Stephen P. Cohen, *The Indian Army: Its Contribution to the Development of a Nation* (Oxford: Oxford University Press, 2001), pp.40–41.

**Table 35 Percent of Madras Army from Different Areas between 1808 and 1829**[326]

| Location | Percentage |
|---|---|
| Bengal | 1.65% |
| Deccan | 1.66% |
| Circars* | 28.32% |
| Carnatic† and Trichinopoly | 35.43% |
| Madura and Dindigul | 7.78% |
| Tanjore | 7.45% |
| Travancore and Tinnevelly | 6.98% |
| Malabar and Bombay | 0.44% |
| Mysore | 9.40% |
| Mahrattas | 0.89% |
| **Total** | **100.00%** |

* Circars is the northern part of the Madras Presidency.
† Carnatic is the southern part of the Madras Presidency.

The recommendations of the Eden Commission were based on the premise that the main problem was internal security and that foreign expeditions were unlikely. The Russian scare made the authorities start thinking about fighting European troops, and military efficiency became more important than internal security and maintaining balance among the presidential armies.[327]

In the Third Burma War of 1887–1889, it was agreed that the Madras regiments did not perform well.[328] The best the Madras sepoy supporters could say about their performance in Burma was, 'it does not appear that more regrettable incidents occurred to Madras troops than to those of other Presidencies'.[329] This author went on to say the Madras incidents were given more publicity than the others.[330] Another factor may have been the age of the Madras soldiers. In 1879, 37 percent of the sepoys in the Madras army had over 15 years of service. This should be contrasted with the Bombay army's 23 percent and the Bengal army's 11 percent.[331] At some point, an army changes from being one of seasoned soldiers to being one of tired old men. Shortly after this war, the process of replacing Madras sepoys with men from the north began.[332]

A glance at the class makeup of the regiments in the Madras range of regimental numbers, 26th to 27th Light Cavalry and 61st to 93rd Infantry, will show how the great majority have northern classes in them. By 1914, only three pioneer regiments and eight understrength – what were in effect garrison regiments – existed that had men from the Madras Presidency.[333]

326 Phythian-Adams, *Madras*, p.263.
327 Cohen, *Indian Army*, p.41.
328 Cohen, *Indian Army*; MacMunn, *Martial*, p.292.
329 Phythian-Adams, *Madras*, p.5.
330 Phythian-Adams, *Madras*, p.5.
331 Omissi, *Sepoy*, p.14.
332 MacMunn, *Martial*, p.292.
333 Phythian-Adams, *Madras*, p.6.

These Madras regiments were normally called 'Carnatic' rather than 'Madras', as if the term 'Madras' was tainted. In 1895, all Madras regiments were changed to a class company organisation.[334] They were set up on a rough class basis of companies of Tamils, Madrasi Muslims, Paraiyans, and Christians. The number varied from regiment to regiment.

Tamil is one of the two major languages spoken in the Madras Presidency. It was spoken by just under 40 percent of the population in the 1890s. The other is Teluga, spoken by 39.5 percent during the same period.[335] These percentages roughly held true in the 1930s.[336] About seven percent of the population was Muslim during this period.[337]

***Madras: Paraiyans***

The Paraiyans were a Tamil untouchable class. In the south of India, not only were untouchables not allowed to touch Brahmins or their food, but they also had to stay a certain distance away from them.[338] The caste acted as gravediggers, watchmen, and scavengers. Most were field labourers, although many owned and cultivated land.[339]

They had a reputation for being dirty, drunken, and somewhat immoral. But, in the military, where they as a class have served for a long time, they are viewed as 'cheerful, brave, and willing soldiers, capable of great physical effort in spite of hardship and danger'.[340]

***Madras: Christians***

The Christians in Madras made up about three percent of the total population in 1931.[341]

***Madras: Others***

The military authorities completely stopped recruiting the Teluga-speaking portion of the population before 1914, just under 40 percent of the total Madras population.[342] This was done in spite of the fact that they had once been 25 percent of the Madras army.[343] However, after the First World War, Telugas were accepted.[344] They also stopped recruiting or never accepted men from the other smaller language groups: Tulu, Kodagu, Toda, Kondi, and Gondhi.[345]

***Madras: Tamils***

The army, under the class system, did not accept all Tamils. Only six classes were accepted in the 1930s for the Queen Victoria's Own Madras Sappers and Miners, a few units of the India Signal Corps, and the 1st Madras Field Battery Indian Army (the last of the Madras infantry

334 Omissi, *Sepoy*, p.87.
335 Bonarjee, *Handbook*, p.151.
336 Mouat, *Madras*, p.18.
337 Bonarjee, *Handbook*, pp.151–52; Mouat, *Madras*, p.62.
338 Mouat, *Madras*, p.59. It appears that the distance they must keep away from higher castes varies by area, because different authors provide different numbers for how far an untouchable must stay away from a Brahmin. Other authors give different distances.
339 Mouat, *Madras*, pp.59, 61.
340 Mouat, *Madras*, p.59.
341 Mouat, *Madras*, p.62.
342 Mouat, *Madras*, p.18; Bonarjee, *Handbook*, p.151.
343 Heathcote, *Indian*, p.104.
344 Mouat, *Madras*, pp.44–58.
345 See Bonarjee, *Handbook*, p.15, for information on these languages.

battalions had been disbanded in 1928).[346] But, since they accepted the same groups as the pre-1914 Madras infantry regiments, the handbook that covered their classes can provide useful guidance.

**Table 36 Tamil Classes[347]**

| Class | Occupation |
|---|---|
| Agamudaiyan | Cultivators |
| Idaiyan (Yadhava) | Shepherds |
| Kammalan (VisvaBrahmin) | Artisans (Goldsmiths, Brass-smiths, Carpenters, Stone Masons, and Blacksmiths) |
| Shanan | Toddydrawers* |
| Vanniyan (or Palli) | Cultivators |
| Vellalan | Cultivators |

* Toddydrawers, also spelled 'toddy-drawers', extract and collect palm sap, which quickly ferments into wine.

### *Madras: Muslims*

Not all Muslims were enlisted. The Madras handbook states that about two-thirds of the Madras Muslims were 'mixed breeds' and converts to Islam and not genuine Muslims at all.[348] The handbook divides the Muslims of Madras into two groups: immigrants from outside or their descendants; and natives of the country who have converted to Islam.

The first group was the bulk of the Muslims enlisted. They spoke only Hindustani and never spoke Tamil. The men were often light in colour, had narrow faces, and had long noses with a pronounced bridge.[349] The second group was only sparingly enlisted. Recent converts, those who spoke only Tamil, and those who had a 'low caste Hindu face' should never be taken.[350]

The best Muslims were hard-working and robust. They came into Madras as fighters, and their fighting spirit remained excellent in their descendants.[351]

**Table 37 Madras Regiments Disbanded and the Year[352]**

| Year | Madras Infantry Regiment | Madras Cavalry Regiment |
|---|---|---|
| 1857 | | 8th |
| 1860 | | 5th, 6th, and 7th |
| 1862 | 47th, 48th, 49th, 50th, 51st, and 52nd | |
| 1864 | 18th, 42nd, 43rd, 44th, 45th, and 46th | |
| 1882 | 34th, 35th, 36th, 38th, 39th, 40th, and 41st | |
| 1890 | 10th* | |

346 Gaylor, *Sons*, p.138.
347 Bonarjee, *Handbook*, pp.26–34.
348 Mouat, *Madras*, p.62.
349 Mouat, *Madras*, p.63.
350 Mouat, *Madras*, p.63.
351 Mouat, *Madras*, p.63.
352 Perry, *Order Part 1*, pp.119, 134–37; Mason, *Honour*, p.361.

| Year | Madras Infantry Regiment | Madras Cavalry Regiment |
|---|---|---|
| 1891 | | 4th |
| 1901 | 11th† | |
| 1902 | 8th | |
| 1903 | 17th‡, 77th (Moplah Rifles), and 25th‡ | |
| 1904 | 5th (65th Carnatic Light Infantry) | |

* Mason, *Honour*, p.361, states that the 10th Madras Infantry disbanded in 1891.
† Changed to Coorg and disbanded in 1904.
‡ Mason, *Honour*, p.361, states that the 17th and 25th Madras Infantry disbanded in 1907.

**Table 38 Regiments Converted to Pioneers and the Year**[353]

| Year | Infantry Regiment* |
|---|---|
| 1883 | 1st (61st) and 4th (64th) |
| 1891 | 21st (81st) |

* The number in parenthesis is the regiment's number in 1914.

**Table 39 Regiments that Had Their Personnel Replaced by Men from Outside Madras (from the Punjab)**[354]

| Infantry Regiment* |
|---|
| 62nd Punjabi Regiment |
| 66th Punjabi Regiment |
| 67th Punjabi Regiment |
| 69th Punjabi Regiment |
| 72nd Punjabi Regiment |
| 74th Punjabi Regiment |
| 76th Punjabi Regiment |
| 82nd Punjabi Regiment |
| 84th Punjabi Regiment |
| 87th Punjabi Regiment |
| 89th Punjabi Regiment |
| 90th Punjabi Regiment |
| 91st Punjabi Regiment |
| 92nd Punjabi Regiment |
| 93rd Burma Regiment |

* Number and short title in 1914.

353 Perry, *Order Part 1*, pp.134–37; Mason, *Honour*, p.361.
354 Perry, *Order Part 1*, pp.134–37.

**Table 40 Regiments with Madras Classes in 1914**[355]

| Infantry Regiment* | Cavalry Regiment* |
|---|---|
| 61st King George's Own Pioneer Regiment | 26th Light Cavalry (formerly 1st Madras Cavalry) |
| 63rd Palamcottah Light Infantry | 27th Light Cavalry (formerly 2nd Madras Cavalry) |
| 64th Pioneer Regiment | 28th Light Cavalry (formerly 3rd Madras Cavalry) |
| 73rd Carnatic Infantry | |
| 75th Carnatic Infantry | |
| 79th Carnatic Infantry | |
| 80th Carnatic Infantry | |
| 81st Pioneer Regiment | |
| 83rd Wallajahbad Light Infantry | |
| 86th Carnatic Infantry | |
| 88th Carnatic Infantry | |

* Number and short title in 1914.

**Table 41 Infantry Regiments with Madras Classes Disbanded Right after the First World War**[356]

| Infantry Regiment |
|---|
| 63rd Palamcottah Light Infantry |
| 80th Carnatic Infantry |
| 88th Carnatic Infantry |

**Table 42 Infantry Regiments with Madras Classes Disbanded in the 1920s and 1930s**[357]

| Year | Old Regiment Number | New Battalion Number |
|---|---|---|
| 1923 | 79th Carnatic Infantry and 83rd Wallajahbad Light Infantry | 3/3rd and 4/3rd Madras Regiment |
| 1926 | 75th Carnatic Infantry and 86th Carnatic Infantry | 2/3rd and 10/3rd Madras Regiment |
| 1928 | 73rd Carnatic Infantry | 1/3rd Madras Regiment |
| 1933 | 61st, 64th, and 81st Pioneers | 1/1st, 2/1st, and 10/1st Madras Pioneers |

When picking what regiments to carry over after the First World War, the old 80th was to have been retained. It had a distinguished history and was the possessor of one of Haider Ali's standards, taken in 1781. However, due to a clerical error, the 86th was carried over rather than the 80th.[358]

355 Perry, *Order Part 1*, pp.134–37; Mason, *Honour*, p.361.
356 Perry, *Order Part 1*, pp.119, 134–37.
357 Gaylor, *Sons*, pp.123, 138.
358 Gaylor, *Sons*, p.138.

**Table 43 Madras Cavalry Regiments Retained after the First World War**[359]

| Old Regiment Number | New Regiment Number |
|---|---|
| 26th Light Cavalry | 8th Light Cavalry (with 30th Lancers) |
| 27th Light Cavalry | 16th Light Cavalry* |
| 28th Light Cavalry | 7th Light Cavalry* |

* These were the two army cavalry regiments selected to be assigned Indian nationals as officers with full powers equal to British officers (Indianisation).[360]

### *Madras: Ethnic Background*

The Madras and other Southern Indian soldiers were often described as shorter and darker than the men of Northern India, almost like they were a different race. In a way, they might have been. In traditional theory, an Indo-European invasion had a heavy influence on the ethnic makeup of Northern India. The Indo-European invasion did not really reach Southern India. That area was populated by small groups who came to India via the Southern Dispersal Route out of Africa. This migration saw people leave Africa about 130,000 and 70,000 years ago and end up peopling Sothern India and Australia.

### *Marathas and Dekhani Muslims*

The Bombay Presidency ran from the borders of Persia (Iran) and Afghanistan to Mysore, near the southern tip of India, and the land across from the city of Bombay, the Dekhan. The Dekhan and the area around it were the home of the Marathas. The borders with Persia and Afghanistan had their own frontier forces. The Baluch regiments formed a major part of these. It included Sind of 'I have sinned' fame.[361]

The wide area of the presidency, its army's tendency to recruit men from outside its presidency, and the movement to a martial-races theory in recruiting all meant that the Bombay army had a wide range of classes in its ranks. Table 44 shows the composition of the army in 1903, after the class company system had fully come into force.

359 Gaylor, *Sons*, pp.73–75, 92.
360 Gaylor, Sons, p.74.
361 The 'I have sinned' statement comes out of Major Sir Charles Napier's actions in the Sind area of India. In 1842, Napier was sent out to ensure that the Amirs in the Sind did not take advantage of British problems in Afghanistan. In 1843, he defeated Amirs at the Battles of Meani and Hyderabad. He then went on to occupy the whole of the Sindh province, thereby far exceeding his orders. The humour magazine *Punch* (1841–2002) printed what seemed to be a factual report that he had sent back to his superiors the Latin message 'Peccavi', meaning 'I have sinned', a pun on 'I have Sindh'. *Punch* got the idea from Catherine Winkworth, a seventeen-year-old schoolgirl. Many people have believed ever since that Napier really sent that message. See Holmes, *Sahib*, pp.59–60.

**Table 44 Number of Companies by Ethnic Composition in the Bombay Infantry, 1903**[362]

| Ethnic Group | Companies |
|---|---|
| Konkani Marathas | 24 |
| Dekhani Marathas | 30 |
| Rajputana and Central Indian Muslims | 12 |
| Punjabi Muslims | 27 |
| Jats | 26 |
| Gujars | 12 |
| Dekhani Muslims | 14 |
| Rajputs | 12 |
| Pathans | 15 |
| Sikhs | 8 |
| Hazaras | 4 |
| Khattaks | 2 |
| Mahsud Wazirs* | 1 |
| Wazirs† | 1 |
| Baluchis and Brahuis | 8 |
| Mers | 6 |
| Hindustani Muslims | 6 |
| **Total (26 Battalions)** | **208** |

* A Pathan tribe.
† A Pathan tribe. This term presumably referred to the other great division of the Waziris, the Darwesh Khel.

By the period 1890–1900, following the abolition of the presidency armies (in 1895), the Bombay army had moved to a class company regimental system.[363] But, for 60 years, the number of classes that were taken into the Indian armies had been growing fewer.[364] Prior to that, both the Bombay and the Madras armies did not pay attention to a man's caste, and all castes stood side by side in the ranks. This also meant that they also ate and slept together.[365] There is a story told of a Bengal army sepoy of high caste from Oudh who asked to be discharged because another sepoy of lower rank had been promoted. Presumably, he thought he should have had the promotion. Upon being discharged, he then went and enlisted in the Bombay army, which did not cater to caste, and he had to face far greater indignities. When asked why he would make such an odd change, he explained that, in the Bengal army, each individual man took pride in his caste but, in the Bombay army, the sepoys took collective pride in the battalion (regiment).[366]

As the Bombay regiments began to develop class companies and regiments, certain ethnic groups that had in the past served in the army began to be dropped. Two examples are the Bene Israel Jews and the Mahars, an untouchable ethnic group that had served as soldiers in the Maratha (also spelled 'Mahratta') armies.

362 Omissi, *Sepoy*, p.22, Table 1.5.
363 Gaylor, *Sons*, p.212.
364 Mason, *Honour*, p.334.
365 Mason, *Honour*, p.23.
366 Mason, *Honour*, p.23.

When the Bombay army was being formed, the Mahars began serving in its ranks. They were hereditary local policemen, and so they seemed to be a natural martial class. It has been estimated that they made up a fifth to a quarter of the pre-Mutiny army.[367] In the famous Battle of Koregan, where a small force of Bombay soldiers held out against odds of 40 to one, they were about half the defending troops. The infantry unit, the 2/1st Bombay Native Infantry, was made a grenadier regiment (in 1914, the 102nd Grenadiers). Since the regiment was now a grenadier regiment and grenadiers were tall, men from the north were recruited, and the short Mahars were no longer enlisted in the unit. Their reward for heroism was the loss of employment in this new, prestigious battalion.[368] They were still serving in the Bombay army in 1880 when a Mahar of the 19th Bombay Infantry was part of a small party that died to the last man holding an outpost in Afghanistan.[369] But, with the abolition of the presidency armies and the move to class companies and regiments, the Mahars were no longer recruited for combat duty.[370] It is believed that there were only a few Mahars in the army in 1900, and they were almost all gone by 1914.[371]

The Mahars felt keenly about this exclusion, fearing a loss of what little status being soldiers had given them and fearful that it was a harbinger of other losses of government employment.[372] They began protesting the cutbacks in 1892.[373] This makes it clear that the process was already well under way by the early 1890s. A formal petition followed in 1910. Other classes – Maharashtrian Brahmins, Telugas, and Coorgs – cut from the army lists were making similar petitions.[374] They did no good, and these classes were not accepted for military service until First World War manpower needs forced the net to be widened for all of India. For example, the 111th Mahar, Anglo-Indian Force, 49th Bengalis, and 71st Punjabs (Punjabi Christians) were all raised during the First World War and disbanded at the end of the war.[375]

The process of changing over to class companies tended to involve a continuing process of restricting what classes were accepted. A good example of this can be seen in the case of the 5th Bombay (Light) Infantry (in 1914, the 105th Maratha Light Infantry), known as the Kali Panchwin, the Black Fifth,[376] because of its unusual black facings, an old and distinguished regiment.

In 1895, when the armies were amalgamated, the 5th had eight companies, each with a different class, namely: Rajputs, Dekhani Marathas, Konkani Marathas, Konkani Muslims, Dekhani Muslims, Bedars, Pardesis, and Sikhs. By 1903, the regiment had only Dekhani Marathas, Konkani Marathas, and Dekhani Muslims.[377]

The Bedars are a forest aborigine tribe of Bombay, Mysore, and Hyderabad (today, Kamataka, Telangana, and Maharashta). They fought in Shivaji's armies and were classified by the British as a criminal class.[378]

367 Cohen, *Indian Army*, p.59. He used two histories of the Bombay army published in 1938 as his sources for this statement.
368 Gaylor, *Sons*, pp.211–12; Mason, *Honour*, pp.16–17, 21.
369 Gaylor, *Sons*, p.212.
370 Gaylor, *Sons*, p.212.
371 Gaylor, *Sons*, p.60.
372 Gaylor, *Sons*, p.60.
373 Gaylor, *Sons*, p.60.
374 Gaylor, *Sons*, pp.60–61.
375 Gaylor, *Sons*, pp.9, 168–69, 211.
376 Mason, *Honour*, p.344.
377 Mason, *Honour*, p.344.
378 Herbert Hope Risley, William Stevenson Meyer, Richard Burn, and James Sutherland Cotton (eds), 'Belgaum District', in *The Imperial Gazetteer of India* (Oxford: Clarendon Press, 1908), vol. 7, p.149.

'Pardesis' is a Bombay term for speakers of Dekhini, a Muslim language spoken in Bombay and the princely states of Hyderabad and Mysore, similar to Urdu. The word, which means 'stranger' or 'foreigner',[379] has been used in several different contexts.

The heart of the presidency was the area behind Bombay. This area consisted of the coastal lands, a chain of mountains, the Sahyadri Range, called the 'Ghats' (steps), and the plateau above them, called the 'Dekhan'. The coast area is called the 'Konkan' and is about 25–50 miles (40–80km) wide. The area is, in most places, rugged and broken with thick jungles. It is interspersed with huge mountains and is intersected by rivers and a large number of rivulets.[380]

The Ghats rise about 305–610m (1,000–2,000ft) above the coastal lands. They have at their crest a zone of rugged hills and countless rivulets. It had high trees and low, impervious brushwood.[381] At the top of and behind the Ghats is the Dekhan, a vast, open, and level area almost without vegetation. It runs from the mountains in the north, the Vindhyas, down towards Hyderabad in the south.[382]

The British, in recruiting Marathas, divided them into two groups, the Konkan and Dekhan, divided by the crest of the Ghats. Men who lived in the crest zone, who were some of Shivaji's best troops, were considered Konkan.[383]

The Marathas claim to be Rajputs. However, because of the history of the Aryan invaders in the area, there are said to be some unique features to their practices. Maharashtra was the last area to be occupied by the Indian Aryans.[384] MacMunn felt that their claim to be Rajputs was not valid. The population was either Aryan with a heavy infusion of the conquered tribes or the original tribes 'only tempered with a leaven of Brahmanism'.[385]

While this may be somewhat of an overstatement written at a time when the Marathas were out of favour as a martial class, even the Maratha proponents acknowledge that the Rajput Maratha family groups or clans have adopted totems. As the Maratha handbook points out, this can 'scarcely be reconciled with a pure Rajput or even Aryan origin'.[386] These clan totems were so important that the handbook lists the totem for over half of the clans.[387]

### *A Maratha Hero: Shivaji*[388]

Just as one must know the history of the Sikhs to understand how they developed into one of the leading fighting classes of India, so one must have a general knowledge of Shivaji, called the 'mountain rat' by his Muslim foes.

He was the son of a Hindu landholder of intermediate rank, a squire, or at most a baron, serving a Muslim ruler of Bijapur.[389] When Emperor Aurangzebe came into Dekhan to break

379 K. S. Singh (ed.), *People of India: Maharashtra* (Mumbai: Popular Prakashan, 2004), vol. 30, part 1, p.408.
380 R. M. Betham, *Handbooks for the Indian Army: Marathas and Dekhani Musalmans* (Calcutta: Office of the Superintendent, Government Printing, India, 1908), p.44.
381 Betham, *Marathas*, pp.44–45.
382 Betham, *Marathas*, pp.46–47.
383 Betham, *Marathas*, p.46.
384 Betham, *Marathas*, p.7; MacMunn, *Armies*, p.165.
385 MacMunn, *Armies*, p.166.
386 Betham, *Marathas*, p.10.
387 Betham, *Marathas*, pp.150–55.
388 The bulk of information on the life of Shivaji comes from Betham, *Marathas*, pp.20–26.
389 Lord, *Maharajas*, p.97.

the Maratha's power, he also destroyed the smaller independent states in the south, including Bijapur, while he was in the area.

At age 20, he was able to gain possession of a fort, Torma, 40 miles (64.4km) west of Poona. The Muslim rulers put little value on this type of fort because they had been so easily captured, but Shivaji thought something could be made of them. Without being able to obtain permission to do so, he began to repair the fort. In the process of doing the repairs, a large treasure was discovered. Shivaji attributed this to a miracle done for his benefit. The funds were used to buy arms and ammunition and to build another fort nearby.

This set Shivaji on a career that, in many ways, is unique in history. Parts of it read like a European mediaeval epic or something out of *One Thousand and One Nights*. He matched wits with emperors in Delhi, was a captive of one of the emperors, and escaped. He snuck past a city full of soldiers to go into a general's house, killing his personal guard and son. And, as noted above, he found a hidden treasure. Perhaps his most famous exploit was breaking a truce by killing an enemy general during a peace conference by stabbing him with a dagger and slashing him with 'tiger's claws' (metal tips that fit on the ends of fingers) that he had managed to smuggle into the conference. It needs to be said that the enemy general planned to kill him. This action, in 1659, followed by the destruction of the general's army by Shivaji's soldiers hidden in the dense vegetation around it, is considered the birth date of the Maratha nation. In history, in terms of creating a nation with a national consciousness, he has few peers except for Shaka Zula and Genghis Khan. He rose from the son of a small landholder to the head of a powerful nation that he had created by playing both ends against the middle among the shifting loyalties in what is now Dekhan and Konkan.

He has been called 'one of the greatest exponents of the skills of guerilla warfare'.[390] He also loved money, and war meant plunder to him. To gain plunder, he led raids into all parts of India against areas that had done him no harm. In 1664, he plundered the English trading town of Surati. Later, one of his raids went as far as the Bay of Bengal.

Today, he is a national hero, but the British took a more jaundiced view of him and the Marathas. They claim both his father and grandfather were soldiers of fortune. Shivaji's father made an arrangement with a local Muslim ruler (of Bijapur), which gave him a land grant and a title. They felt Shivaji had the instincts of his forefathers and delighted in predatory exploits. He grew up to be a leader of brigades and built up his rule on the basis of plunder and blackmail. Every year, he collected vast numbers of Maratha horsemen under his standard and scoured the countryside, near and far. They also claimed the name 'Shivaji' became a terror far and wide.[391]

During this period, his army consisted of about 50,000 infantry and 7,000 cavalry. The army consisted of all classes, including low-class untouchables, serving side by side.

Following Shivaji's death, his kingdom quickly fell apart. It ended up being ruled by Peshwas (prime ministers), who were the power behind the throne. This arrangement was not unheard of. The same thing happened in Japan, where the shoguns ruled on behalf of the emperors for centuries, and, in mediaeval France, where the Mayors of the Palaces (originally a nobleman who was head of

390 John Keegan and Andrew Wheatcroft, *Who's Who in Military History: From 1453 to the Present Day* (London: Weidenfeld and Nicolson, 1976), p.301, which has Shivaji's name spelled 'Sivaji'.

391 James Wheeler, *The History of the Imperial Assemblage at Delhi: Held on the 1st January, 1877, to Celebrate the Assumption of the Title of Empress of India by Her Majesty the Queen, Including Historical Sketches of India and Her Princes, Past and Present* (Jalandhar: R. K. Publishing House, 1982), pp.25–28.

the royal household, the *major domus*) were the powers behind the throne until one of them, Pepin the Short (714–768), stepped forwards and seized the crown. Charlemagne was the son of Pepin.[392]

After Shivaji's death, Emperor Aurangzebe personally led a large army to the Dekhan to bring his breakaway lords and the Maratha under control. He spent the rest of his life – 27 years – working towards this goal. But all he succeeded in doing was deepening the anarchy in the Dekhan and weakening the empire by not properly ruling it.[393] He besieged and conquered the two Muslim principalities that existed in the area, but he could not destroy the Marathas, who waged a war against him, putting armies in the field when it was safe and retreating to their mountain forts when necessary.[394] The death of the emperor in 1700 found the Mughal Empire weaker and the Marathas, without rivals in the Dekhan, stronger.

The Marathas began to play a part in the political battles around the throne in Delhi. In 1720, a Maratha army marched to Delhi to help depose one emperor and replace him with another who ruled until 1748. During these years, the Brahmin advisors to the illiterate Maratha chiefs, the Peshwas, became the true rulers of the land. The office of Peshwa became hereditary. The existence of the Peshwa gave a certain unity to the Marathas, which counterbalanced the fact that they had split up into a number of different principalities. During this time, the Marathas continued to send out wide-ranging plundering expeditions.[395]

In 1742, the English in Calcutta built a defensive work, the Maratha Ditch, to protect themselves from possible Maratha attacks.[396] The remains of the ditch could still be seen up to 1892–1893, when the last of the ditch was filled in.[397] There were also forts at Cuttack and Saharanpur that were built during the period for protection against their attacks.[398] In 1740, the Marathas were the most powerful nation in India.[399]

In 1761, they, together with a large number of Hindus, fought a Muslim Afghan army at Panipat, near Delhi. It was in part a battle to see which religion would control upper India and in part to see what group would control that area. The Marathas lost badly. The real winners were the rising English of the EIC, which was expanding into the Indian power vacuum.[400] After they were done with Tipu Sultan of Mysore in 1799, they fought two wars against the Marathas (first, 1803–1806; second, 1817–1819).[401]

The major part of the Maratha army was supplied by the five great states of the Maratha Confederacy: Baroda, Indore, Gwalior, Kolhapur, and Berar. Berar did not survive past the mid-1800s.

In December of 1803, the size of the Berar was greatly reduced by the Treaty of Deogaon, one of several treaties that marked the end of the first phase of the Second Anglo-Maratha War. Under its terms, Berar surrendered coastal territory (Cuttack) on the Bay of Bengal to form part of Orissa, which allowed continuous connection between Bengal and Madras. Berar also

392 Will Durant, *The Age of Faith: A History of Medieval Civilization–Christian, Islamic, and Judaic–from Constantine to Dante: A.D. 325–1300* (New York: Simon and Schuster, 1950), vol. 1, pp.460–61.
393 Betham, *Marathas*, pp.26–27.
394 Betham, *Marathas*, pp.27–28.
395 Betham, *Marathas*, pp.30–33.
396 P. T. Nair, 'The Growth and Development of Old Calcutta', in S. Chaudhuri (ed.), *Calcutta: The Living City, Volume 1: The Past* (Calcutta: Oxford University Press, 1990), p.12.
397 Nair, 'Growth', p.12.
398 Betham, *Marathas*, p.34.
399 Betham, *Marathas*, p.32. Opinion cited.
400 Betham, *Marathas*, pp.35–37.
401 For a good overview of these wars, see MacMunn, *Armies*, pp.37–81.

surrendered to Hyderabad all of Berar west of the Wardha River.[402] After this, the diminished state tended to be called 'Nagpur' after its capital city.

From 1853 on, the income from parts of the Hyderabad Province of Berar was used to support the infantry and cavalry regiments of the Hyderabad Contingent.[403] The proper term for the territories turned over to the company was the 'Hyderabad Assigned Districts', because they were a bit different from the Berar of the Nizams of Hyderabad and the old Mogul province.[404] But everyone called it 'Berar'. Then its Raja died without an heir, and an adopted heir was not allowed. The state was annexed by the company for want of a ruler in 1853.[405]

Information on the surviving states is shown in Table 45.

**Table 45 The Great Maratha States in 1901**[406]

| State | Gun Salute | Population in 1901 | Size in Square Kilometres | Size in Square Miles |
|---|---|---|---|---|
| Baroda* | 21 | 1,952,692†† | 13,034.1 | 8,099 |
| Indore† | 19 | 850,000¶ | 15,288.8 | 9,500 |
| Gwalior‡ | 19 | 2,933,001** | 40,299.6 | 25,041 |
| Kolhapur§ | 19 | 910,011 | 5,093.6 | 3,165 |

* The founder of the ruling house distinguished himself at the Battle of Balpur (1720) between the Marathas and Hyderabad,[407] and, as a reward, he was given permission to collect revenue in the area that is now Baroda.[408]

† The founder started life as the son of a shepherd. He went into the Maratha cavalry and rose through the ranks to earn the track of land that became Indore for the support of his troops.[409]

‡ The founder started as a slipper-bearer. Having won approval for performing this work, he moved on to the military and rose through the ranks.[410]

§ This state was ostensibly ruled by Shivaji's descendants. But there were several adoptions in the ruling line during the nineteenth century.[411] Thus, there is some question as to whether or not any of Shivaji's DNA was in the ruler in 1914.

†† Fell by 19 percent between 1891 and 1901 because of plague and famine.

¶ Fell by 23 percent between 1891 and 1901 because of famine.

** Fell by 13 percent between 1891 and 1901 because of famine.

402 Jac Weller, *Wellington in India* (Harlow: Longman, 1972), p.227.
403 Devendra Nath Dutt, *A Brief History of the Hutwa Raj, with a Genealogical Table of the Hutwa Family* (Calcutta: K. P. Mookerjee and Co., 1909), p.185.
404 'Berar Province', *Wikipedia*, <https://en.wikipedia.org/wiki/Berar_Province>, accessed 31 Dec. 2023.
405 Mason, *Honour*, p.254; Dutt, *Brief History*, p.186.
406 Herbert Hope Risley, William Stevenson Meyer, Richard Burn, and James Sutherland Cotton (eds), 'Baroda State', in *The Imperial Gazetteer of India* (Oxford: Clarendon Press, 1908), vol. 7, pp.25–79, 'Indore State', in *The Imperial Gazetteer of India* (Oxford: Clarendon Press, 1908), vol. 12, pp.333–49, 'Gwalior State', in *The Imperial Gazetteer of India* (Oxford: Clarendon Press, 1908), vol. 12, pp.416–37, and 'Kolhāpur State', in *The Imperial Gazetteer of India* (Oxford: Clarendon Press, 1908), vol. 15, pp.380–86.
407 H. H. The Maharaja of Jaipur, *A History of the Indian State Forces: Their Lineage and Insignia* (New Delhi: Orient Longmans, 1967), p.6.
408 Betham, *Marathas*, p.31.
409 Betham, *Marathas*, p.31.
410 Betham, *Marathas*, p.31.
411 Hope Risley, Stevenson Meyer, Burn, and Sutherland Cotton (eds), 'Kolhāpur', p.383.

### *Marathas: Composition of the Bombay Army*

The fighting against the Marathas was, in great part, done by the Bengal and Madras armies. Bombay, during this period, situated as it was on a group of small islands across from Maratha territory, did not have much recruiting territory. As a result of this, Bombay had to recruit soldiers from the north, among men from Oudh and Behar (the Purbiyas) and Rajputana, because the Marathas were enemies.[412]

At the time of the Mutiny, roughly one-third of the Bombay army consisted of Purbiyas, often from the same villages as the soldiers who were revolting in the Bengal army. Only about a third was Maratha.[413] The balance would have been Rajputs and men from 'non-military' classes.

The Bombay army had a history of recruiting northern men. The commissions that studied recruitment and regimental composition in 1859 and 1879 tried to stop this poaching of men from outside an army's territory.[414]

Both the Peel Commission of 1859 and the Eden Commission of 1879 had recommended the regiments draw soldiers from a wide range of caste backgrounds, that they serve together in the ranks, and that recruits come only from within the area of the presidency. A large part of their thinking was that the Indian army would, for the most part, only be used in India fighting other Indians.[415] The Russian scare of 1885 introduced a new situation: the possibility of fighting Russian troops. Was the Indian army, as constituted in 1885, able to do this?

The answer many feared was no, and a series of reforms were made. These changed the base of recruiting to race and caste and away from territory.[416] About this time, in the late 1880s and early 1890s, the British began to use the term 'class' to mean one particular ethnic caste or religious group.[417]

One of the main driving forces behind this change was Lord Roberts, who was commander-in-chief of the Indian army from 1885–1893 after being commander-in-chief of the Madras army beginning in 1881. During his long years of service in India, he had come out to serve in the army of the EIC, and he had formed definite views about the different classes serving in the army. His dislike of the Madras soldier is well known. What is less known is his low opinion of Marathas as a class.[418]

Roberts, by being in command of the Madras army, had been able to see the Madras soldiers up close and form judgements based on his experiences. Although Mason felt he went to Madras with his mind already made up, Roberts found the poor soldiers he was expecting.[419] He had almost no direct dealings with the Bombay army or the Marathas. He just assumed that the years of peace had killed their ancient military spirit. He lumped them together with the ordinary Hindustani of Bengal as a group that could no longer be pitted against the war-like races or employed outside the limits of Southern India.[420]

412 Mason, *Honour*, p.21.
413 Heathcote, *Military*, p.106.
414 Cohen, *Indian Army*, pp.38–41.
415 Cohen, *Indian Army*, pp.38–41.
416 Cohen, *Indian Army*, pp.41–42.
417 Cohen, *Indian Army*, p.42, footnote 28.
418 Mason, *Honour*, pp.342, 439.
419 Mason, *Honour*, p.345.
420 Frederick S. R. Roberts, *Forty-One Years in India: From Subaltern to Commander-in-Chief* (London: Richard Bentley and Son, 1898), vol. 1, p.499.

MacMunn, in his 1911 book, *The Armies of India*, had good things to say about most of the classes enlisted in the Indian army. The most he could bring himself to say about the Marathas was that 'they have long served with credit and distinction in the Bombay Army', and they 'have a reputation for great wiriness and endurance'.[421]

Others were scathing. For example:

> The Mahrattas in days gone by had courage; but it was the courage of the freebooter rather than the genuine soldierly instinct. They were at the best bold freebooters who were capable at times of courage because it paid them to be so; but the moment the prospect of gain was taken away, their courage oozed out. The highest instincts of the soldier were never theirs ... The Mahratta all through his history has never risked a whole skin unless there was something very tangible and substantial to be got thereby.[422]

That they once were freebooters would explain why Roberts and the others could discount the fighting value of the Marathas at the turn of the twentieth century in spite of their great military past – that and the old standby, the softening effect of long periods of peace on oriental peoples.

The author of the 1908 official army handbook noted that the popular classes were Sikhs, Pathans, and Punjabi Muslims. He noted that the Marathas were good infantry soldiers and the Dekhani were unsurpassed as cavalrymen. These qualities were not recognised. He complained that the Marathas had been given very little opportunity to show their worth through active service. He then said plaintively, 'It is hard that they should be misjudged without a fair trial.'[423]

The labelling of the Marathas as a class of poor fighters affected their numbers in the Bombay army, as shown in Table 46.

**Table 46 Infantry Units from Bombay, 1862–1914[424]**

| Year | 1862 | 1885 | 1892 | 1914 |
|---|---|---|---|---|
| Number of Infantry Units | 30 | 26 | 26 | 18 |

These numbers do not reflect the true state of affairs because of Bombay poaching from the northwest of India and the Punjab. For example, in 1879, of the 16,034 soldiers in the Bombay infantry, 5,032 were from outside the presidency.[425]

When the First World War came, the Marathas had a chance to prove themselves in Mesopotamia, and they did very well. In 1916, an article in the *Civil and Military Gazette of Lahore* stated, 'one of the surprises of the war had been the Maratha'. The newspaper continued, 'the less conspicuous types have made good. In France we were always hearing of the Garhwalis, in Mesopotamia it is the Marathas'. It then covered the exploits of the 103rd, 110th, and 117th Regiments.[426]

421 MacMunn, *Armies*, p.167.
422 Bonarjee, *Handbook*, p.216.
423 Betham, *Marathas*, p.76.
424 Cohen, *Indian Army*, p.44.
425 Cohen, *Indian Army*, p.44.
426 Mason, *Honour*, p.439.

After the First World War, the 117th was made a royal regiment for its performance in Mesopotamia. It was one of three Maratha regiments captured at Kut (the other two were the 103rd and the 110th) and the only one reformed during the First World War.[427] In the Battle of Sharqat in 1918, the 114th won two Distinguished Service Orders (DSOs), four Military Crosses (MCs), six IOMs, and 15 Indian Distinguished Service Medals (IDSMs), perhaps the highest number of awards granted to any unit following a single action.[428]

In 1923, six regiments, the 103rd, 105th, 110th, 116th, 117th, and 114th, went to form the 5th Mahratta Light Infantry.[429]

The Dekhani Marathas pursued agriculture almost exclusively. He was said to be unsurpassed as a cavalry soldier. But the handbook states he did not like to leave his home, and the pre-First World War army had only one squadron of them in the 31st Lancers.[430] However, large numbers went into the infantry. So it may have been less an unwillingness to leave home than an inability or unwillingness to produce the buy-in payment required by the cavalry's Silladar system.

The Konkani Marathas, which include those who live in the Konkan Ghat Mahta area, went only into the infantry.[431] They were Shivaji's infantry and the foundation of his power.[432] In the Konkan proper, men were not accepted from the parts of the Konkan that were north of Bombay, as the people there showed no taste for soldiering. South of Bombay, the population had been fond of the army life since Shivaji's time. The handbook states that, 'of late years', the army stopped recruiting men on the south who lived within 10 or 12 miles (16.1–19.3km) of the coast. The reason for this action was that it was felt that the seaboard climate undercut good physiques.[433]

### *Marathas: Konkani Muslims*

Once, the army had Konkani Muslims in its ranks. This is shown in the discussion of the composition of the 5th Bombay Infantry in 1895 and in Table 44. By 1914, this class was no longer recruited.

### *Dekhani Muslims*[434]

There had been Muslim missionaries in India from an early date, but they had not made much headway. Islam was put on a firm footing in the Dekhan by the Muslim invasion in the latter part of the thirteenth century. During the Bahmani dynasty (1347–1526), large numbers of foreign fighters, such as Persians, Tartars, Moghuls, and Arabs, were brought in. Later, Afghans came in. Some of these settled in the area, and, through unions with local women, they produced a new class – the Dekhani Muslims. In addition, there have been converts to the religion over the years. Many of these were from the lower Hindu castes, who, in addition to genuine belief, saw the Muslim classless religion as a way out of their low status in the Hindu religion. But such is

427 Gaylor, *Sons*, p.146.
428 Gaylor, *Sons*, p.146.
429 Gaylor, *Sons*, p.145.
430 Betham, *Marathas*, p.75.
431 Betham, *Marathas*, pp.46, 75.
432 Betham, *Marathas*, pp.46, 75.
433 Betham, *Marathas*, p.91.
434 Betham, *Marathas*, pp.103, 112–13, 115, 117–20.

human nature that many of these lower-status converts then tried to gain status by claiming to be descendants of one of the foreign troops.

### *Dekhani Muslims: Recruiting*

For recruiting, the British divided the Dekhani Muslims into three groups:

- Converts, descendants of converts, and mixed parentage
- Four classes who claim some strain of foreign blood
- Special communities.

Recruits from the army were drawn mostly from the first two groups. Occasionally, a man would be taken from the third group.

The converts were, of course, of the same racial stock as the Hindu Marathas. They were said to be half Hindu in their feelings, thoughts, speech, lifestyle, and manner of dress. They knew little of the Muslim religion, observed Hindu festivals, and worshipped idols, some would not eat beef, and they were not circumcised. The handbook says, 'They can hardly be distinguished from Hindus except for wearing a beard.'

The second group, like Muslims in the Punjab and indeed all over India, were or claimed to be descendants of Fatima, the daughter of the prophet Mohammad; certain ancient Muslim leaders; the Moghuls; Pathans from Afghanistan; or a combination of these claims. However, most of the people in these groups were converts who either took the name and religion of their leaders or were trying to gain status by claiming exalted heritage. By and large, they looked just like the local Marathas, but many of them were larger, fairer-skinned, and 'better featured' than the general Marathas. The Pathan group were generally taller than average.

The special communities were artisans who had developed manners, customs, and so on that slightly set them apart. Examples of these communities were perfumers, shoemakers, elephant drivers, mutton butchers, beef butchers, bricklayers, papermakers, farriers, and so on.

The converts had the same characteristics as Marathas, in that they were orderly and amenable to discipline. Those with more foreign blood (or DNA) were more likely to be unruly, unclean, and turbulent and to resist discipline. They were said to soon tire of routine duty, as they had a more adventurous spirit than the normal soldier. 'But, for all of this the men (with foreign blood) make fine soldiers and can be relied upon in times of trouble.'

The Muslims in general would eat anything except pigs and buffalo. The men did not seem to lead as moral lives as the Marathas, and a large number of recruits were rejected for having venereal disease.

### *Characteristics of Maratha Sepoys*

The characteristics of the Marathas were said to be hardworking, law-abiding, and frugal. Theft was almost unknown, and great stress was placed on living a virtuous life. Their history of guerrillas and raiders showed up in their preference for strategy over force, although the Maratha handbook credits this preference to their timidity. When roused, they were not a contemptible enemy, as they were not without courage. Only 39 Marathas out of every 1,000 were classified as literate (3.9 percent). On entering the army, every man went to school until he could sign his name.

They were short and lacked swagger. The Dekhan Marathas were dark with a shaved head, except for a topknot of hair. The Konkani Maratha was generally slightly fairer, taller, and without as good a physique as the Dekhani. Their topknot was longer. Both wore moustaches and often whiskers, but they never had a beard. That was left to the Muslims.[435]

### *Brahmins*

It is well known, even by people who know nothing about India, that Brahmins are at the top of the religious hierarchy. Those who know just a little more understand that they are the priestly class of India, much like the Levites were in ancient Israel. All of this is true, which makes it strange to be considering the priestly Brahmins' place in the Indian army. Blame it on human nature. Over the centuries, priests had more children than there were openings for priests. A given population can only support so many holy men who do not do economically beneficial work. Many of the surplus children who could not find employment as priests turned to farming and service as soldiers. Being a soldier was the one form of employment that could be undertaken without loss of caste.[436]

They had served in Muslim armies since the fifteenth century. When the EIC began to raise an army in Bengal in the 1760s, it enlisted the groups that had served in the Muslim armies. By the early 1800s, the company drew most of the men for the Bengal army from the Brahmins and Rajputs of Bihar and Oudh (also spelled 'Awadh'). It has been claimed that, by 1857, some three-fourths of the Bengal army's infantry were high caste, probably Brahmins, from Oudh.

Because they were so important to the army, the high-caste men made demands that would have been rejected out of hand in the armies of Bombay and Madras. In Bengal, the authorities, aware of the high-status group's importance to the army, tended to acquiesce to the soldiers' demands. The sepoys were able to insist on a strict observance of religious ritual prohibitions. High-caste sepoys would not take orders from sepoys of a lower caste. This led to lower-caste men rarely being promoted. In time, the high-caste sepoys were able to get the lower-caste men excluded from the Bengal army. At first, this was just by custom, but, in 1855, regulations to this effect were adopted.[437]

The high-caste men resisted serving overseas, as they felt it would break their caste standing. Only six regiments in the entire 72-regiment-strong Bengal army were enlisted for general service (that is, could be sent anywhere, even overseas).[438] Talk of sending one regiment overseas by ship led to mutiny. A law enacted in 1856 that men enlisted in the future could be sent anywhere, even overseas by ship, was felt to have contributed to the Indian Mutiny.[439]

When the Mutiny broke out, it was centred among the high-caste men of Bihar and Oudh that the Bengal army had for years catered to. It was one of the great traumas of British history, and its causes and the course of the Mutiny have been covered in great detail in many excellent works since the Mutiny's end. Comments about the causes of the Mutiny are limited here to noting that there was more behind it than cartridge grease. The company annexed Oudh in 1856, thereby depriving the sepoys of their influence at the court of the king of Oudh and their favourable arrangements with Oudh administrators. This was especially harmful, as Oudh was the home of 90 percent of sepoys.[440]

435 Betham, *Marathas*, pp.73–76.
436 Bingley and Nicholls, *Brahmans*, p.8.
437 Omissi, *Sepoy*, p.4.
438 Omissi, *Sepoy*, p.4.
439 Omissi, *Sepoy*, p.5; Mason, *Honour*, pp.242–45, 261–62.
440 Mason, *Honour*, p.231.

After conquering the Sikhs, the Punjab was annexed just as Sind had been earlier. Upon being annexed, they became part of the company's possessions, and the men no longer received extra pay ('batta') for active service or when stationed outside the company's territory. The men's reward for victory was a loss of pay. Batta could be important. In Afghanistan in the 1840s, it was four rupees a month on top of the regular pay of eight rupees a month.

The British took steps that made the landowning sepoys lose income, or fear its loss, as landowners and family members that received incomes and status from an endowment to charities or religious buildings and schools. A group of company officials, called the 'Levellers', did this by strictly examining all documents that formed the basis for the claim to such income. Often, such documentation did not exist. In one case, a landowner claimed income from 189 villages. But, when the documents were closely studied, it was found that he had a valid legal claim for only 51 villages. This meant a nearly three-fourths drop in income. This happened all over India. In 1852, the Southern Maratha Country Commission looked at the titles of 35,000 estates, and three-fifths were held invalid. The invalid estates were taken away from the landlords and left in the hands of the peasants who tilled the land.

Not all company officials believed in this legalistic approach to land titles. Many, foreseeing trouble by meddling, felt things should be left just as they were. Often, they overruled the actions of a Leveller. Then, sometimes, the original action of a Leveller was upheld by a Leveller in an even higher rank in the company bureaucracy. The whole process was capricious, uncertain, and most upsetting to the landowning Purabiya Brahmins.[441]

### *Brahmins: After the Mutiny*

In 1858, after the Mutiny, a British government commission was formed in London under Secretary of State for War Major General Jonathan Peel. The commission was to examine the organisation of the Indian army and determine how it could be improved. It heard from 47 witnesses, who gave conflicting advice.

Some wanted to do away with the high-caste soldiers of the old Bengal army, while others said they made the best soldiers. Some wanted an army of only Sikhs and Muslims, and others said that was too risky. Others wanted no Indian soldiers and to hold India with troops from outside India. It heard conflicting advice on how the regiments should be constituted.[442]

In the end, the British did not try to construct a new Indian army on the cool, rational grounds of advice from the Peel Commission but rather went with facts on the ground. A few regiments of the Bengal army had not mutinied or been disarmed. Those were retained and given new numbers. Table 47 shows these units.

441 Mason, *Honour*, pp.248–52.
442 Omissi, *Sepoy*, pp.6–8.

**Table 47 Bengal Regiments that Survived the Indian Mutiny**[443]

| Old Regimental Number | New Regimental Number |
|---|---|
| 21 | 1 |
| 31 | 2 |
| 32 | 3 |
| 33 | 4 |
| 42 | 5 |
| 43 | 6 |
| 47 | 7 |
| 59 | 8 |
| 63 | 9[*] |
| 66 | 11[†] |
| 70 | 13 |

* Later 9th Gurkhas.
† Later 1st Gurkhas.

In addition, several other regiments remained loyal. They were the Kelat-i-Ghilzie (old Shah Shujah's Infantry) and Shekhawatee Regiments (Shekhawati Local Force). They were also two Sikh regiments raised in territory taken from the Sikhs after the First Sikh War. They were the Regiments of Ferozepur and Ludhiana. These regiments, after the Mutiny, became the 12th, 13th, 14th, and 15th Regiments, respectively.[444]

In 1850, the Sirmoor (Local) Battalion was made part of the Bengal army. After the Mutiny, it became the 2nd Gurkha Rifles.[445]

During the war, elements of the 13th, 48th, and 71st and the 3rd, 36th, and 61st Regiments remained loyal. The first group helped with the defence of Lucknow during the Mutiny. After the Mutiny, they were formed into the 16th (Lucknow) Regiment. After the Mutiny, the second group was formed into the 17th (Loyal Purbiya) Regiment.[446] A local unit, the Alipore Regiment, which had started life as the Calcutta Native Militia, came in as the 18th Regiment.[447]

All of the Bengal regular cavalry regiments (11) either mutinied or were disbanded as a safety precaution during the Mutiny. In addition, 10 of the 18 corps of the Irregular Horse mutinied or were disbanded. The surviving corps and the regiments they became are shown below.

Any of these units could have Brahmins in their ranks. One table presented to the Peel Commission showed the Bengal army had 8,526 Brahmins under arms on 1 April 1858 (that is, just after the Mutiny). This broke down to 6,549 regulars and 1,882 irregulars.[448] Other reports gave somewhat different but roughly similar numbers.[449]

443 Perry, *Order Part 5B*, pp.127–29; MacMunn, *Armies*, p.108.
444 Perry, *Order Part 5B*, p.129.
445 Perry, *Order Part 5B*, p.129; Marrion and Fosten, *Tradition*, p.1.
446 MacMunn, *Armies*, p.109.
447 MacMunn, *Armies*, p.109; Perry, *Order Part 5B*, p.130.
448 Omissi, *Sepoy*, p.7, Tale 1.1.
449 Omissi, *Sepoy*, p.7, footnote 4.

**Table 48 Bengal Irregular Cavalry Corps that Survived the Mutiny**[450]

| Irregular Corps Number | New Regiment Number |
|---|---|
| 1 | 1 |
| 2 | 2 |
| 4 | 3 |
| 6* | 4 |
| 7 | 5 |
| 8 | 6 |
| 17 | 7 |
| 18 | 8 |

* A similar list shown in MacMunn, *Armies*, p.111, does not show the 6th Irregular Corps as surviving. However, in A. H. Bowling, *Indian Cavalry Regiments, 1880–1914* (London: Almark Publishing Co., 1971), p.12, where the history of the 4th Cavalry is given, the regiment is shown as coming from the 6th, which survived the Mutiny.

In 1864, five of the Bengal cavalry regiments had several different classes mixed together in several troops. Brahmins were one of the seven classes in the regiments. In the same year, among the Bengal infantry, seven regiments continued to be staffed more or less as they had before the Mutiny, with chiefly Hindustani Muslims, Brahmins, and Rajputs. Seven regiments were organised on a class company basis, with one or two companies composed of Hindustani (Purabiya) Brahmins and Rajputs. In addition, seven of the new Punjab regiments, the 34th and 35th through 41st Regiments, had one or two class companies of those men. The 42nd through 44th could be composed of up to one-fourth Hindustanis. It is easy to see that the Brahmins continued to play a part in the Bengal army despite adding Sikhs and other western classes.

After the 1883 Russian war scare, the Bengal army changed over to a class company organisation. The Brahmins were effectively removed from the cavalry. They served in only one squadron in the entire Bengal cavalry. The troop was in the 7th Cavalry Regiment. They served in the 7th up to 1901,[451] but, by 1914, with four squadrons in a cavalry regiment, they had disappeared. The British cavalry had been reorganised shortly before the outbreak of the Boer War in 1899. The cavalry troop was replaced by the squadron as the basic unit in a cavalry regiment.[452] Fourteen of the infantries had one or two companies of Brahmins (although the 3rd had three companies). These were, by and large, a carry-over from the regiments that had Brahmins in their ranks in 1864.

In 1892, as part of a general move to organise the Purbiya soldiers into class regiments, the Brahmins were concentrated into the 1st and 3rd Regiments, which henceforth had only Brahmin sepoys.[453] The 1st and 3rd Brahmins were recruited from the United Provinces of Agra, Oudh, and Berar, the centres of the Indian Mutiny. The talk of banning Brahmins from the company's Bengal army was completely gone.[454]

450 Perry, *Order Part 5B*, pp.116–17.
451 Bowling, *Indian Cavalry*, p.19.
452 Marquess of Anglesey, *A History of the British Cavalry, 1816–1919* (Barnsley: Leo Cooper, 1986), vol. 4, pp.360–61.
453 Heathcote, *Indian*, p.95.
454 Bingley and Nicholls, *Brahmans*, p.54.

Brahmins continued to soldier on in regiments that were not part of the old Bengal army. In 1914, two companies served in the 9th Bhopal Infantry, which, up to 1903, had been a local battalion and more or less set its own rules. The 89th and 90th Punjabis each had one Brahmin company. These regiments were both Madras regiments that had been designated as Burma battalions and had their Madras classes replaced by northern classes in the early 1890s.[455]

***Brahmins: Characteristics***

There were many things in the Brahmin character that were attractive to the British. He was said to be more intelligent than any other class. Indeed, most classes in the army were considered rather thick. He was easily disciplined, trustworthy on money matters, frugal, and free from debauchery. Being naturally clean and tidy, he looked good on parade. They also looked good on parade because, as a group, they were tall men. Men of a height of 1.73m (five feet, eight inches) could be recruited in large numbers, and they had splendid physiques. He could stand severe and protract privations and was a match for anyone in endurance.[456]

There were other things the British liked about them. One recruiting officer made the following comments about Brahmins:

> A high caste Brahmin may be distinguished by his appearance. He is fair complexioned, and far more intelligent than any caste in the country, has nearly always good features and an air of breeding about him, his nose too is distinctively aristocratic in type and the nostrils narrow, the width at the base being less than any other caste in the country.[457]

Reading comments like this makes one want to check to be sure he is not reading Heinrich Himmler describing one of his SS cohorts.

The Brahmins, as a class, had some strong negative traits that went far towards off setting their good points. The soldiering classes of the Brahmins were described as deep and tricky.[458] They had a love of intrigue and litigation and an unwillingness to deviate in even the smallest degree from the religious rules of his caste and the customs of his race.[459] The love of intrigue could set men within a mixed-class regiment at one another's throats. It was hoped that, when the two Brahmin-class regiments were formed, the sepoys' intrigues would be exhausted on each other.[460] Of course, the intra-regimental intrigues made it harder to manage the regiment. However, the unifying factor of men's pride in their caste had the makings for a strong *esprit de corps*.[461]

The Brahmin was frugal. He spent as little as possible on himself and his family and then splurged on public displays for weddings and festivals. In the army, he often did not eat his full ration and saved the balance. One of the most important duties of his officers was to inspect regimental records to see that the men were eating all their provided food.[462]

455 Nevins, *Forces*, p.241.
456 Bingley and Nicholls, *Brahmans*, pp.42, 45, 48.
457 Bingley and Nicholls, *Brahmans*, p.52.
458 Bingley and Nicholls, *Brahmans*, p.54.
459 Bingley and Nicholls, *Brahmans*, pp.47–48.
460 MacMunn, *Martial*, p.272.
461 Bingley and Nicholls, *Brahmans*, p.42.
462 Bingley and Nicholls, *Brahmans*, p.42.

The rules requiring the cooking and eating of food by Brahmins are very complex. Near female relatives may cook his food, but only his wife may eat with him. In the Bengal army, the families did not live with the sepoys, so having the food cooked by a family member was not an option. When a Brahmin soldier was away from female relatives, he cooked his food and ate it alone. This made having mess halls practically impossible.[463]

The process of cooking was quite complex. A space of about five square feet (0.46 square metres), called a '*chauka*', was marked off, and within it was set a fireplace. This was then leeped with mud or cow dung. After collecting the food for the meal and placing it inside the *chauka*, the Brahmins bathed and prayed. He then went into the *chauka* to cook and eat his meal, wearing only his loincloth. Special cooking utensils were used, and only certain foods could be eaten. These foods varied by tribe. When the meal was finished, he left the *chauka* and washed his hands and feet. All food was eaten with the fingers, and only the right hand was used. If anyone who is not a Brahmin touched the *chauka* or its contents after they had been prepared, all the food in it was considered defiled and thrown away.[464]

These rituals could be steps taken to avoid having one's food infected and to avoid disease. They may date back to the days when the Aryan invaders first came into India and found it home to many diseases they had not experienced before.[465] Current theory in India discounts the idea of an Aryan invasion and holds that the caste system arose spontaneously out of wholly local Indian conditions. Again, this may be because of the influence of Hindutva theory.

When the Brahmins were being transported by ship and setting up a *chauka* for each man was impossible, a special ration of parched gram, salt, and sugar was issued.[466] When on service on the Northwest Frontier when the weather was cold, the Brahmins of the 1st Regiment gave up bathing and cooked and ate their food while wearing wool garments. It seems only wool was acceptable. The wool field service jersey of the army met the requirements.[467]

The Brahmins, who had taken up agriculture, did not touch the plough.[468] They had people under them do the work.

The Brahmins, like many other Hindus, were addicted to lawsuits, often pursuing them beyond all logic. Their love of litigation led to much perjury.[469] This was not limited to the Brahmins. Most Indians thought nothing of lying under oath, and it was common practice to hire people to serve as lying witnesses.[470]

The army did not take just any Brahmins. Rather, it took only certain groups within the larger Brahmin class. Generally speaking, the Brahmins were divided into two broad groups: Gaur, the tribes that lived north of the Dekhan, which was the home of the Marathas (the dividing line was the Vindhya and Berbudda Mountains); and Dravira, the tribes to the south of the Vindhya and Nerbudda Mountains, among Telugas, Marathas, Tamils, and peoples of the Carnatic.

463 Bingley and Nicholls, *Brahmans*, p.42.
464 Bingley and Nicholls, *Brahmans*, pp.42–43.
465 William H. McNeill, *Plagues and Peoples* (New York: Anchor Books, 1998), p.91.
466 Bingley and Nicholls, *Brahmans*, p.48.
467 Bingley and Nicholls, *Brahmans*, p.43.
468 Bingley and Nicholls, *Brahmans*, p.47.
469 Bingley and Nicholls, *Brahmans*, p.47.
470 Allen, *Plain Tales*, pp.222–23.

The Dravira Brahmins did not supply any men to the army. Three of the five Gaur groups supplied men for the army. They were Kanaujia, Saraswat, and the Gaur Proper.

Of these, the Kanaujia were the largest and most important. They supplied three-fourths of the Brahmins in the army. The Kanaujia were divided into five sub-tribes, which the Brahman handbook describes in loving detail. Some were almost total vegetarians, which was thought to lessen their value as soldiers, and others would only eat certain meats, such as sheep, goats, fish, game animals (deer and hare), and game birds (pigeon, partridge, and duck).[471]

While the Saraswat could be enlisted, few were, except a very few enlisted as Dogras.[472] The Gaur Proper were dismissed as ignorant and bigoted and said to 'not make very good soldiers as they are strict vegetarians and will neither touch meat or fish nor drink liquor'. The Brahmin handbook gives them less than a page of coverage.[473]

During the First World War, the 1st Brahmins served on the Northwest Frontier in India and in Aden. The 3rd was in Mesopotamia as part of the 14th Division troops, as well as serving in Egypt, India, and the Persian Gulf.[474]

The 1st Brahmin's flexibility on the Northwest Frontier in 1884–1885 about bathing before meals and wearing wool clothing while eating gave hope that the Brahmins would be flexible about their religious rules in times of war.[475] However, the First World War dashed this hope. In Mesopotamia, the 3rd Brahmins unexpectedly refused to abrogate their washing and cooking rules and, thus, starved as a consequence.[476]

The need for special cooking pots was not limited to Brahmins. In Mesopotamia, cavalry following the Battle of Es Sin (Essinn) outside Kut in September 1915 did not pursue the beaten Turks because they would not use captured Arab cooking pots (there had not been room in the transport to bring theirs).[477] The official war history of Mesopotamia blandly states that the cavalry spent their time after the battle trying to find water. It does not come right out and say they did not pursue the Turks.[478] But the British war histories are often careful not to criticise the conduct of British officers or units.

The cavalry consisted of two squadrons of the 7th Lancer and one-and-a-half squadrons of the 16th Cavalry. The 7th consisted of one squadron of Jats, Sikhs, Dogras, and Muslims. The 16th had two squadrons of Sikhs and one each of Jats and Dogras. There is no way to tell what classes were at the battle.

After the Great War, the 3rd Brahmins was one of nine regiments to be disbanded in 1921–1922.[479] The 1st Brahmins was made the 4th Battalion of the 1st Punjab Regiment, which otherwise contained all old Madras regiments whose personnel had been replaced before the First World War by men from the Punjab. The Brahmins in the 4th Battalion were from the

471 Bingley and Nicholls, *Brahmans*, pp.13–18.
472 Bingley and Nicholls, *Brahmans*, p.19.
473 Bingley and Nicholls, *Brahmans*, pp.18–19.
474 Perry, *Order Part 5B*, pp.254, 269–72, 284–86, 295–98, 300–01, 311–12, 322.
475 Bingley and Nicholls, *Brahmans*, p.43, footnotes.
476 MacMunn, *Martial*, p.272.
477 Marquess, *History*, vol. 6, p.20; F. J. Moberly, *History of the Great War Based on Official Documents: The Campaign in Mesopotamia 1914–1918* (London: HMSO, 1923), vol. 1, Appendix IV; A. J. Barker, *The Neglected War: Mesopotamia 1914–1918* (London: Faber and Faber, 1967), pp.114–15. Barker doesn't believe Townshend ever intended to use his cavalry as a pursuit force.
478 Moberly, *Campaign in Mesopotamia*, vol. 1, p.334.
479 Gaylor, *Sons*, p.19.

Gaur Proper clan, which was not recruited before the First World War, as they were strict vegetarians and did not eat fish or meat. They were deemed ignorant and bigoted.[480] After the war, their simpler cooking and feeding caused them to be the only class recruited.[481] In 1931, as part of a retrenchment in the Indian army, the 4th Battalion of the 1st (the old 1st Brahmins) was disbanded.[482] This was the sad end of a class that had formed the heart of the army that had conquered most of India for the British.

### *Other Classes: Christians*

Christian missionaries have a surprisingly long history in India, and Indian Christians live in every part of India. During the First World War, the British were able to raise a regiment of Punjabi Christians, the 71st.[483] However, it was only in South India that they were taken into the army in peacetime. In the south, the Indian Christians were divided into two main groups: St Thomas Christians and other Christians.

St Thomas Christians (also called Syrian Christians) lived mostly in Transcore and Cochin. In Transcore, Christians were about 24 percent of the population. The St Thomas Christians numbered 227,670, or about 33 percent of Transcore's total indigenous Christian population.[484] In Cochin, Christians totalled 24 percent of the population.[485] The St Thomas Christians numbered about 514 in 1901 and were 0.26 percent of the total indigenous Christian population in Cochin.[486] Christians made up a little more than three percent of the Madras population.[487] Some St Thomas Christians lived across the border in the Madras Presidency and went into the Madras army as part of their Christian troops.

The St Thomas Christians may be considered almost native to India. They trace their origins to Thomas, one of the apostles of Jesus, who was charged to go out and spread the Gospel in India. Legend says he was martyred for his faith but was unsuccessful in winning many converts. Prosecutions drove the early Christians into the mountains of the western Malabar Coast. There, they grew in number. In time, they became one of the recognised classes of South India.

At some point, the community adopted the Nestorian branch of Christianity. The Portuguese, when they came, viewed the Nestorian belief as heresy and introduced the Inquisition to help convert them to Roman Catholicism. The Portuguese were able to stamp out Nestorianism and bring in Roman Catholicism in the Malabar area. But, when the Portuguese left, Nestorianism came back in a modified form from Syria. This left the southern Christians partly Catholic and partly Nestorian in their beliefs.[488]

480 Bingley and Nicholls, *Brahmans*, p.18.
481 MacMunn, *Martial*, p.272.
482 Gaylor, *Sons*, p.132.
483 Gaylor, *Sons*, p.9.
484 Herbert Hope Risley, William Stevenson Meyer, Richard Burn, and James Sutherland Cotton (eds), 'Transcore State', in *The Imperial Gazetteer of India* (Oxford: Clarendon Press, 1908), vol. 24, p.9.
485 Herbert Hope Risley, William Stevenson Meyer, Richard Burn, and James Sutherland Cotton (eds), 'Cochin State', in *The Imperial Gazetteer of India* (Oxford: Clarendon Press, 1908), vol. 10, p.344.
486 Hope Risley, Stevenson Meyer, Burn, and Sutherland Cotton (eds), 'Cochin State', pp.345–46.
487 Mouat, *Madras*, pp.22, 24.
488 Bonarjee, *Handbook*, p.206.

An Israeli sociologist who studied the St Thomas Christians found they shared many customs in common with the local Jewish community. To mention a few, they eat unleavened bread at a special nightfall meal on Maundy Thursday, they bury their dead facing Jerusalem, and their priests wear black velvet caps similar to Jewish headgear.[489] The priesthood was practically hereditary in two families for several centuries. They also do not make any effort to convert others.[490]

The very great majority of Christians in India and Madras are people who have been converted or their descendants. The Christians had been enlisted in the Madras army for many years. Since it was only in Madras that Christians were taken into the army, a look at the breakdown of Christian religions in that presidency is in order. In 1931, Roman Catholics were about 47 percent of the total Christian population. All other Christians, excluding St Thomas Christians, were about 51 percent of the total. The early Christian missionaries accepted the rules of caste, maybe hoping that, in time, it would wither away. It did not, and they still applied among the converted Christians, particularly among the Roman Catholics.[491]

It was estimated that 75 percent of the Christians enlisted were converts or descendants of converts from low-caste families.[492] The Madras class handbook notes that, while the missionaries could convert low-caste individuals and give them new hope and ideals, some did not immediately improve their morals and actions. For this reason, the handbook says it was wise to recruit from among those whose families had been Christians for several generations rather than taking new converts.[493] The Christian soldier was said to often receive a good elementary education at mission schools. They were said to be courageous, hard-working, and physically robust, as well as cheerful and amenable to discipline. They were happy to leave behind the caste prejudices found in civil life.[494] The numbers and percentages used above are for 1931, but there is no reason why they would not be roughly the same before 1914.

### *Other Classes: Ahirs*

The Ahirs were originally a pastoral tribe, and the name 'Ahirs' is said to come from the word 'milkman'.[495] While the Ahirs were originally herders of cattle, the disappearance of grazing grounds forced many of them to turn to agriculture, although many of them in the 1890s were still engaged in a pastoral life.[496]

It was felt that the main difference between the Jats, Gujars, and Ahirs was social status rather than ethnicity.[497] All three groups had the same appearance, and all would eat and smoke together. The Ahir language was different from that of the Jats, but their customs were the same except for a minor difference in which widows could remarry.[498]

489 Nathan Katz, *Who Are the Jews of India?* (Berkeley: University of California Press, 2000), p.19.
490 Katz, *Who Are the Jews*, p.19.
491 Mouat, *Madras*, p.61.
492 Mouat, *Madras*, pp.61–62.
493 Mouat, *Madras*, p.61.
494 Mouat, *Madras*, p.62.
495 Christie, *Jats*, p.44.
496 Bonarjee, *Handbook*, p.209.
497 Christie, *Jats*, p.7.
498 Christie, *Jats*, p.44.

The Ahirs were split into three divisions, which usually did not eat together or intermarry. They are Jadubansi, Nandbansi, and Gwalbansi.[499]

Prior to 1878–1880, Afghan Ahirs were enlisted in both the Bengal and Bombay armies. There were 15 companies of Ahirs in the Bengal army (they were found in regiments 33 through 40), and there were many Ahirs in the Bombay army's mixed companies. After the change over to a class company organisation, there were four companies of Ahirs in the army in 1914. This made them the smallest caste serving in the infantry and cavalry. There were also many in the other branches of service, notably the artillery.[500] The regiments that had Ahir companies in 1914 were the 95th Russell's and 98th Infantry Regiments (each had two companies of Ahirs).

The British felt the Jadubansi made the best soldiers. They felt that soil and climate played a key role in alteration in physique and martial character and that the Ahirs of the Gangenetic Plain and the east had lost their edge and were inferior to those in the west. The west – the Punjab, Rajputana, and the Western United Provinces – was the home of the Jadubansi. Before 1914, the Jadubansi almost monopolised the few Ahir openings in the army.[501]

The other groups were called upon in the First World War but stopped being taken again after the war was over. Having tasted and enjoyed military life, many Nandbansis began to try to pass themselves off as Jadubansis to army recruiters.[502]

In the reorganisation of the post-First World War army, the Ahirs went into the 19th Hyderabad Regiment. After 1923, each battalion had one of its four companies composed of Ahirs from the Eastern Punjab.[503]

While hardworking husbandmen, the Ahir was not well thought of. Several sayings reflect these views. 'Do not trust a jackal, spear grass, or an Ahir.' 'Three castes are without mercy. When opportunity occurs, they have no shame – the prostitute, the Bania, and the Ahir.' (Banias are moneylenders.)

This poor view is perhaps because of their hard work and resulting prosperity. The British felt 'in this part of India (Rajputana), they take the palm as peaceable, industrious, and prosperous cultivators'.[504]

They were said to be conscientious and painstaking as soldiers and of a bold and stubborn disposition. They had soldiery instincts and great endurance. Their largest failing was that they were a little lacking in initiative.[505]

### *Other Classes: Gujars*

The Gujars were traditionally nomadic pastoralists, moving their animal charges from one feeding ground to another as the seasons changed. They were found in all parts of India but only recruited in Rajputana, and MacMunn said that often the term 'Gujar' was applied to grazing people irrespective of their real race.[506] In British times, they concentrated on cattle, and, by the

499 Christie, *Jats*, p.45.
500 Christie, *Jats*, p.44.
501 Christie, *Jats*, p.45.
502 Christie, *Jats*, pp.45–46.
503 Gaylor, *Sons*, p.197.
504 Cole, *Rajputana*, p.40.
505 Cole, *Rajputana*, p.40.
506 MacMunn, *Armies*, pp.161–62.

First World War period, they were chiefly cattle dealers and breeders.[507] As the population in India grew, the countryside filled up with people, and there was less room to graze their cattle. This forced many of them to turn to agriculture. Very often, they were poor cultivators.[508] This may have been because, for centuries, they had been cattle herders, and their real love was cattle. This caused them to steal cattle on a regular basis.[509]

Their neighbours did not appreciate their cattle being stolen and bore a heavy sense of antagonism towards the Gujars. A folk saying reflects this: 'The dog and the cat, the Rangher,[510] and the Gujar, if it were not for these four, you might sleep with your doors open.'[511] They were also considered fickle. 'A dog, a monkey, and a Gujar change their minds with every step.'[512]

The British felt they were quarrelsome and very thick-headed.[513] However, one handbook posits that the Gujar soldier's seeming lack of intelligence might be caused by his lack of school. Much of the time of a young Gujar was devoted to being a herdsman with the cattle.[514]

Before 1878–1880, Gujars had served in both the Bengal and the Bombay armies. The handbook for Gujars states that, by 1914, there were only three companies of them in the army.[515] However, there were six companies of them in the army in 1914. The regiments they served in were the 102nd Grenadiers, 112th Infantry, 113th Infantry, 119th Infantry, 120th Infantry, and 122nd Infantry.

While the army did not take many, it felt the Gujars made good soldiers. They could make long marches without losing stamina. They were very phlegmatic. On active service, they showed a marked degree of courage. They had the determination to hold out.[516] They also had an excellent physique. Before the First World War in Rajputana, their average height was nearly 1.73m (five feet, eight inches), and their mean chest measurements were 86.36cm (34in).[517]

### *Other Classes: Jews and Parsis*

The Parsis of India are followers of the Zoroastrian religion, which was once the dominant religion of Persia. When Persia was conquered by Muslim invaders in the eighth century, some Persians who still followed the Zoroastrian religion moved to the Gujarat–Sind area of India. ('Parsis' is the Persian word for Persian.) Legend has it that one of the conditions set by the local Hindu ruler for allowing the Parsis to settle in India was that they not carry weapons.[518] The conditions set by the ruler vary from account to account. However, this one appears in all of them, as does the condition that Parsi women dress in local dress (sari) and the Parsis speak the local language (Gujarati).

507 Cole, *Rajputana*, p.37.
508 Christie, *Jats*, p.38.
509 Christie, *Jats*, pp.38–39; Cole, *Rajputana*, p.37.
510 Ranghers were generally Rajputs who had converted to the Muslim religion.
511 Christie, *Jats*, p.38.
512 Cole, *Rajputana*, p.37.
513 Cole, *Rajputana*, p.37.
514 Christie, *Jats*, p.37.
515 Christie, *Jats*, p.37.
516 Christie, *Jats*, p.37.
517 Cole, *Rajputana*, p.38.
518 Margaret A. Mills, Peter J. Claus, and Sarah Diamond (eds), *South Asian Folklore: An Encyclopedia* (Abingdon: Routledge, 2003), p.462.

When the British came to West India and operated out of Surat, Parsis from Gujarat began to move to the British territory for the new jobs offered and the new trading opportunities. When the British acquired Bombay, they moved there.

The Parsis were able to fill many job niches, as they had an inherent advantage over Hindus. The rules of caste meant that a Hindu would perform one job but not another. This swelled the number of servants in households and the army.[519] The army also had a large number of servants (camp followers). For example, the grooms who took care of a regiment's horses would not go out and cut grass for their feed; another class of men did that. Other classes brought water, cooked the food, tended the wounded, and removed bodily waste. Businesses had the same problem. An employee would do this but not that; they would deal with this fellow employee but not that one. With Parsis, who had no caste in their community, the British employers had none of these problems. Naturally, they were only too happy to hire Parsis. It was like union busting.

A few Parsis became very rich by taking part in the opium trade with China. They acted as intermediaries in collecting opium from Central India (grown mostly in princely Indian states) and set up trading stations in Canton (in 1837, there were 11 Parsi companies, four European, and nine American ones).[520] They set up firms in Bombay and operated shipping fleets to carry opium. In the first half of the nineteenth century, their ships were a third of the ships in the trade.

Bombay, in the last quarter of the eighteenth century, developed an extensive trade with China, selling raw cotton. Opium replaced cotton as the most profitable Indian export to China by the 1820s, and the Parsis were right in the middle of it.[521]

However, not every Parsi got rich in the opium trade. Most lived a life of doing common jobs, trying to make a living. Many were employed by the rich Parsis; others found other work. In Herman Melville's *Moby-Dick*,[522] one of the great American novels, a Parsi (spelled 'Parsee') is one of the crew members of the doomed American whaling ship *Pequod* on its hunt for the great white whale, Moby-Dick.

A Parsi named Jamsetji Tata built the Taj Mahal Palace Hotel in Bombay. It opened in 1903 and is still one of the great luxury hotels in the world. The Tata conglomerate (the Tata Group), owned by the modern Tata family, is one of the largest in India.

A few seem to have enrolled in the Bombay army at one time. But, with the changeover to class companies, they must have been removed from the army.

## History of Sepoys and Regiments

The rank-and-file Indian soldiers serving under British officers of the Governor and Company of Merchants of London trading to the East Indies ('East India Company', 'EIC', 'John Company', or 'Company'), starting from small toeholds, conquered all of India.[523] They did so with the aid of locally raised regiments, a few company European regiments, and, after 1754, British

519 Allen, *Plain Tales*, pp.90–91. For example, one man would dust the inside floor, but another man would sweep the veranda.

520 Jesse S. Palsetia, *The Parsis of India: Preservation of Identity in Bombay City* (Leiden: Brill, 2021), pp.53–56.

521 Palsetia, *Parsis*, p.55.

522 Published in 1851.

523 Heathcote, *Indian*, p.14.

regiments.[524] The story of how this was accomplished is one of desperate battles against overwhelming odds, self-sacrifice, long marches, privations cheerfully borne, and huge impregnable fortresses captured. Unfortunately, the regiments and men of the Indian army of 1880–1914 are not the regiments and men who accomplished those feats. In fact, in many cases, even the regiments have disappeared. In other cases, normally in the old Madras and Bombay armies, the regimental names were retained, but a new breed of men was placed in them.

The Indian Mutiny wiped out the Bengal army. Table 49 shows the number of regiments in each category that survived the Mutiny.

**Table 49 Survival Rate of Indian Regiments in 1857[525]**

| Unit | Number of Regiments | |
|---|---|---|
| | **Prior to 1857 Mutiny** | **After Mutiny** |
| Bengal Regular Cavalry | 10 | 0 |
| Bengal Irregular Cavalry | 18 | 3 |
| Bengal Infantry | 74 | 12*† |
| Punjab (Frontier) Cavalry | 5 | 5 |
| Sikh (Frontier) Cavalry | 4 | 4 |
| Guides (Infantry and Cavalry Elements) | 1 | 1 |
| Punjab (Frontier) Infantry | 6 | 6 |
| Bombay Regular Cavalry | 3 | 3 |
| Bombay Irregular Cavalry | 5 | 5 |
| Bombay Infantry | 30‡ | 28 |
| Bombay Baluch Regiments | 2 | 2 |
| Gwalior Contingent Cavalry | 2 | 0 |
| Gwalior Contingent Infantry | 10 | 1 |
| Oudh Irregular Cavalry | 3 | 0 |
| Madras Cavalry | 8 | 7 |
| Madras Infantry | 52 | 52 |
| Hyderabad Contingent Cavalry | 4 | 4 |
| Hyderabad Contingent Infantry | 6 | 6 |

* Includes a Gurkha regiment that was moved to be listed with the Gurkhas as the 9th Gurkhas.

† In addition, loyal elements of the 13th, 48th, and 71st Bengal Infantry went to form the 16th (Lucknow) Rajput Infantry, and loyal elements of the 3rd, 36th, and 61st Regiments went to form the 17th Infantry (The Loyal Regiment). Both groups helped in the defence of the Residency at Lucknow.

‡ Counts the 21st (Marine Battalion) and 21st Native Infantry.

The mutinous Bengal regiments had been largely recruited from higher castes of Rajputs and Brahmins living in Oudh, Agra, and Behar. The so-called 'Poorbeahs' or 'Purbiya', men of

524 The first British regiment sent to India was the 39th Regiment (later 1st Dorsetshire Regiment). It earned the motto 'Primus in Indis'. The 39th fought at Plassey in 1757.

525 Perry, *Order Part 1*, pp.118–24, 127–39, 148–50.

the eastern provinces,[526] were very careful of their caste. Even in modern India, this is an area of strong Hindu religious feeling and is known in India as the Cow Belt, much as the area of strong religious feeling in America is known as the Bible Belt. During elections, some modern politicians in the Cow Belt will cater to these religious feelings in much the same way some American politicians do.

A memorable example of the strong religious beliefs found in these areas is found in *Life of Sir Henry Lawrence*. A Bengal army Brahmin subadar was badly wounded and dying of thirst and loss of blood. General James Skinner offered him a drink of water. The Brahmin would not take it, saying, 'My caste, sir! My caste!' Skinner urged him to take a sip, saying, 'We are alone, no one will see you.' The Brahmin would not drink. He was just able to say, 'God sees me!'[527]

The Poorbeah Hindu sepoys (there were also Muslim and a relatively few Sikh ones) took their religion and caste requirements very seriously. Just how serious can be seen in the life of Sita Ram, a native officer in John Company's Bengal army. Twice, his service caused him to become ritually unclean, and, on these occasions, his family had to pay Brahmins large amounts of money to perform the ceremonies that would restore his caste standing. For one, they took all the money that he had saved during his five years of army service.[528]

The Muslims were just as strong in their religious beliefs. Lord Roberts, in his biography, told the story of a Muslim, Subadar Major Aziz Khan, who dated back to the Indian Mutiny days. In 1878, he was wounded in the knee. After a few days, the wound became infected, and the doctors told him his leg would need to be amputated and he would need to drink some wine to undergo the operation. Aziz Khan refused, saying both were against his religion, and he would accept death rather than disobey the precepts of his religion. He died accordingly.[529]

These were the men who reacted to the stories that the British had coated the paper holding the cartridges they needed to bite into to load their rifles with grease from cows and pigs. To load a rifle, the man would bite off one end. The powder inside was then poured into the rifle barrel, and the cartridge paper was rammed down to form a wad with the bullet resting on it. The paper was greased for ease of insertion.[530]

Researchers have teased out many other additional reasons. These included the loss of extra pay (batta) for serving in a foreign area as more and more of India came under direct British rule. The reform of property rights has also been listed as a reason. These threatened the well-being of the sepoys, who were almost all landowners. On paper, the reforms may have been helpful to them, but, in practice, they did not like them and did not trust the process. Another reason was the annexation of princely states. Lord Dalhousie, who was in charge of India during the period 1848–1856, felt that British rule was far better than that of an Indian prince. He and the company therefore tried to annex princely states whenever they could. There was a fairly narrow set of rules limiting what states were subject to annexation. He also claimed the right to take over a state in cases where there had been prolonged misgovernment. These cases were also few in number. But the mere fact that it was being done at all upset the other princes. During Dalhousie's eight years in office, he wanted to seize seven states. In one case, the directors of

526 MacMunn, *Armies*, pp.83–84.
527 Herbert B. Edwardes and Herman Merivale, *Life of Sir Henry Lawrence* (3rd edition, London: Smith, Elder and Co., 1873), p.50, footnote 13.
528 Lunt (ed.) and Norgate (trans.), *Sepoy*, pp.49–50, 126.
529 Roberts, *Forty-One*, vol. 1, p.354, footnote.
530 Heathcote, *Indian*, p.86.

the EIC in London decided against annexation. In two others, the decision was overruled by his successor.

The hardest blow was the annexation of the state of Oudh in 1856 on grounds of corruption and incompetence in the state's administration. It was one of the two great Muslim states in India. The king had been a loyal ally for 80 years, and Oudh was the main recruiting area for the company's Bengal army. This move, in one blow, upset the other princes and the sepoys. It showed the princes that not even loyalty to the British would always protect them. It added to the unease of the sepoys, as it changed one more factor in their heretofore stable world. They also lost the benefits they had been able to secure at the court of the ruler of Oudh.[531]

One other reason scholars have suggested is the attack on Hindu religion. England was going through a religious revival, which we think of as being associated with the Victorian period.[532] To the ever-increasing religious British of the mid-1800s, India was a country full of heathens who literally worshipped in front of false idols. In the early days, the company had kept most missionaries out of India. But, with the passage of the Charter Act of 1834, the company lost the right to do so, and, in the 1840s and 1850s, missionaries of all sects proliferated.[533] Individuals, both civilian and military, fired with religious zeal, made efforts to convert the native population. Officers were known to preach on the virtues of Christianity to their sepoys drawn up on parade, and some operated projects to have the orphan children of sepoys given to missionaries so they could be raised as Christians.[534] In 1856, they began to force future newly enlisted soldiers to agree to serve overseas, which was likely to mean the loss of caste standing.[535]

Prophecy is one additional reason mentioned by researchers. There was said to be a prophecy that the rule of the *Feringis* (Europeans) would last 100 years. The Battle of Plassey, which set the John Company on its path of conquest, was fought in 1757. One hundred years later, the soldiers, because of the above factors, were unhappy with their lot,[536] so it only took a local spark to set off the Great Mutiny.

After the Second Anglo-Sikh War, the company had enlisted some Sikhs in the Bengal army and in the frontier irregulars. Many had been against doing this. The Sikhs had just been conquered; they had been a most difficult foe, and many felt they could not be trusted.

When the Mutiny came, many, but not all, of the Sikhs in the Bengal army mutinied along with their messmates.[537] With their Bengal army in almost total revolt, the British turned to the one source of fighting men available, the Punjab. If this meant accepting Sikhs into the new regiments, that was a risk that would have to be run in this emergency.

531 Mason, *Honour*, pp.226–27, 247–57.
532 However, many of its traits began early in the nineteenth century. For example, Thomas Bowdler published his bowdlerised version of Shakespeare's writings in 1818. The British outlawed sati – the burning alive of widows of high status on their husbands' death – and allowed widows to remarry in 1829. The *Thagi* (Thugs), ritual murderers in Central India, were eradicated by William Sleeman in the 1830s. This was one of Britain's proudest accomplishments. However, there is a modern suggestion that Sleeman was nothing more than a prosecutor with unlimited powers on a witch hunt, seeing Thuggees behind every tree. See *Children of Kali* by Kevin Rushby.
533 Heathcote, *Indian*, p.84.
534 Heathcote, *Indian*, p.85.
535 Heathcote, *Indian*, p.85.
536 Mason, *Honour*, p.214.
537 MacMunn, *Armies*, p.85.

## Post Bengal Army

The Bengal cavalry regiments 9 through 19 were units that were raised for service in the Mutiny. In addition, some 15 other units were raised and disbanded after the Mutiny. The first eight regiments were continuations of loyal regiments of irregular Bengal cavalry regiments.[538] In the infantry, the first 11 regiments were renumbered continuations of old regiments that had stayed loyal when so many others had mutinied. Twelve had stayed loyal, but one of them, the old 66th Infantry, the new 11th Infantry, was made up of Gurkhas, and, within five months, it was moved to a separate Gurkha list as the 1st Gurkhas.[539] Several other Gurkha regiments remained in the Bengal line up until the 1890s, when they were moved to a separate Gurkha list.[540]

Bengal regiments 12 through 18 consisted of local units brought out to fight the mutineers and composite regiments created out of the loyal elements of regiments that had mutinied or been disarmed. Regiments 19 through 48 in 1861 were continuations of units that had been raised during the Mutiny years to help put down the Mutiny. Almost all of the men in them came from the Punjab, and their personnel primarily consisted of Sikhs, Muslims, and Dogras. The years following 1861 saw some of these regiments disband and undergo other changes. In addition, the British raised three infantry levies that did not live on after 1861.[541]

Only the first eight cavalry regiments and 10 of the 11 infantry regiments (except the ninth, which was Gurkha) were still recruited in Oudh, Agra, Behar, and the east. The rest of the Bengal line came from the Punjab, Rajputana, and the frontier areas.

## Manning the Bengal Army

Following the Mutiny, a commission, the Peel Commission, sat in London to consider the lessons of the Mutiny and how the Indian army should be manned. They recommended what is known as the 'plum pudding' system, that is, have all the different classes mix in each regiment as was done in the Madras and Bombay armies. However, when it came to the Bengal army, which was the main target of this advice, it was a bit too late. The Bengal authorities on the ground, in the heat of the emergency, raised regiments on whatever basis they could, and it would be a bit hard, to say nothing of dangerous, to start tinkering with these loyal men's livelihoods.

In 1861, five of the 19 cavalry regiments were mixed the way the Peel Commission wanted, as were 18 of the 45 Bengal infantry line regiments (plus an additional four single-class Gurkha regiments). In 1861, the army had a large number of different classes in its ranks, and several of these were low-status classes. By 1884, before the heyday of the martial classes theory, the number of different classes in the regiments had been reduced, many lower classes had been dropped, and all the mixed-class regiments had been converted into class troop or company regiments. The tables below show this evolution.

538 Perry, *Order Part 1*, pp.116–17.
539 Perry, *Order Part 1*, pp.127–33; Marrion and Fosten, *Tradition*, p.8.
540 See Marrion and Fosten, *Tradition*.
541 Perry, *Order Part 1*, pp.127–33.

**Table 50 Bengal Native Regiments' Composition in 1864 – Cavalry**[542]

| Regiments | Multanis | Hindustani Muslims | Trans-Indus and Border Tribes | Punjabi Muslims | Hindustani Hindus | Sikhs | Dogras and Hillmen | Bundelas | Jats | Total Troops | Remarks |
|---|---|---|---|---|---|---|---|---|---|---|---|
| 1st Bengal Cavalry | The composition of the corps to remain as previously, namely, entirely Hindustani Muslims. | | | | | | | | | | |
| 2nd Bengal Cavalry | To be composed gradually, but eventually, of Muslims, Dogras, Sikhs, Jats, Rajputs, Brahmins, and Mahrattas, in equal numbers and mixed together in several troops. | | | | | | | | | | |
| 3rd Bengal Cavalry | The same as the 2nd Bengal Cavalry Lancers. | | | | | | | | | | |
| 4th Bengal Cavalry | The same as the 2nd Bengal Cavalry Lancers. | | | | | | | | | | |
| 5th Bengal Cavalry | The same as the 2nd Bengal Cavalry Lancers. | | | | | | | | | | |
| 6th Bengal Cavalry | – | 1 | 1 | – | 1 | 1 | – | 1 | 1 | 6 | That is, class troops. |
| 7th Bengal Cavalry | The same as the 2nd Bengal Cavalry. | | | | | | | | | | |
| 8th Bengal Cavalry | – | 1 | 1 | 1 | 1 | – | – | 1 | 1 | 6 | |
| 9th Bengal Cavalry | – | – | 1 | 2 | – | 2 | 1 | – | – | 6 | |
| 10th Bengal Cavalry | – | – | 1 | 1 | – | 2 | 1 | – | 1 | 6 | |
| 11th Bengal Cavalry | – | – | 1 | 1 | – | 3 | 1 | – | – | 6 | |
| 12th Bengal Cavalry | – | – | 1 | 1 | – | 2 | 1/2 | 1/2 | 1 | 6 | |
| 13th Bengal Cavalry | – | – | 1 | 2 | – | 2 | 1 | – | – | 6 | |
| 14th Bengal Cavalry | To remain as formerly a class regiment of Jats only. | | | | | | | | | | |
| 15th Bengal Cavalry | To remain as formerly a class regiment of Multanis, Duranis,* Pathans, Baluchis, and so on. | | | | | | | | | | |
| 16th Bengal Cavalry | – | 1 | 1 | – | 2 | – | 1 | – | 1 | 6 | |
| 17th Bengal Cavalry | – | 1 | 1 | 1 | 1 | – | 1 | – | 1 | 6 | |
| 18th Bengal Cavalry | – | 1 | – | 1 | 1 | 1 | – | – | 2 | 6 | |
| 19th Bengal Cavalry | 1 | – | 1 | 1 | – | 2 | 1/2 | – | 1/2 | 6 | |

* Duranis (normally spelled 'Durranis') were an Afghanistan Pashtun tribe. Elements of this tribe had come into India as part of invading armies. Their descendants lived as settled farmers on Indian land that had been given to them as booty.

542 F. G. Cardew, *The Bengal Native Army* (London: Leonaur, 2008), p.329.

**Table 51 Bengal Native Regiments' Composition in 1864 – Infantry[543]**

| Regiments | Brahmins and Rajputs | Hindustani Muslims | Jats | Fas and Hillmen | Bundelas | Ahirs | Pasis | Lodhs | Dhanuks | Kurmis | Gujars | Chumars | Mehtars | Hindus of the Interior Castes | Punjabi Muslims | Trans-Indus and Border Tribes | Dogras and Hillmen | Trans-Sutlej Sikhs* | Cis-Sutlej Sikhs† | All Races and Castes |
|---|---|---|---|---|---|---|---|---|---|---|---|---|---|---|---|---|---|---|---|---|
| 1st Native Infantry | To be recruited as formerly, a predominance of Rajputs, with large numbers of Brahmins and Hindustani Muslims, some Sikhs and low-caste men. | | | | | | | | | | | | | | | | | | | |
| 2nd Native Infantry | As formerly, chiefly of Hindustani Muslims, Brahmins, and Rajputs, a few low-caste men. | | | | | | | | | | | | | | | | | | | |
| 3rd Native Infantry | The same as the 2nd. | | | | | | | | | | | | | | | | | | | |
| 4th Native Infantry | The same as the 2nd. | | | | | | | | | | | | | | | | | | | |
| 5th Native Infantry | 2 | 1 | 1 | 1 | 1 | – | – | – | – | – | – | – | – | 1 | – | – | – | 1 | – | – |
| 6th Native Infantry | 1 | 1 | 2 | – | – | – | – | – | – | – | – | – | – | 1 | 1 | | 1 | 1 | – | – |
| 7th Native Infantry | As formerly, chiefly Hindustani Muslims, Brahmins, and Rajputs, with an admixture of Cis-Sutlej Sikhs† and low-castes. | | | | | | | | | | | | | | | | | | | |
| 8th Native Infantry | 2 | 1 | – | – | – | – | – | – | – | – | – | – | – | 1 | – | 1 | 1 | 1 | – | 1 |
| 9th Native Infantry | 2 | 1 | 1 | 1 | 2 | – | – | – | – | – | – | – | – | – | – | – | 1 | – | – | – |
| 10th Native Infantry | 2 | 1 | 1 | – | 1 | – | – | – | – | – | – | – | – | 1 | 1 | – | 1 | – | – | – |
| 11th Native Infantry | To be recruited as formerly, much the same as the 2nd. | | | | | | | | | | | | | | | | | | | |
| 12th Native Infantry | As the 2nd, with an admixture of Punjabi Muslims. | | | | | | | | | | | | | | | | | | | |
| 13th Native Infantry | 1 | 1 | 2 | 1 | 2 | – | – | – | – | – | – | – | – | 1 | – | – | – | – | – | – |
| 14th Native Infantry | As formerly, principally Cis-Sutlej Sikhs, with a small admixture of Punjabi Muslims and Trans-Sutlej* Sikhs. | | | | | | | | | | | | | | | | | | | |
| 15th Native Infantry | As the 14th. | | | | | | | | | | | | | | | | | | | |
| 16th Native Infantry | As formerly, of Hindustani Muslims, Brahmins, and Rajputs, with a few Ahirs, Sikhs, and low-castes. | | | | | | | | | | | | | | | | | | | |
| 17th Native Infantry | As formerly, much the same as the 2nd. | | | | | | | | | | | | | | | | | | | |
| 18th Native Infantry | 2 | 2 | – | 2 | 1 | – | – | – | – | – | – | – | – | 1 | – | – | – | – | – | – |
| 19th Native Infantry | To be composed of Punjabi Muslims and Trans-Sutlej* Sikhs in nearly equal proportions, with a few Dogras. | | | | | | | | | | | | | | | | | | | |
| 20th Native Infantry | | | | | | | | | | | | | | | | | | | | |
| 21st Native Infantry | | | | | | | | | | | | | | | | | | | | |
| 22nd Native Infantry | | | | | | | | | | | | | | | | | | | | |

543 Cardew, *Bengal Army*, pp.330–31.

| | | | | | | | | | | | | | | | | | | | | |
|---|---|---|---|---|---|---|---|---|---|---|---|---|---|---|---|---|---|---|---|---|
| 23rd Native Infantry | A class regiment of Mazbi Sikhs. | | | | | | | | | | | | | | | | | | | |
| 24th Native Infantry | The same as the 19th Native Infantry. | | | | | | | | | | | | | | | | | | | |
| 25th Native Infantry | | | | | | | | | | | | | | | | | | | | |
| 26th Native Infantry | | | | | | | | | | | | | | | | | | | | |
| 27th Native Infantry | | | | | | | | | | | | | | | | | | | | |
| 28th Native Infantry | | | | | | | | | | | | | | | | | | | | |
| 29th Native Infantry | | | | | | | | | | | | | | | | | | | | |
| 30th Native Infantry | | | | | | | | | | | | | | | | | | | | |
| 31st Native Infantry | The same as the 19th Native Infantry, but Cis-Sutlej† Sikhs may be entertained. | | | | | | | | | | | | | | | | | | | |
| 32nd Native Infantry | A class regiment of Mazbi Sikhs. | | | | | | | | | | | | | | | | | | | |
| 33rd Native Infantry‡ | – | 1 | – | – | – | 3 | 1 | – | – | – | – | 1 | – | 1 | – | – | – | – | – | 1 |
| 34th Native Infantry‡ | 1 | – | – | – | – | 1 | – | 1 | 1 | – | – | 1 | 1 | 1 | – | – | – | – | – | 1 |
| 35th Native Infantry‡ | – | – | – | – | – | 2 | – | 2 | 1 | – | – | 2 | 1 | – | – | – | – | – | – | – |
| 36th Native Infantry‡ | 2 | – | 1 | – | – | 2 | – | – | – | 2 | – | – | – | – | – | – | – | – | – | 1 |
| 37th Native Infantry | 1 | 1 | 1 | – | – | 1 | – | – | – | 1 | 2 | – | – | – | 1 | | | | – | – |
| 38th Native Infantry | 2 | – | 2 | – | – | 2 | – | – | – | 1 | – | – | – | – | – | – | – | – | – | 1 |
| 39th Native Infantry | 1 | – | 1 | 1 | – | 1 | – | – | – | – | – | 1 | | 1 | – | – | – | – | 1 | 1 |
| 40th Native Infantry | 2 | – | – | – | – | 3 | – | – | – | – | – | – | – | 1 | – | – | – | 1 | – | 1 |
| 41st Native Infantry | 2 | 1 | 2 | 1 | – | – | – | – | – | – | 1 | – | – | – | – | – | 1 | – | – | – |
| 42nd Native Infantry | Chiefly of Gurkhas and Hillmen (Assamese), with a proportion, not exceeding one-fourth of its strength, of Hindustanis. | | | | | | | | | | | | | | | | | | | |
| 43rd Native Infantry | The same as the 42nd. | | | | | | | | | | | | | | | | | | | |
| 44th Native Infantry | | | | | | | | | | | | | | | | | | | | |
| 45th Native Infantry | As formerly, to be composed entirely of Punjabis and Sikhs. | | | | | | | | | | | | | | | | | | | |
| 1st Gurkha Regiment | Class regiments, entirely of Gurkhas and Hillmen. | | | | | | | | | | | | | | | | | | | |
| 2nd Gurkha Regiment | | | | | | | | | | | | | | | | | | | | |
| 3rd Gurkha Regiment | | | | | | | | | | | | | | | | | | | | |
| 4th Gurkha Regiment | | | | | | | | | | | | | | | | | | | | |
| Sappers and Miners | Five-eighths Hindustani, two-eighths Punjabis and Sikhs, and one-eighth Trans-Indus tribes. | | | | | | | | | | | | | | | | | | | |

* 'Trans-Sutlej' means Punjab.
† 'Cis-Sutlej' means Eastern Punjab.
‡ Low-caste levies.

In 1883, a war scare with Russia led to concerns about having an army able to fight the Russians, who were drawing ever closer to India, and the new martial-races theory joined together to cause a change in a way the regiments were manned. Plum pudding went out, and groupings of the martial classes in the regiments began.

**Table 52 Bengal Native Regiments' Composition in 1883 – Cavalry**[544]

| Corps | Class Regiment (CR) or Class Troop (CT) | Muslims | | | Hindus | | | | Remarks |
|---|---|---|---|---|---|---|---|---|---|
| | | | | | Punjabi | | Hindustani | | |
| | | Hindustani | Punjabi | Trans-Indus and Border | Sikhs | Dogras | Rajputs | Other Hindus | |
| 1st Bengal Cavalry | CR | 6 | – | – | – | – | – | – | |
| 2nd Bengal Cavalry | CT | 2 | – | – | 1 | – | 1 | 2* | |
| 3rd Bengal Cavalry | CT | 3 | – | – | 1 | – | 1 | 1* | |
| 4th Bengal Cavalry | CT | 3 | – | – | 1 | – | – | 2* | |
| 5th Bengal Cavalry | CT | 2 | – | – | 1 | – | 1 | 2* | |
| 6th Bengal Cavalry | CT | 2 | – | – | 2 | – | 1 | 1* | |
| 7th Bengal Cavalry | CT | 2 | – | – | 1 | – | 1 | 2† | |
| 8th Bengal Cavalry | CT | 3 | – | – | 1 | – | 1 | 1 | |
| 9th Bengal Cavalry | CT | – | 2 | 1 | 2 | 1 | – | – | |
| 10th Bengal Lancers | CT | – | 1 | 1 | 2 | 2 | – | – | |
| 11th Bengal Lancers | CT | – | 1 | 1‡ | 3 | 1 | – | – | |
| 12th Bengal Cavalry | CT | – | 2 | – | 3 | 1 | – | – | |
| 13th Bengal Lancers | CT | – | 1 | 1 | 2 | 2 | – | – | |
| 14th Bengal Lancers | CR | – | – | – | – | – | – | 6* | |
| 15th Bengal Cavalry | CR | – | 2 | 4 | – | – | – | – | |
| 18th Bengal Cavalry | CT | – | 4 | – | 2 | – | – | – | |
| 19th Bengal Lancers | CT | – | 1 | 1 | 2 | 1 | – | – | One troop of independent trans-border tribes. |

* Jats.
† One troop of Jats and one of Brahmins.
‡ One-fourth of the troop might consist of Afridis.

544 Cardew, *Bengal Army*, p.405.

**Table 53 Bengal Native Regiments' Composition in 1883 – Infantry**[545]

| Corps | Class Regiment (CR) or Class Company (CC) | Muslims | | | | Hindus | | | | | | Northeast Frontier | | Jarwahs of Assam |
|---|---|---|---|---|---|---|---|---|---|---|---|---|---|---|
| | | | | | | Punjabi | | | Hindustani | | | | | |
| | | | | | | Sikhs | | | | | | | | |
| | | Hindustani | Punjabi | Independent Trans-Border | Trans-Indus and Border | Jats and so on | Mazbis | Dogras | Brahmins | Rajputs | Other Hindus | Gurkhas | Hillmen | |
| 1st Bengal Infantry | CC | 2 | – | – | – | – | – | – | 2 | 3 | 1 | – | – | – |
| 2nd Bengal Infantry | CC | 2 | – | – | – | – | – | – | 2 | 3 | 1 | – | – | – |
| 3rd Bengal Infantry | CC | 2 | – | – | – | – | – | – | 3 | 2 | 1 | – | – | – |
| 4th Bengal Infantry | CC | 2 | – | – | – | – | – | – | 2 | 3 | 1 | – | – | – |
| 5th Bengal Infantry | CC | 2 | – | – | – | – | – | – | 1 | 2 | 3[*] | – | – | – |
| 6th Bengal Infantry | CC | 2 | – | – | – | – | – | – | – | 2 | 4[*] | – | – | – |
| 7th Bengal Infantry | CC | 2 | – | – | – | – | – | – | 1 | 3 | 2 | – | – | – |
| 8th Bengal Infantry | CC | 2 | – | – | – | – | – | – | 1 | 3 | 2 | – | – | – |
| 9th Bengal Infantry | CC | 1 | – | – | – | – | – | – | 1 | 2 | 2[†] | – | 2 | – |
| 10th Bengal Infantry | CC | 2 | – | – | – | – | – | – | 1 | 2 | 3[*] | – | – | – |
| 11th Bengal Infantry | CC | 2 | – | – | – | – | – | – | 2 | 3 | 1 | – | – | – |
| 12th Bengal Infantry | CC | 3 | – | – | – | – | – | – | 1 | 2 | 2 | – | – | – |
| 13th Bengal Infantry | CC | 2 | – | – | – | – | – | – | – | 1 | 4[*] | – | 1 | – |
| 14th Bengal Infantry | CR | – | 1 | – | – | 7[‡] | – | – | – | – | – | – | – | – |
| 15th Bengal Infantry | CR | – | 1 | – | – | 7[‡] | – | – | – | – | – | – | – | – |
| 16th Bengal Infantry | CC | 2 | – | – | – | – | – | – | 1 | 3 | 2 | – | – | – |
| 17th Bengal Infantry | CC | 3 | – | – | – | – | – | – | 2 | 3 | – | – | – | – |
| 18th Bengal Infantry | CC | 2 | – | – | – | – | – | – | 1 | 2 | 1 | – | 2 | – |
| 19th Bengal Infantry | CC | – | 2 | 1 | 1 | 4[§] | – | – | – | – | – | – | – | – |
| 20th Bengal Infantry | CC | – | 1 | 2[**] | 1 | 2[§] | – | 2 | – | – | – | – | – | – |
| 21st Bengal Infantry | CC | – | 2 | 1[**] | 1 | 3[§] | – | 1 | – | – | – | – | – | – |
| 22nd Bengal Infantry | CC | – | 3 | – | – | 4[§] | – | 1 | – | – | – | – | – | – |
| 23rd Bengal Infantry | CR | – | – | – | – | – | 8 | – | – | – | – | – | – | – |
| 24th Bengal Infantry | CC | – | 2 | – | 1 | 3[§] | – | 2 | – | – | – | – | – | – |
| 25th Bengal Infantry | CC | – | 3 | – | – | 3[§] | – | 2 | – | – | – | – | – | – |
| 26th Bengal Infantry | CC | – | – | 1[**] | 2 | 4[§] | – | 1 | – | – | – | – | – | – |
| 27th Bengal Infantry | CC | – | 2 | – | 2 | 3[§] | – | 1 | – | – | – | – | – | – |
| 28th Bengal Infantry | CC | – | 2 | – | 2 | 3[§] | – | 1 | – | – | – | – | – | – |
| 29th Bengal Infantry | CC | – | 2 | – | – | 4[§] | – | 2 | – | – | – | – | – | – |
| 30th Bengal Infantry | CC | – | 2 | – | – | 4[§] | – | 2 | – | – | – | – | – | – |
| 31st Bengal Infantry | CC | – | 2 | – | – | 4[§] | – | 2 | – | – | – | – | – | – |
| 32nd Bengal Infantry | CR | – | – | – | – | – | 8 | – | – | – | – | – | – | – |

545 Cardew, *Bengal Army*, pp.406–07.

| 33rd Bengal Infantry | CC | 2 | – | – | – | – | – | – | 2 | 2 | 2[¶] | – | – | – |
|---|---|---|---|---|---|---|---|---|---|---|---|---|---|---|
| 38th Bengal Infantry | CC | – | – | – | – | – | – | – | – | 2 | 4[*] | – | 2 | – |
| 39th Bengal Infantry | CC | – | – | – | – | – | – | – | 1 | 1 | 4[*] | – | 2 | – |
| 40th Bengal Infantry | CC | – | – | – | – | – | – | – | 1 | 3 | 4 | – | – | – |
| 42nd Bengal Infantry | CR | – | – | – | – | – | – | – | – | – | – | 7 | – | 1 |
| 43rd Bengal Infantry | CR | – | – | – | – | – | – | – | – | – | – | 7 | – | 1 |
| 44th Bengal Infantry | CR | – | – | – | – | – | – | – | – | – | – | 7 | – | 1 |
| 45th Bengal Infantry | CR | 1 | – | – | – | 6 | – | 1 | – | – | – | – | – | – |
| 1st Gurkha Regiment<br>2nd Gurkha Regiment<br>3rd Gurkha Regiment<br>4th Gurkha Regiment | CR | – | – | – | – | – | – | – | – | – | – | 8 | – | – |

* Two of Jats.
† Jats.
‡ Cis-Sutlej Sikhs chiefly.
§ Cis-Sutlej Sikhs prohibited.
** Afridis.
¶ Jats and so on.

## Changes Up to 1889[546]

By 1889, there had been sufficient changes to issue new tables. In the Bengal native cavalry, a squadron was added to each regiment. The addition did not significantly impact the class makeup of the regiments, as the men added to most regiments were added within already-present groups. Three exceptions exist where a new class was added to those groups already establishing the makeup of the regiment. They include the 7th Bengal Cavalry (a company of Dogras was added), the 8th Bengal Cavalry (a company of Punjabi Muslims was added), and the 19th Bengal Lancers (a company of trans-frontier tribes was added).

In addition, the 16th and 17th Bengal Cavalry were re-raised in 1885 after being disbanded as an economic move in 1882.[547] The 1st through 4th Punjab Cavalry and the Guides cavalry were now listed as part of the army cavalry because of their 1886 transfer of control from the civil government of India – under the government of the Punjab – to the army under the control of the commander-in-chief.[548]

In the Bengal native infantry, the changes were minor. The makeup of the infantry regiments was, except in a few cases, almost identical with that ordered in 1883, the only difference being that the companies of 'other Hindus' (exclusive of Jat companies) were entirely eliminated and extra companies of Rajputs substituted in their place; the Assam Gurkha regiments exchanged their Jarwah companies for an eighth company of Gurkhas, while the Jarwahs were distributed throughout the regiment, 15 to each company; the 45th became a class regiment of Sikhs

546 Cardew, *Bengal Army*, p.408.
547 Perry, *Order Part 1*, p.118.
548 MacMunn, *Armies*, p.126; Cardew, *Bengal Army*, p.409.

only, recruiting from Cis- and Trans-Sutlej; the 38th Bengal Infantry, retaining its two Rajput companies, became otherwise a class regiment, having six companies of Jats.[549]

Four infantry regiments, the 34th Pioneers (Mazbis Sikhs), 35th (Jat Sikhs), 36th (Jat Sikhs), and 37th (Dogras), were re-raised as class regiments after being disbanded in the economic changes of 1882.[550] There were also added to the list the Guides infantry, the four Sikh infantry regiments (1–4), and the five Punjab infantry regiments (1, 2, 4, 5, and 6) to reflect them now being under army control.

## 1892 Changes

After these changes, the cavalry had 14 single-class troops and three single-class regiments. The infantry, including the Frontier Force, had 16 single-class regiments, and the balance was multi-class regiments. Then, in 1892, 'Purbiya' infantry regiments, those recruited from the Eastern Punjab, Oudh, Agra, and Behar, were reorganised as single-class regiments as follows:

- 1st and 3rd – All Brahmins
- 2nd, 4th, 7th, 8th, 11th, 13th, and 16th – All Rajputs
- 5th, 12th, 17th, and 18th – All Muslims
- 6th and 10th – All Jats
- 9th – All Gurkha.

## Fighting Reputation

The regiments produced by this system were always somewhat brittle tools. Sometimes, they would fight heroically; other times, they would let you down. Under John Company, a type of political correctness was held, and one could not express poor opinions of the sepoys. Anyone who dared to tell the truth would be persecuted and ruined.[551]

One can find many examples of the most tenacious and heroic actions, as well as examples where regiments failed to meet minimum standards of combat performance. A few examples follow.

In 1805, an army under Lake attempted to capture the almost impregnable city of Bhurtpore. It was guarded by a moat and thick walls between 80 and 100ft (24.4 and 30.5m) high. The British did not have heavy siege artillery. Lake could not make breaches in the walls, and his ladders were not long enough to reach the top of the walls. Nevertheless, the British and sepoy regiments tried three times to capture the city. They failed each time with terrible losses. A fourth assault was tried. Men drove their bayonets into the walls and used the hilts to climb. The 31st Bengal Native Infantry almost made it to the top of the wall on the fourth attack before they were driven back.

Their colours were so full of holes from the gunfire from Bhurtpore and the campaigns prior to it that they were ordered replaced. The colours were stored the night before their retirement

549 Cardew, *Bengal Army*, pp.408–09.
550 Perry, *Order Part 1*, p.131.
551 Holmes, *Sahib*, pp.293–94.

next to the new colours. The next morning, the old colours were gone, and the British officers could not learn what had happened to them.

In 1826, the British came back to Bhurtpore with a stronger army and a siege train of heavy guns. The 31st was in this army. Breaches were made in the walls by mines, and the troops rushed into the city. Among the troops surging into the city was the 31st, carrying their colours. Attached to these colours were many ribbon strips. The ribbons were pieces of the old colours of the 31st that had been preserved and passed down to the sons of the sepoys who had been at Bhurtpore in the failed attack of 1805. They were brought out as the regiment's honour had been redeemed.[552]

The 31st stayed loyal during the Mutiny and became the 2nd Bengal Infantry. When the Purbiya regiments were turned into class regiments in 1897, they became the 2nd Rajput Light Infantry. They had that title in 1914.

In 1778, a small force from the Bombay army was sent out into Maratha country. The force was soon set upon by a Maratha army 30 times their size, and the Bombay army retreated. The British, in large part, were saved by a combination unit of grenadiers, which acted as a rear-guard. This composite unit was formed from the six grenadier companies of the three battalions in the force. It was standard practice at the time to detach the grenadier and light infantry companies from battalions or regiments and form separate ad hoc units.

Later, the detached grenadier companies, joined by some others, were formed into the 8th Bombay Infantry. The men were upset because they were not given the designation of grenadiers, as being called 'infantry' was a step down in status.

Soon thereafter, the new 8th Regiment and the 2nd Battalion, 42nd (Royal Highland) Regiment of Foot (in 1914, 2nd Battalion, the Black Watch), were besieged in Mangalore by Tipu, the Tiger of Mysore (also known as Tippoo), and an army of some 150,000. The siege lasted from 16 May 1783 until 30 January 1784. At the end, men were dying at a rate of 15 a day, and others were going blind. The British started with 1,900 men and had 236 Europeans and 618 Indians fit for duty when the commander capitulated with the honours of war. Both regiments were awarded the battle honour 'Mangalore' – one of the very rare times when a battle honour was granted for a defeat. In addition, the 8th was now named the 8th Grenadiers. In this, it beat the 1st Regiment of Foot Guards by 32 years.[553] The 8th Grenadiers survived the Mutiny and post-Mutiny cutbacks. In 1914, it was the 101st Grenadiers.

The 13th (1st Somersetshire) Regiment (Light Infantry) was heaped with honours after undergoing a four-month siege at Jellalabad, a small city just inside Afghanistan, in 1842. It was granted a Mural Crown, superscribed with the word 'Jellalabad', and given the name and monogram of Prince Albert.

During the siege, earthquakes knocked down great lengths of the newly improved walls and the protective walls, and a third of the town was demolished. The soldiers ran short of food and ammunition. After the siege, the regiment had the nicknames 'Jellalabad Heroes' and the name 'Illustrious Garrison' from Ellenborough, governor general of India from 1842 to 1844.[554]

552 Mason, *Honour*, pp.128–30.
553 Mason, *Honour*, p.127.
554 Ian Knight, *Go to Your God Like a Soldier: The British Soldier Fighting for Empire, 1837–1902* (London: Greenhill Books, 1996), p.58.

There were Indian units there also, notably 750 men of the 35th Bengal Infantry to go with the 13th's 700 men. The 35th also earned the battle honour 'Jellalabad' and the name 'Illustrious Garrison'. The other units were a handful of cavalry and 150 sappers and miners out of a levy of 600 that had been raised for Shah Soojah. The 35th Regiment at Jellalabad seems to have gone down Orwell's memory hole, and it is seldom mentioned in accounts of the siege.

The 35th shared all the fighting and privations of the siege. A loose siege began on 12 November 1842, and a closed siege by a large army in late February. The garrison regularly sallied out of the walls to drive off advancing siege parties. In one of the sorties, the troops managed to round up 500 sheep and goats (some say cattle) held by the attackers. When it came time to divide up the flock, the men of the 35th gave their share to the 13th, saying meat was not as necessary for them as it was for the British, a noble gesture when food was short. After the siege, the 13th, to honour this act, gave the 35th a silver potpourri bowl, the Attar Dan. (It was misplaced when the 35th was disbanded, but it is now in the National Army Museum, Sandhurst.)[555] Then, on parting, the 35th threw a feast for the 13th.[556]

The reason the 35th has been largely airbrushed from history is that the regiment disappeared during the Mutiny. It is not clear whether they actually mutinied or were disarmed as a safety measure.[557] During the Mutiny, there were very few British regiments stationed in the area where the mutinies were occurring. No one could predict which regiments would revolt. In every regiment, the officers swore that their men were loyal right up to the time the men turned on them. Given these facts, the British adopted the policy of better safe than sorry. They started disarming every sepoy regiment they could unless there was iron-clad proof that the regiment was loyal. The 35th may have been caught up in one of these prophylactic disarmings.

A similar example of an Indian regiment feasting their British comrades occurred during the Second Sikh War. The British Commander Gough presented the 5th Bengal Light Cavalry with 500 rupees (present value: £5,380 or $6,310),[558] though other sources state the payment was higher. The 5th used the money to throw a feast for its comrades, the 14th Light Dragoons (in 1914, the 14th Hussars).

The religion of the men of the 5th forbade them from eating with the British, who, after all, were untouchables, but 'they stood by the tables, superintending the feast, and literally dispensing their hospitality to their guests'.[559] The 5th also bought and presented to the 14th's sergeants' mess an impressive ornate tankard. The sergeants' mess has kept this tankard, known as the Ramnuggur Cup, down to the present. Each year on the anniversary of the Battle of Ramnuggur, 22 November, a commemorative dinner or dance is held in the sergeants' mess. The 'cup' will hold over a bottle of champagne. It has the names of 28 battles and engagements that the 14th took part in during wars in the Peninsula, Punjab, Persia, and Central India engraved on it.[560]

The fate of the 5th was a sad one. The 5th was one of three out of 10 Bengal light cavalry regiments that did not mutiny in whole or in part during the Mutiny.[561] It never had a chance

555 Holmes, *Sahib*, p.301.
556 MacMunn, *Armies*, p.94.
557 MacMunn, *Armies*, p.94; Perry, *Order Part 1*, p.148.
558 Calculated using the 1831 statistic of 10 rupees to £1.
559 Holmes, *Sahib*, pp.300–01.
560 Henry B. Hamilton, *Historical Record of the 14th (King's) Hussars from A.D. 1715 to A.D. 1900* (London: Longmans, Green and Co., 1901), p.213.
561 Perry, *Order Part 5B*, pp.116, 149.

to be tempted to do so, as it, along with all Bengal regiments in the Punjab and the Northwest Frontier, was disarmed within a few days of hearing about the fall of Delhi to the mutineers when the British did not know who they could trust.[562] The reason for this action was that, when the Indian Mutiny of 1857 broke out, John Lawrence decided to send every soldier he could from the Punjab and the frontier to retake Delhi. He could not hold back British soldiers to watch Bengal regiments that might mutiny.[563] So it became his policy, and that of the British, to disarm all Bengal regiments in the Punjab and on the frontier, even if no civil disobedience had occurred.[564] Then, all these units were later disbanded.[565] Better safe than sorry.

One more example of heroic conduct by Indian troops should be mentioned: the Guides fighting to the last man at the British Residency in Kabul on 3 September 1879. The political situation was once again in turmoil in Afghanistan. The Russians had extended their empire to the borders of Afghanistan. The British wanted to bind Afghanistan to them and place a Residency in Kabul, which was refused. Afghanistan was again invaded by India, and the Second Afghanistan War broke out. The sitting Amir fled, and a new Amir took the throne. Negotiations led to peace and, among other clauses, gave the British the right to establish a Residency in Kabul. The envoy and an escort of 25 Guides cavalry and 52 Guides infantry arrived in Kabul in July. From the beginning, the British were greeted with a mix of friendliness and hospitality. On 3 September, Afghan regular army regiments mustered for their pay. When they did not receive the full amount of back pay owed to them, they reacted by attacking the British Residency. In a fight that lasted all day, every soldier in the Residency fought to the death. The men even fought on after the British officers had been killed.

Of the 80 men in the escort, only nine were not killed in the attack on the Residency. One had died the day before the attack, one was on leave, four were away collecting supplies, and one had been sent out through the attackers' lines with a request for help to the king of Afghanistan.

Roberts recommended that the IOM, the highest medal Indian sepoys could be awarded, be conferred on all members of the escort and that the regiment be given the battle honour 'Residency Kabul'. Neither happened because of technicalities. During that period, the medal was not awarded posthumously. The battle honour was not awarded because too small a portion of the regiment had been at the Residency.[566]

While the sepoys have fought well on many occasions, they have also shirked and outright run away from others. The first example is the Battle of Maiwand in 1880. The battle is more well known for the last stand of the 66th Regiment (in 1914, for the 2nd Battalion, Princess Charlotte of Wales' Royal Berkshire Regiment) and the saving of the guns.

The battle was the result of a man named Ayub Khan, the brother of the Amir of Afghanistan, Yakub Khan, who had been deposed in 1840 by British actions. Ayub Khan raised an army to seize Kandahar Province in Afghanistan and then planned to move on to become king of Afghanistan. The Indian army had occupied Kandahar, so conflict was inevitable.

After some half-measures, the British sent out a field force of the 66th (British) Infantry, the 1st Bombay Infantry (Grenadiers), the renumbered 8th Bombay Grenadiers, who had done

562 Mason, *Honour*, pp.290–91; see Perry, *Order Part 5B*, pp.148–49.
563 Mason, *Honour*, p.290.
564 Mason, *Honour*, p.291.
565 See Perry, *Order Part 5B*, pp.116, 127–29.
566 W. E. H. Condon, *Frontier Force Rifles 1849–1946* (East Sussex: Naval and Military Press, 2015), pp.29–36.

so well at Mangalore (in 1914, the 101st Grenadiers), and the 30th Bombay Infantry (Jacob's Rifles; in 1914, the 130th Baluchis Jacob's Rifles). The cavalry consisted of the 3rd Sind Horse (who was disbanded in 1882), the 3rd (the Queen's Own) Bombay Light Cavalry (in 1914, the 33rd Queen Victoria's Own Light Cavalry), and a company of the Bombay Sappers and Miners. E Battery, B Brigade of Royal Horse Artillery, supplied the force's artillery.

The battle was joined at about 11:00 a.m. on 27 July 1880. The 66th beat off several attacks on the left of the line. However, such was the pressure, artillery on the left flank was moved to the centre for additional support. Then, the left flank came under attack by a mass of Ghazis (irregular religious fanatics). The sight of this screaming mass of men waving nearly metre-long (three-foot) knives unnerved the two companies of the 30th Bombay on the left of the battle line, which had lost most of the British and Indian officers (the rest of the 30th were in the centre of the battle line). The two companies of the 30th, in their panic, sought protection in the ranks of the 1st Bombay Grenadiers as if for shelter. The 1st was then thrown into confusion.

The commander of the 1st and his officers tried to rally the sepoys. But the commander was badly wounded, and the sepoys continued to stream off the battlefield. Part of the horse artillery was overrun. But most of it was limbered up, and they removed their guns from under the noses of the on-rushing Ghazis and Afghan regulars. The company of Bombay Sappers held steady. They fired several volleys at the oncoming Afghans, and they marched in formation to the rear.

As the mass of Afghans continued to charge forwards from the left, the rest of the 30th, stationed in the centre of the battle line, panicked and retreated towards their right, away from the attackers. This brought them to the left and rear of the 66th (British) Infantry, who were at the right end of the battle line. This disrupted the formation of the 66th at the very time they were under attack on their front from the Afghans. The 66th, unlike the 30th and 1st Grenadiers, preserved its cohesion and moved to the right while holding off the Afghans. At this point, to try to bring relief to the 66th, a cavalry charge was ordered. The 3rd Sind Horse and the 3rd Bombay Light Cavalry, despite the best efforts of their officers, failed to do their duty. Most would not even line up for a charge. One hundred and thirty charged, but they veered off before the moment of impact and left the battlefield.

Most of the 66th made a fighting withdrawal to the small village of Khig. The men fought from inside Khig for a while. At last, 11 men charged outside the walls of Khig. It was just outside the village that these men made their last stand.

The 66th took heavy casualties at Maiwand. The six companies that went into the battle numbered 19 officers and 427 other ranks. Ten officers and 275 enlisted men were killed. In addition, two officers and 31 men were wounded. The reason for the low number of wounded is that the wounded could not be removed from the battlefield and were killed where they lay by the Afghans. One of the wounded officers was Surgeon Major Preston. The regiment believes he was the basis for Arthur Conan Doyle's Dr Watson, who, in the Sherlock Holmes stories, was wounded with the 66th Berkshires at Maiwand. A few men were able to leave the battlefield and retreat 40 miles (64.7km) to Kandahar. There, they and other members of the Maiwand army were besieged until relieved by a force under Roberts in an operation that made Roberts famous.[567]

567 Michael Barthorp, 'Disaster at Maiwand, 27 July 1880: Part I', *Tradition*, 64 (n.d.), pp.17–19, and 'Disaster at Maiwand, 27 July 1880: Part II', *Tradition*, 65 (n.d.), pp.18–20, 28; Frederick Myatt, *The Royal Berkshire Regiment (the 49th/66th Regiment of Foot)* (London: H. Hamilton, 1968), pp.59–68.

Two companies of the 66th were not at the battle because they had been detached elsewhere in Afghanistan. A monument was built to the 66th in Reading, which lists the names of all the regiment's men killed at Maiwand. It was the first time the names of enlisted men were memorialised on a monument.

The failure of the Bombay regiments, the 1st Grenadiers, the 30th Jacob's Rifles, the 3rd Sind Horse, and the 3rd Bombay Horse, to do their duty in the battle did not add lustre to the name of the Bombay soldier. It doubtless added support to those who said the southern sepoys were inferior to sepoys from the martial classes of the north.

The British, in late 1884, sent troops into the Sudan to rescue 'Chinese' Gordon, who was under siege in Khartoum by the Mahdists, named for a Dervish chief who was considered the 'Mahdi' (Messiah) and wanted Egyptians and all foreigners out of the Sudan.

A second front was opened based in eastern Sudan on the port of Suakin with the goals of ensuring the security of the seaport, supporting the eastern flank of the troops marching to rescue Gordon, and building a road inland from the port. To accomplish this, a force consisting of three infantry brigades was landed: (1) Guards, (2) line infantry and Royal Marines, and (3) Indian. There were also elements of three British and one Indian cavalry regiments.

The Indians, two British regiments, and a squadron of the 8th (Irish) Lancers were sent out to bring the Dervishes to battle. The force had to march through dense mimosa shrubs that covered the countryside. After a tiring march of six-and-a-half hours, they had gone only eight miles (12.87km).

At about 2:00 p.m., a halt was called to the first day's march. The force, as was standard practice in the Sudan, began to build zaribas. Zaribas are mini-forts whose walls are made of cut thorn bushes and shrubs. The walls are necessary because the Dervishes would charge through the heaviest rifle fire.

The plan was to build three zaribas. A large one was for the Indian troops: the 15th (Bengal) Sikhs, the 28th (Bombay) Infantry, and the 17th (Loyal Purbian) Bengal Infantry. The 17th Regiment was the descendant of a composite force that had helped defend the Lucknow Residency during the Mutiny.

The two British units were the 1st Berkshires (the old 49th Foot, now joined with the old 66th of Maiwand fame to form the Princess Charlotte of Wales' Berkshire Regiment) and a battalion of the Royal Marine Light Infantry. They were each to have their own smaller zaribas. The Berkshires were to build theirs off the southwest corner of the large zariba. Each of the smaller zaribas was to have two Gardner machine guns manned by sailors.

The soldiers spent the time after the march stopped building the zaribas. Half of the Berkshires worked on their zariba off the southwest corner of the large zariba. The 15th Sikhs and the 28th Bombay Infantry were stationed on the northwest side of the large zariba, presumably helping to build the walls on that side. The Marines were building their zariba off the northeast side of the large zariba. The other half-battalion of the Berkshires was stationed in the open to the northeast of the Marines' zariba so as to be able to protect the force from attack from that direction. While there, they were cutting down thorny bushes and shrubs to be used in the zaribas. The 17th (Bengal) Infantry was off the southeast corner of the large zariba, with the transport animals on its left. It is not clear why the 17th was there – perhaps to provide a guard or maybe to gather material for zaribas.

The squadron of the 5th Irish Lancers was scouting off to the south. However, they did a poor job, perhaps because of the thick mimosa shrub. The British got word from them that hostiles were in the area. A second report had hardly been made when some 5,000 screaming Fuzzy-Wuzzies swept onto the scene from the southwest.[568] The 17th Bengal Infantry was in their direct line of attack, and they made ready to deal with it. However, the fleeing lancers, just ahead of the Dervishes, hit them first. The 5th Lancers rode right over the 17th and threw them into confusion. The infantry attempted one wild volley and then turned and ran. Their CO was killed as he tried to rally them. The Dervishes also killed and drove back the camels, horses, and mules in the transport lines. The 17th ran through the British camp and out into the shrub on the other side. The Dervishes were just behind them, killing the sepoys who had thrown away their rifles to allow them to run better.

The unarmed working parties of the four companies of Berkshires just had time to run into their zariba, unpile their rifles, and form squares before thousands of Dervishes swarmed over the zariba's southeast side angle. The Gardner guns were overrun. The Berkshires fought it out inside the zariba with rifle fire and hand-to-hand combat.

A good many of the enemy bypassed the Berkshires and were dealt with by the 15th Sikhs, who behaved with steadiness and gallantry. They stopped the Dervishes' forward movement on the right side of the battlefield after the fighting with the Berkshires had taken the heart out of the enemy in this area of the battlefield. The Marines were in their completed zariba and thus relatively safe. Their fire kept the Dervishes away from them and halted their advance in the centre.

The other half-battalion of the Berkshires was caught in the open. But they had enough warning that they could unpile their arms and open fire well before the attack reached them. Their fire was so heavy and accurate that the foe never got close to them. The Dervishes drove stampeding baggage animals towards the Berkshire lines in an effort to break them up, but the Berkshires killed everything that moved in front of them, and, after a bit, the enemy veered off. Soon thereafter, the Madhi's forces left the area.

For their gallant conduct in preventing what could have been a debacle, the Berkshires were made a royal regiment. They, the 15th Sikhs (in 1914) and the 28th (Bombay) Infantry (in 1914, the 28th Pioneers), were given the battle honours of Tofrek and Suakin 1885. The goat of the battle, the 17th (17th Loyal Regiment in 1914), even managed to obtain these two battle honours. The Battle of Tofrek was sometimes unofficially known as the Battle of McNeill's Zariba.[569]

## Tanga[570]

The British attack on the port of Tanga in German East Africa may be the best-known failure of the Indian troops in the early twentieth century. The attack was made by two brigades: the 27th Bangalore from the south of India and an Imperial Service Brigade. These brigades were

568 However, these Fuzzy-Wuzzies did not have an extreme puffed-out Afro hairstyle. The local leader of the Madhis, Osman Rigna, had ordered all hair be shaved off, because he had had a vision where the prophet told him that this would make his men bulletproof.

569 Myatt, *Royal Berkshire*, pp.69–76; Keown-Boyd, *Good Dusting*, pp.85–87.

570 See Charles Hordern, *History of the Great War Based on Official Documents by the Direction of the Historical Section of the Committee of Imperial Defence: Military Operations in East Africa, August 1914–September 1916* (London: HMSO, 1941), vol. 1.

selected after other divisions and brigades had been chosen for service in France, Egypt, Persia, and the Northwest Frontier. The 27th Brigade was selected mostly because it was stationed far from the Northwest Frontier, and the Imperial Service Brigade was a new formation made of state troops with the 13th Rajputs for stiffening. Richard Meinertzhagen, who was a captain on the force's intelligence staff, was scathing about these troops, as was his wont. He called the troops 'the worst in India' and the senior officers fossils in his diary before they left India. They may be considered bad in that most of the regiments were not made up of men from the northern martial classes.

The composition of the brigades was as follows:

**Table 54 Tanga Brigade Composition**

| Brigade | Regiments | Companies |
|---|---|---|
| 27th Brigade | 2nd Loyal North Lancashire | |
| | 63rd Palamcottah Light Infantry | 4 Madrasi Muslims<br>2 Tamils<br>2 Mixed Paraiyans and Christians |
| | 98 Infantry (Old 5th Hyderabad Infantry) | 3 Rajputs<br>3 Hindustani Muslims<br>2 Ahirs of Eastern Punjab |
| | 101st Grenadiers (Old 1st Bombay Grenadiers) | 2 Dekhani Mahrattas<br>2 Konkani Mahrattas<br>2 Rajputana Muslims<br>2 Punjabi Muslims |
| Imperial Service Brigade | 13th Rajputs* | |
| | 2nd Kashmir Rifles | |
| | One-half 3rd Kashmir Rifles† | |
| | One-half 3rd Gwalior Rifles‡ | |
| | 61st KGO Pioneers | 4 Tamils<br>2 Madrasi Muslims<br>2 Mixed Paraiyans and Christians |

* All Rajputana Rajputs.
† Mostly Dogras but some Gurkhas.
‡ The Gwalior state troops had to be recruited from men who lived in that state. This was about 85 percent Hindus and some four percent Muslims. The rest were untouchable tribes, most of whom lived in jungles.

The Indian Force, Expeditionary Force B, arrived off Mombasa, Kenya. These British Royal Navy officers announced they had a local truce with the Germans, and they needed to go to German East Africa to tell their authorities that the truce was off before landings could be made. This meant a loss of surprise. It was not a telling loss because the German military commander, Lieutenant Colonel Paul von Lettow-Vorbeck, who would later in the war win fame as a guerrilla commander, had, based on captured mail, already reached the conclusion that the British would attack in the Tanga area. Accordingly, he ordered additional *Feld-Kompanies* (FKs) to move to Tanga to support the one FK at Tanga, the 17th FK.

The force commander landed his first troops, the 13th Rajputs and the 61st King George's Own (KGO) Pioneers, as darkness fell on 2 November. Along with them landed African porters from Zanzibar. The object of the attack was the port town of Tanga. The advance to it would take the British and Indian troops through dense plantations of rubber and sisal and, after them, a strip of land where crops were grown. In both zones, visibility was limited, and it was hard for the units to maintain contact with each other. After the crop zone came railroad tracks. This was a clear area but exposed to German fire. After the railroad tracks, there was the town itself.

Shortly after dawn on 3 November, half a battalion of the 13th and three companies of the 61st went forwards. As they came into the open fields, the 17th FK's machine guns opened fire on them. They cut great swaths in the ranks of both regiments. The African porters threw down their loads of ammunition and supplies and ran to the rear. The two Indian units started to waver and then began to fall back. Five out of the 12 British officers in the 13th and four companies of the 61st had two British officers killed in the fighting. At this point, the 16th FK arrived and went on the attack. At this, the sepoys' nerves gave way, and they turned and ran towards the beach, dropping everything, including the machine guns. (The official war history says these units 'fell back some distance' and 'had begun to give way'. In the withdrawal, surviving British and Indian officers controlled the retirement as best they could. The war history is consistently more favourable than modern writers to the Indian regiments in describing their actions in the battle.) Once they got back to the beach, some even tried to wade back to the lighters.

There was still time to mount another attack, but Brigadier General Tighe reported that the 13th and 61st were so shaken that they could not be relied upon. He would not contemplate using them for further action that day. Tighe thought about using the North Lancashires, who were in the process of being landed, to mount an attack. He elected not to do this, fearing the adverse moral effect if a second weak attack failed.

The British command decided to land all their combat regiments before another attack was attempted. This took the rest of 3 November and until 9:30 a.m. the next day. During this time, no one bothered to reconnoitre the German position. If they had, they would have found the Germans had pulled out of Tanga except for a few scouts.

Shortly after 12:00 p.m. on 4 November, the attack began. (The delay between 9:30 a.m. and noon was caused by giving everyone a good breakfast.) The Loyal North Lancashires (LNL) were in the centre of the attacking line and were to give direction to the attacking force. On their right were the 2nd Kashmir Rifles and half of the 3rd Kashmir Rifles. To the LNL's left was the 63rd Light Infantry, and on the 63rd's left was the 101st Grenadiers. Aitken considered the LNL and the 101st his two best units, and he sandwiched the 63rd, in whom he had little confidence, between these units. The 13th Rajputs and 98th were placed in support behind the fighting line. The 61st Pioneers was the force's general reserve. Aitken hoped that the success and good example of the front line might put a new heart into the 13th and 61st. The Gwalior half-battalion was used to guard the stores on the beaches.

The Kashmir units, during the march forwards, had edged to the right and outside their assigned path. When they came into the clearing around the railroad tracks, they came under heavy fire. The LNL moved to its right to help the Kashmiris and keep in contact. This left the 63rd far behind and out of contact with the LNL. The companies of the 63rd began to disintegrate from the moment that German machine guns opened fire on them. The 63rd was one of the Madras regiments kept understrength, and, to bring it up to war strength, batches of men and officers were imported from the 83rd Wallajahbad Light Infantry. Only six out of the original officers were with the regiment. The rest came from the 83rd and other regiments.[571] This meant that many of the regiment's officers were strangers, and their words had little effect on the men. The soldiers pulled back and dispersed into the thick undergrowth of the rubber plantation. The regiment, as a fighting force, ceased to exist without firing a shot.

Two results flowed from this. First, the 101st was ordered to move to the right to maintain contact with the LNL. This meant that the entire course of attack, when combined with the Kashmiris moving to the right, was farther to the right than originally planned.

Second, the 98th Infantry, which was still behind the fighting lines, was shaken by the sight of men moving to the rear and the sound of machine-gun fire. They also came under attack by wild bees.[572] Within a few minutes, they, without a shot being fired at them, broke and scattered in all directions. It took a long time to reassemble them. Another regiment ceased to exist as a fighting force without firing a shot.

The 61st, who was the force's general reserve, does not seem to have ever been brought into combat with the exception of its two machine-gun teams.

On the right flank, the two Kashmir Rifles intermixed with the LNL, and some of the 13th Rajputs who had not gone to the rear charged across the railroad, cutting into the town. There, they undertook house-to-house street fighting.

On the left flank, the 101st Grenadiers was still isolated in spite of its moving to the right. It moved forwards in the thick vegetation. Some of the German native troops began to give way, but their officers were able to hold them together. The German lines were extended southwards by the 1st and 17th FKs. Then, a fresh unit, the 13th FK, mounted an attack on the grenadiers' open left flank. The men of the 101st were forced back, fighting the entire time. The remnants of the regiment eventually broke up into small groups in the bush, still fighting. These scattered groups, by 4:00 p.m., no longer protected the left flank of the LNL.[573]

While the 101st were being forced back, the LNL and the Kashmiris were beginning to encounter ever stiffer opposition in the town as the Germans received reinforcements. It was difficult for the LNL and the Kashmir troops to communicate because they spoke different languages and, as a state force, the Kashmiris had only three British with them. As fighting progressed, all became casualties.

The LNL in the town, at around 4:00 p.m., after hearing firing farther behind their left flank and not being able to discover how the Kashmiris were doing, decided to withdraw to the railway cutting. They took heavy losses in doing so. The Kashmiris withdrew in conformity with the LNL. A defensive line was established along the railway cutting. A left flank was created with companies of the LNL and two machine guns, the 61st Pioneers and two of the 13th Rajputs.

The stragglers in the thick vegetation were thrown into a panic. The carriers taking ammunition forwards from the beaches had come under long-range fire. They at once dropped their

571 In the same way, the 61st was brought up to strength with drafts from the 81st Pioneers.

572 All units, British and German, came under bee attack at different times during the day. The others found ways to keep fighting. One man, Conductor Preston, was stung 300 times on his head and continued taking a message. He was awarded the Distinguished Conduct Medal (DCM).

573 Hordern, *Military Operations in East Africa*, pp.87–88. This is the war history version. Other authors dealing with the German counterattack quote Lettow-Vorbeck: 'Our machine guns opened fire and our men dashed forward. In wild disorder, the enemy fled in dense masses. Our machine guns… mowed down whole companies to the last man'.

loads and ran. Dressed in khaki and fezzes, they were mistaken for German native soldiers breaking through. The Indian troops panicked and ran for the ships at the beaches.

Aitken at first planned a moonlight counterattack with the LNL, the Kashmiris. He was doubtful about the 13th and 61st, who, in theory, could be used in the counterattack, as they had not been committed to battle that day. Since there was no water near the railway tracks, the units were temporarily withdrawn to a line resting on the German hospital and a landing site.

After a reconnoitring patrol went into Tanga and found it occupied by an unknown number of German troops, the night attack was cancelled. After considering different options, it was decided to evacuate the force. The troops and carriers would be loaded on the ships at first light on the next day, 5 November.

During the morning of 5 November, the Indian troops showed just how spooked they were. The covering force fired a few shots at a German patrol. Indian troops standing on the beach, waiting to be landed on the boats to be taken to the larger ships, panicked. Rifles were thrown away, and the Indians rushed into the sea up to their necks. Meinertzhagen said to see whole battalions standing in deep water with only their heads showing was too dreadful. And the enemy had not fired a shot.

After being loaded, the ships sailed to Mombasa. The low morale made them unfit to fight for some time.

Aitken suggested that the 63rd and 98th Regiments be sent back to India in disgrace. This suggestion was not followed.

Major General Aitken was sent to England in disgrace and reduced to his substantive rank of colonel. He never had another command. The news of the defeat of the Tanga Expeditionary Force was hushed up for several months. The War Office even issued an order prohibiting any mention of the Tanga expedition in private correspondence.

The Indian troops were kept in Kenya and used to guard lines of communication. In 1915, a bridge on the railroad from Kenya to Uganda, ostensibly guarded by men of the 98th (Indian) Infantry, was blown up. They had not posted sentries or prepared defensive positions. The men of the 98th were lounging about without their rifles, and the Germans just rushed up in broad daylight. It turned out the men had been ordered to carry rifles at night but not by day.[574]

The 2nd Battalion of the LNL fought in the Lake Victoria region and in the campaign to capture the Kilimanjaro area of German East Africa.[575] Then, in May 1916, it began a move to South Africa to recover from ill health. In December 1916, it was moved to Egypt to take part in the fighting in the Middle East.[576]

## Contractions and Expansions

The armies of all three presidencies and the Frontier Force saw the disbanding of regiments in 1882 after the war in Afghanistan. Reductions in forces had been seriously considered in

574 J. R. Sibley, *Tanganyikan Guerrilla: East African Campaign 1914–18* (London: Ballantine Books, 1971), p.42.

575 Michael Langley, *The Loyal Regiment (North Lancashire): The 47th and 81st Regiments of Foot* (London: Leo Copper, 1976), pp.64–65.

576 James, *British*, p.88.

1878, but the Afghan War of 1878–1879 had sidetracked the work, and, after the war, it had taken time to work through the military bureaucracy. Then, in 1885, an Anglo-Russian crisis that seemed like it would lead to war caused a few of the reduced regiments to be restored to the army lists.[577] For example, this disbanding and recreation happened to the 16th and 17th Bengal Cavalry.

***Madras Army***

The Madras army was almost totally unaffected by the Mutiny. Seven of its eight cavalry regiments survived, as did all 52 of its infantry regiments. During the Mutiny, the Madras Presidency raised a new regiment, the Madras Rifles, but it was disbanded in 1858.[578] But soon thereafter, adjustments were made. In 1860, three of the youngest cavalry regiments were disbanded. (They only dated back to 1799–1800.) Twelve infantry regiments were disbanded during the years 1862–1864.[579]

Then, in 1882, another wave of disbanding saw seven infantry regiments disbanded. In addition, between these two waves, there were four individual regiments disbanded at different times between 1890 and 1903. One regiment had its composition changed to Coorg personnel in 1901 as an experiment. The experiment failed, and the regiment was disbanded in 1904.[580] The Coorgs were Muslim descendants of Arab traders and local women who lived on the Coromandel Coast. Moplahs were the Muslim descendants of Arab traders and local women who lived on the Malabar Coast. In 1891, another cavalry regiment, the 4th Madras Cavalry, was disbanded.[581]

In addition to disbanding regiments, authorities let some 15 regiments live on but purged their ranks of Madras personnel and replaced them with men from the Punjab. This allowed the regiments to keep their battle honours and badges. This normally involved changing the regimental name to include 'Punjab' to recognise the new situation. These changes were made for the most part in the 1890s and were identified by new names in 1903.

In addition to these changes, three regiments suffered the dignity of being converted to pioneer regiments: two in 1883 (became the 61st and 64th Pioneers in 1903) and one in 1891 (became the 21st Pioneers in 1903). That left nine non-pioneer regiments that drew from the people of the Madras Presidency. However, these regiments were understrength. They were more peacekeeping units than fighting regiments.[582] The Carnatic garrison peacekeeping regiments had 600 men,[583] and a fighting regiment had about 900 other ranks.[584] They were also, after 1903, given the name 'Carnatic', an old name for a part of the Madras Presidency, as if the very name 'Madras' carried a negative connotation.

This meant that, after 1903, there were only 12 infantry regiments with Madras classes left of the 52 that had existed in the Madras army in 1857 and only three of the eight cavalry regiments

577 Heathcote, *Military*, pp.136–41; MacMunn, *Armies*, pp.123–24.
578 Perry, *Order Part 1*, p.137.
579 Perry, *Order Part 1*, pp.119, 134–37.
580 Perry, *Order Part 1*, pp.134–37.
581 Perry, *Order Part 1*, p.119.
582 Gaylor, *Sons*, p.138.
583 Gaylor, *Sons*, p.138.
584 Heathcote, *Indian*, p.55.

the army had in 1857. The old Madras army had been almost as completely wiped out as the Bengal army.

The Hyderabad Contingent cavalry and infantry were typical of the type of unit the John Company liked to form. They were based in or near a princely state, and that state provided the funds for the upkeep of the regiments. However, the regiments were under the command of British company officers, and the company controlled these regiments. In addition to the Hyderabad Contingent, such contingents were maintained at Oudh and Gwalior. However, the latter two groups mutinied, and the Hyderabad regiments remained loyal, with only a part of one regiment being disarmed.[585]

The Hyderabad regiments at first were supported by payments to be made by the company to the Nizam of Hyderabad ('Nizam' is the title of the ruler of the state of Hyderabad) for the rent of five of the Nizam's provinces.[586] From the rent, the company would deduct the cost of their troops that were kept on hand to 'aid' the Nizam. The cost of the troops always equalled the rent due, and the Nizam received nothing. At the same time, the company was loaning money to the Nizam. He was chronically behind and short on repaying the loans. Finally, to solve this problem, the company was given the management of one of his richer provinces, Berar. The company was to pay for the upkeep out of monies collected from Berar and turn the balance over to the Nizam. But it was remarkable how the company and later the government, which inherited the arrangement when it assumed responsibility for India after the Mutiny, never had any funds to turn over to Hyderabad despite now having five provinces and Berar to cover the troops' costs. Finally, in 1902, the viceroy, Curzon, by fiat told the Sixth Nizam that the British government would pay him a flat fee of 25 lakhs (£67,000; current value: £6,973,800 or $8,192,600) a year and take permanent control of Berar.[587] In legal theory, they were to hold it in trust for the Nizam.[588]

All Hyderabad regiments remained loyal during the Mutiny: four cavalry regiments and six infantry regiments. They all continued to exist up until the beginning of the twentieth century. In 1903, one of the four Hyderabad cavalry regiments, the 3rd Cavalry, later the 3rd Lancers, was disbanded.[589]

In the reorganisation of 1903, when all the regiments in India were given continuous numbers, the Hyderabad cavalry regiments were used as fillers in the numbering system so other groups of regiments, such as the Bombay cavalry and Frontier Force cavalry, could at least have their second number remain as a tie to their old regimental numbers. Thus, the Hyderabad cavalry regiments were renumbered as follows:

585 Perry, *Order Part 1*, p.150.
586 'Nizam' comes from Nizam al-Mulk, (regulator) of the state. He was an official of the Mughals in Delhi and was then able to break free of Mughal control.
587 Anon., 'Hyderabad, India (State)', in *Encyclopædia Britannica* (Edinburgh: Encyclopædia Britannica, 1911), vol. 14, pp.31–32.
588 Lord, *Maharajas*, pp.67–78.
589 Bowling, *Indian Cavalry*, p.45.

**Table 55 Change of Numbers for Hyderabad Cavalry Regiments in 1903 (and Short Titles)[590]**

| Old Number and Name | New Number and Name |
|---|---|
| 1st Lancers, Hyderabad Contingent | 20th Deccan Horse |
| 2nd Lancers, Hyderabad Contingent | 29th Lancers (Deccan Horse) |
| 4th Lancers, Hyderabad Contingent | 30th Lancers (Gordon's Horse) |

The 1st through 6th Hyderabad Contingent Infantry came through the Indian Mutiny unscathed. In the 1903 reorganisation, they were given the regimental numbers 94 through 99. The 1st Infantry, Hyderabad Contingent, was given the number 94, and then regiments 2 through 6 adopted numbers 95 through 99 in numerical order. Most of the regiments were also given new names that related to their earlier histories. The 97th and the 99th were given the rather Germanic name 'Deccan' (which is the name of the area) because they were formed fresh in 1854. The 98th did not have a subsidiary name because its history lay in the Nizam's army. The 94th and 95th carried the name 'Russell', the name of an earlier resident at the Nizam's court who first established this type of subsidiary force. The 97th was given the name 'Berar', a name it had carried between 1797 and 1826.[591]

The Hyderabad cavalry and infantry were originally recruited from the local population. The cavalry had taken a heavy portion of Muslims. But, over time, as the southern peoples fell into disfavour, the composition of these regiments changed. The 20th Deccan Horse and the 29th Lancers had Dekhani Muslims in their ranks. In the 20th, they were 50 percent, and, in the 29th, they were only 25 percent of the ranks. The 30th Lancers no longer recruited Dekhani Muslims.

It was the same story with the infantry. Only the 94th and 97th recruited Dekhani Muslims, and they were a minority in those regiments. All the regiments recruited either Rajputs or Jats. However, these are not classic southern classes and probably came from the Punjab or Rajasthan.

### *Frontier Force: Cavalry*

The five cavalry regiments raised in 1849 to help hold the new Punjab frontier not only remained loyal during the Mutiny but also played a major part in putting the Mutiny down. One regiment, the 4th, was disbanded in the general retrenchments of 1882. The other four lived on until 1914. Three of the four – the 1st, 2nd, and 5th; later the 21st, 22nd, and 25th – carried the battle honours of Delhi and Lucknow. The 3rd – later the 23rd – was left home to guard the always volatile frontier.[592]

### *Frontier Force: Infantry*

In 1846, four regiments of Sikh infantry were raised to help maintain order on the newly acquired Punjab western frontier. They were not a Sikh-class regiment but took their name from the fact that their men came mostly from the old Sikh army. In 1849 (other sources say 1847), the famous Guides were raised to perform the same function. The reason for two different

590 Bowling, *Indian Cavalry*, pp.43–45.
591 Perry, *Order Part 1*, p.137.
592 Perry, *Order Part 1*, p.119.

formation dates being cited is that, in 1847, Lieutenant Lumsden raised a small force of 100 horsemen and 200 infantry, consisting of Gurkhas, Sikhs, and mostly frontier tribesmen. Then, in 1849, the Guides were increased to a full regiment of cavalry and a full infantry battalion.[593]

Five regiments of Punjab infantry were also raised in 1849 to provide additional help with maintaining peace in this lawless area. Further reinforcements were received in 1853, when the Scinde Camel Corps of the Bombay army was converted into the 6th Punjab Infantry (Scinde Rifle Corps).[594]

During the Mutiny, only a few regiments, the 4th Sikhs and the 1st, 2nd, and 4th Punjab Infantry, could be spared to help at Delhi.

All but one of the frontier infantry continued in existence until 1914. The exception was the 3rd Punjab Infantry, which was disbanded in the cutback of 1881. These regiments in 1903 were given numbers ranging from 51 to 59.[595] The Corps of Guides were put outside the Indian regimental list in the same fashion as was done with the Rifle Brigade and the British regimental list.

In 1858, a Gurkha regiment, the 25th Punjab Infantry, Hazara Gurkha Battalion, was raised to help during the Mutiny and made part of the Frontier Force. In 1861, it became the 7th Punjab Infantry, and, later in 1861, it was named the 5th Gurkha Regiment.[596]

The Frontier Force regiments, especially the Guides, were considered by themselves, and, in fairness, by many others, as elite corps. Therefore, it never went through an adjustment of personnel.

### *Bombay Army: Cavalry*

The Bombay army suffered very little disruption during the Mutiny years. All three of the regular cavalry regiments remained loyal, as did its five Silladar irregular cavalry regiments.

The three regular regiments survived until 1914. Four regiments of the irregular regiments were included in the new army in 1861–1862. They were, in 1862, the 1st Poona Horse and the 1st through 3rd Scinde Horse. A south Mahratta Horse existed in 1862, but it was disbanded in 1865. The above irregular regiments, except for the 3rd Scinde Horse (disbanded in 1882), lasted until 1914. The 3rd's place in the Bombay cavalry list as the 7th Bombay Cavalry (later 37th Lancers – Baluch Horse) was taken by a 'Baluch' unit raised in 1885. As is normal for these regiments, the term 'Baluch' refers to the area and not the tribe. The Baluch ethnic group was a minority in the regiment.

### *Bombay Army: Infantry*

Of the 30 Bombay infantry regiments in existence prior to the Mutiny, only two were disbanded: the 21st and 27th. The Bombay army also had two extra Baluch regiments, which were loyal during the Mutiny.

In 1861, several adjustments were made to the Bombay line. The 1st Baluchs were given the disbanded 27th's number. There was no need to do anything about the disbanded 21st's number

593 J. B. R. Nicholson (ed.), '10th Queen Victoria's Own Corps of Guides Cavalry (Frontier Force)', *Tradition*, 73:Special Indian Cavalry Issue 2 (n.d.), pp.11–12.
594 Perry, *Order Part 1*, p.133.
595 Perry, *Order Part 1*, p.133.
596 Perry, *Order Part 1*, p.133.

because two regiments had a tie to the number 21 before the Mutiny: the Marine Battalion and the 21st. The 21st was disbanded, and the Marines took the number 21, which they had carried in the 1820s.[597]

Also in 1861, the 29th Infantry was disbanded, and the 2nd Baluch Regiment was given its number. There were five regiments raised for Mutiny service, and four of these were disbanded in 1861. One, the 1st Baluch Rifles, was added to the Bombay line as the 30th Infantry (later, in 1914, 130th Baluchis – Jacob's Rifles).[598]

In the reductions of 1882, the Bombay army lost the 6th, 11th, 15th, and 18th Infantry Regiments. The gaps created in the run of numbers in the Bombay line lasted down to 1914, except in 1904 when the 106th Hazara Pioneers was raised, which filled in the gap left by the loss of the 6th Infantry.[599]

While a large percentage of the Bombay regiments survived the Mutiny and the reductions in the 40 years that followed the Mutiny, there were changes made at the personnel level. As the martial classes theory became more popular, the classes that had made up the Bombay army found themselves outside the charmed circle. The Mahars, an untouchable caste who had served in the armies of Shivaji and at one time made up 20–25 percent of the Bombay army, were dropped around 1900.[600]

They even went so far as to drop classes such as the Dhangar and Mali, who were clearly of the Maratha stock, although not of the fighting Ksatriya class. This was done through pressure from both the British with their new martial class theory and other Maratha classes who no longer wished to serve next to the wrong sort of soldiers.[601] Also dropped were outcaste Parwaris, the Bhandari, the Koli, native Christians, and the Bene Israel.[602]

The Bene Israel (or Beni Israel) was a small native Jewish community that originally lived near the city of Bombay and served in the army.[603] They were also dropped in the early twentieth century. The Jewish community in Britain, beginning in 1890, put out a *Jewish Year Book*, which, among other entries, lists Jewish officers in the British Empire's army and navy. An entry for 1902 shows five Jewish native officers, subadars, or subadar majors serving in four different Bombay infantry regiments, one each in the 3rd, 8th, and 17th and two in the 22nd.[604] By 1907, there were only two serving Jewish native officers. Both were in the old 22nd, now titled the 122nd Rajputana Infantry.[605] The *Year Book* notes that, prior to the reorganisation of the Indian army into class companies, there had been more than 100 of the Bene Israel serving in the rank and file of the Bombay infantry.[606]

597 Perry, *Order Part 1*, pp.138–39.
598 Perry, *Order Part 1*, p.139.
599 Perry, *Order Part 1*, pp.137–38.
600 Cohen, *Indian Army*, p.57.
601 Heathcote, *Military*, p.93.
602 Heathcote, *Military*, p.93.
603 See Katz, *Who Are the Jews*, pp.90–120, in regard to the Bene Israel.
604 Isadore Harris (ed.), *The Jewish Year Book: An Annual Record of Matters Jewish, #5663, 2nd October, 1902 – 21st September, 1903* (London: Greenberg and Company, 1902), p.235.
605 Harris, *Jewish #5668-9*, p.277.
606 Harris, *Jewish #5668-9*, p.277. Opinion cited.

### *Central India Horse*

During the Mutiny, Central India was an area that saw heavy support for those who turned against company rule. Consequently, there was a great deal of fighting in the area, and several ad hoc cavalry regiments were raised. Among them were Meade's Horse, Beatson's 1st and 2nd Horse, and Mayne's Horse, which drew loyal troopers from the Malwa, Bhopal, and Gwalior contingents. In 1860, these were formed into the 1st through 3rd Central India Horse to serve as a local force that was willing to serve anywhere. Then, in 1861, the 3rd Regiment was disbanded. The other two served until 1914. In 1914, they had the numbers 38 and 39.[607] The two regiments, after the Mutiny, began to discharge their low-caste men, in spite of the fact that these were the type of men who had been there for the British in the emergency.[608] Over time, the regiment's enlisted men ceased to come from Central India and came from the north. By 1914, it was manned by Sikhs, Muslims, Rajputs, Pathans, and Punjabi Muslims and, as such, was indistinguishable from an average Bengal cavalry regiment.

### *Gurkhas*[609]

Almost all the early Gurkha units served in the Bengal army. That was the army that fought them in the Nepal War and first discovered their worth as fighters under the influence of martial caste theory.

What became three Gurkha regiments had their origin in units that were raised following the war with Nepal in 1814–1815. In 1815, there were four battalions: the 1st and 2nd Nasiri (friendly or local battalions) and the Sirmoor and Kamaon battalions. In 1826, the 2nd Nasiri was merged into the 1st Nasiri to form what became the 1st Gurkhas (the Malaun Regiment). The men for the Nasiri battalions had come from prisoners captured at the fall of the Gurkha fortress of Malaun. They went by different names until 1850, when they became the 66th Bengal Infantry. In 1861, they were moved to a separate Gurkha list as the 1st Gurkha Light Infantry. In 1891, they became the 1st Gurkha Rifles.

Another Gurkha battalion was raised in 1815 at the town of Sirmoor, and it went by different names until 1861, when it was moved to a separate Gurkha list as the 2nd Gurkha Regiment.

The third of the Gurkha battalions raised in 1815 was the Kamaon battalion. It recruited men from the Garhwal and Kumaon Districts. These were the districts that would later supply the men for the 39th Garhwal Rifles. The districts, up until the peace treaty ending the Nepal War, had been part of Nepal, and men from this area had served in the Nepalese army. The battalion went by different names until 1861, when it was moved to a separate Gurkha list as the 3rd Gurkha Regiment.[610]

The Extra Gurkha Regiment was raised during the Mutiny. In 1861, it was moved to the Gurkha list as the 4th Gurkha Regiment.

Another Gurkha battalion was raised in 1858 for Mutiny service. It had the title '25th Punjab Infantry', or 'Hazara Gurkha Battalion' (sometimes the names were combined), and was

607 Perry, *Order Part 1*, p.121.
608 Heathcote, *Military*, p.88.
609 Perry, *Order Part 1*, pp.141–42; Marrion and Fosten, *Tradition*, pp.8, 11, 17, 19, 21, 25, 28–29, 31, 36–37.
610 Marrion and Fosten, *Tradition*, pp.8, 11, 16.

considered to be part of the Frontier Force. In 1861, it was moved to the Gurkha list as the 5th Gurkha Regiment.

In 1817, a Gurkha regiment was raised as the Cuttack Legion in the area of the modern Indian state of Odisha. It is just to the southeast of Bengal on the Bay of Bengal. Cuttack was the old capital of a native kingdom in this region. In 1823, the battalion moved to the Assam area to control the local tribes on the Northeast Frontier. It had different names until 1861, when it was given the title of 42nd Bengal Infantry. In 1903, it was moved to the Gurkha list as the 6th Gurkha Rifles.

Two other Gurkha battalions were added to the Bengal army in 1861 as the 43rd and 44th Bengal Native Infantry. What became known as the 44th Bengal Native Infantry was originally raised in 1824 for the Northeast Frontier as a Gurkha battalion to serve as a protection force. It served as a local force. In 1861, it was given a number in the Bengal army. Then, in 1903, it was put on the Gurkha list as the 8th Gurkhas.

Another Gurkha local battalion was given a Bengal regimental number in 1861. It was created in Assam out of ex-detached companies and served in Assam until at least 1861 under different titles. In 1861, it was designated the 43rd Bengal Native Infantry. In 1903, it was moved to the Gurkha list as the 7th Gurkha Rifles. Then, in 1907, it was made the 2nd Battalion of the 8th Gurkha Rifles.

What became the 9th Gurkhas had its foundations in the Fategarh Levy, raised in 1817, and the Mainpuri Levy, raised in 1819. In 1823, these were joined as the 1st Battalion of the 32nd Bengal Native Infantry. During the Mutiny, the 32nd came under suspicion, and the regiment stood down for two years. However, in the end, it was judged to be loyal, and it lived on post-Mutiny as the 3rd Brahmins.[611] The Gurkha element was formed into a company of the 9th Bengal Native Infantry. In 1892, the regiment was made an all-Gurkha regiment. In 1901, it was named the 9th Gurkha Rifles on the Gurkha list.

By 1914, there were 20 Gurkha battalions. Many of these did not have a history of contact with the Bengal army.

The 7th Gurkha Rifles was originally formed in 1902 as the 8th Gurkha Rifles. In 1903, it was made the 2/10th Gurkha Rifles, and, in 1907, it was named the 7th Gurkha Rifles and took the place of the old 43rd Bengal Native Infantry.

In 1887, what became the 10th Gurkha Rifles was raised as the Upper Burma Military Police. In 1890, it became the 10th Madras Infantry (1st Burma Rifles). In 1901, it was made the 10th Gurkha Rifles on the Gurkha list.

At different times, each of the 10 Gurkha regiments raised second battalions. Below is a list of when these second battalions were raised.

611 Perry, *Order Part 1*, p.128.

**Table 56 Date of Raising Second Battalions by Gurkha Regiments**

| Battalion | Date |
|---|---|
| 2/1st | 1886 |
| 2/2nd | 1886 |
| 2/3rd | 1891* |
| 2/4th | 1886 |
| 2/5th | 1886 |
| 2/6th | 1904 |
| 2/7th | 1907 |
| 2/8th | 1907 |
| 2/9th | 1904 |
| 2/10th | 1908 |

* An earlier second battalion raised in 1887 became the 39th Garhwal Rifles in 1891.

## Indian Regiment Mutinies, 1860–1914 (Plus One More)[612]

Between 1860 and 1914, there were six mutinies of regiments in the Indian army. The mutinies were normally made to protect the rights of the soldiers that they saw as being under threat. This could range from the withdrawal of rice batta to the introduction of new eating arrangements to the perceived favouritism of one class over another in mixed-class regiments. Table 57 shows the six mutinies, the regiment's units, and the dates and places the mutinies took place.

**Table 57 Indian Army Mutinies, 1858–1914**

| Unit | Date | Place | Troops Involved |
|---|---|---|---|
| 3rd Gurkhas | April 1886 | Almorah (India)* | Majority of 1 Battalion |
| 17th (Loyal Purbiya) Bengal Infantry | May 1894 | Agra (India)† | A and E Companies |
| 25th Madras Infantry (Disbanded in 1903) | October 1894 | Shwebo (Burma) | 4 Hindu Companies |
| 14th Bombay Infantry (Later the 114th Mahrattas) | September 1897 | Bareilly (India)‡ | 170 Konkani Mahrattas |
| 17th Bombay Infantry (Later the 117th Mahrattas) | November 1897 | Bhuj (India)§ | 1 Company |
| 27th Madras Infantry (Later the 87th Punjabis) | September 1897 | Moulmein (Burma) | 30 Men |
| 76th Punjabis | April 1910 | Tientsin (China) | 200 Men |

* Almorah was located in the Kumaon District (currently in Uttarakhand).
† Agra Division was located in Hindustan (currently in Uttar Pradesh).
‡ Bareilly Division was located in Hindustan (currently in Uttar Pradesh).
§ Bhuj was located in the princely state of Cutch in the Bombay Presidency (now part of Gujarat).

612 See Omissi, *Sepoy*, pp.134–52.

It is unusual for these mutinies to be addressed, and one can read through a great many books on the Indian army without this touchy subject being mentioned. A good part of the reason they are not mentioned is that they were only technically mutinies.

To the average person, a mutiny is what happened during the Indian Mutinies or the Russian Revolutions of 1905 and 1917. The soldiers seize weapons and go wild, killing their officers and, at times, the officers' families and other civilians.

However, the 1879 Army Act states that mutiny is 'collective insubordination or a combination of two or more persons to resist or induce others to resist lawful military authority'. This means that, to have a mutiny, all that is needed is a group, although it can be as small as two soldiers. Furthermore, the group need not be violent, just fail to follow orders, such as orders to disperse.[613]

Many of the mutinies involved soldiers gathering to present grievances to the commander of their unit rather than presenting grievances individually up the chain of command. Any old soldier knows that trying to send a complaint up through the NCOs and the junior officers normally does not work. These worthies normally kill the complaint, lest it somehow reflect badly on them.

There very well could have been more of these technical grievance mutinies. Regimental officers did not like to report mutinies in their regiments. Firstly, it would likely cause an investigation of the officer's conduct. Secondly, it would reduce the status of the regiment. Thirdly, the men's actions, while technically a mutiny, could be viewed as a passing outburst of temper or sudden fit, which natives sometimes give into. Lastly, the higher authorities were reluctant to admit in public that a mutiny had taken place, lest other units imitate the action or the prestige of the British Raj be damaged. For these reasons, a lesser charge than mutiny was often found against the soldiers.[614]

### *Mutinies*

The 3rd Gurkhas acted in 1886 because their colonel reduced the rice batta. This was the final addition to a list of grievances: the men had to cook outside, so they could not eat when it rained; there had been no furlough for nine months; the new colonel was unpopular; and the native offices would not or could not respond to complaints sent up normal channels of command. Their mutiny took the form of troops gathering in a tumultuous manner.[615]

The disorder among the Gurkhas was unusual. Most mutinies during this period were orderly. For example, some in the 17th Bombay protested against new mess arrangements in 1897. Ten men were picked up by a native subadar, and he marched them to a regimental CO so a formal complaint could be made. As the party of 10 was on their way, a group of 42 men joined the march and ignored orders to disperse. Other men from the Konkani Mahratta portion of the regiment also gathered in support and would not disperse.

In 1894, the four Hindu companies of the 25th Madras Infantry mutinied over cooking plans for the Dussehra festival.[616] The commander was thought by the Hindus to be under the influ-

613 Omissi, *Sepoy*, p.134.
614 Omissi, *Sepoy*, p.135.
615 Omissi, *Sepoy*, p.142.
616 Dussehra is a major Hindu festival that is normally celebrated twice a year, during mid-March and early October. The celebrations typically last for nine or 10 days and take place in all parts of India.

ence of the Muslim subadar major.[617] This type of intergroup dispute was one of the weaknesses of the class company regiments. But the tendency of the different classes towards disputes was also why the British favoured class company regiments. If a regiment's different classes were unhappy with each other, they were unlikely to unite against the British.

It is interesting to note how the situation spiralled out of control. The Hindus of the 25th sent a single sepoy spokesman to present their point of view to the authorities. His arrest led to his entire company following in military formation and refusing to disperse. When the company was arrested, the three other Hindu companies of the regiment refused to turn out for parade. The units sent word that they were just like the company that had been arrested and, therefore, they should be made prisoners too.[618]

### *British Officers' Reactions*

The first reaction of the British officers to their men was to try to talk them into dispersing. This was normally done by promising to look into the complaints and that the improper gathering, qua mutiny, would be viewed leniently if they dispersed now. This was often combined with a reference to army regulations and its harsh treatment of mutinies. If that did not work, and normally it did not, the authorities would then arrest the 'ringleaders'. This was based on the theory that the men in the regiment were basically sound and had been led astray by a few mischievous individuals. To the British, it was less important that they arrest the actual ringleaders than that they be seen taking some strong, responsive action.

Some of the sepoys, for their part, tried to avoid British efforts to fragment them by taking oaths before they began their collective action. The night before the 3rd Gurkhas acted, the soldiers took an oath that if they did not join in the mutiny, their mothers would be dishonoured seven times. They also swore another oath while touching the Gurkhas' book (*Suhk Sagar*) that they would mutiny and to curse all the female relatives of those who did not mutiny. Once the soldiers were assembled, they took another oath with their arms extended towards the *Suhk Sagar*.[619] In the 17th Bombay Infantry, the men swore an oath to stay with the mutiny or they would drink their wives' urine.[620]

Once the complaint had been made, the sepoys seemed to have been willing to accept whatever punishment the military system handed out to them. Having made their point, they normally went back to their duties within a few hours or a day. The British, for the most part, tended to show clemency in handing out punishment. During the period 1861–1914, no mutineers were executed. Prominent ringleaders normally received sentences of transportation (sent to a penal colony) from seven years to life, and those who had shown less initiative normally were sentenced to between three and seven years or were dismissed from their regiment.[621] Of the 170 sepoys in the 14th Bombay Infantry, some 141 received no penalty at all.[622]

Quite often, the mutinies achieved their goals. Those that mutinied to avoid particular tasks were normally successful because the authorities were prudent enough to not further provoke the soldiers by forcing the issue. Unpopular COs were removed on at least two occasions.

617 Omissi, *Sepoy*, p.140.
618 Omissi, *Sepoy*, p.144.
619 Omissi, *Sepoy*, p.144.
620 Omissi, *Sepoy*, p.144.
621 Omissi, *Sepoy*, p.145.
622 Omissi, *Sepoy*, p.146.

Face-saving reasons other than that they were unpopular with their soldiers were found for the commander leaving.[623]

### *Singapore, 1915*[624]

In contrast to the peaceful mutinies mentioned above, the mutiny of the 5th Light Infantry (5th LI) in Singapore in 1915 was very violent. The 5th LI had been stationed in Singapore in 1914, when the First World War began. The Yorkshire Light Infantry, also stationed there when the war began, was sent to France. This left the 5th as the only regular army troops in the town. The Malay State Guides had been brought into the city to provide extra military manpower.

The 5th consisted of Muslims from the Eastern Punjab and Hindustan. There are many different theories about why a part of the regiment mutinied and why the mutiny became so lethal. The new commandant was very unpopular with some of the British officers. These had formed into two cliques. The Indian officers were divided over a disagreement about promotion. Preachers at a local mosque attended by the sepoys preached against the British and urged an uprising by the troops. The British had lost prestige by having their ships sunk in the area by the German warship *Emden* and by battlefield setbacks in Europe and Africa.

The regiment was slated to leave Singapore. An address to the regiment by the CO left the men uncertain as to where they were to be sent. The rumour mill soon filled this vacuum. The word went out that the regiment was being sent to France, where thousands were being killed each week, or to the Middle East (Egypt or Mesopotamia), where they would have to fight the Turks, their coreligionists, near the Holy Places of Islam.

It has also been suggested that Julius Lauterbach, a German naval officer and prisoner in the POW camp at Tangling Barracks on the outskirts of Singapore, was, in part, behind the mutiny. Tangling, at the time, was guarded by sepoys of the 5th, and Lauterbach, who spoke English, made friends with some of the guards. He had been making plans to escape, and he and a small group of other prisoners had been digging a tunnel out of Tangling. When a sergeant of the 5th told Lauterbach that the regiment was to go to France and did not want to go, he asked what they should do. Lauterbach drew up step-by-step plans for a mutiny on the spot, knowing the mutiny's mayhem and confusion would be the perfect cover for his escape effort. The next day, the 5th was replaced as guards by Malay soldiers, and the Germans lost contact.

About half of the 5th LI mutinied on the afternoon of 15 February 1915. The sepoys began by shooting down four of their own officers. Two officers escaped and ran to a nearby group of 83-man-strong Malay State Rifles. They were sent out to fight the mutineers but were forced back by the large number of mutineers. They found refuge in an officer's bungalow and began to undergo what would be a 20-hour siege.

The other mutineers set out of the barracks and shot any Englishmen they encountered. In some cases, they spared women, although one woman who did not leave her husband was killed with him.

623 Omissi, *Sepoy*, p.147.
624 Omissi, *Sepoy*, p.149; Edwyn Gray, 'While World War I Raged in Europe, a Cunning German Naval Officer Touched Off a Bloody Rebellion in Singapore', *Military History*, 15:5 (1998), pp.30, 32, 84, 86, 88, 90; George F. MacMunn, *Turmoil and Tragedy in India: 1914 and After* (London: Jarrolds, 1935), pp.105–13.

One group went to capture Tangling Barracks. They surprised the Malay guards, who thought the advancing Indians were taking part in a training exercise. It was only when they opened fire on the guards that the truth came out. Twenty-three British officers and Malay men were killed at Tangling.

The prisoners were invited to join with the men of the 5th, but the prisoners said no. It is not clear whether they did not want to take part in killing fellow Europeans or if they just had enough foresight to know that the 5th's venture in the middle of the British Empire would not end well. The Tangling prisoners picked up the weapons of their dead guards and took over the defence of the camp. They even gave shelter to some British refugees until order was restored.

Lauterbach used the confusion to escape. He and eight comrades escaped across the Strait of Malacca to the Dutch-held island of Sumatra. Via Honolulu and New York, he returned to Germany in October.

At dusk on 15 February, the British imposed martial law and disembarked an armed landing party from the sloop HMS *Cadmus*. Armed civilians were sent out to patrol the streets, and women and children were removed from the suburbs and placed on ships.

At dawn, a force made up of the seamen and armed civilians set out to the 5th's barracks. There, they rescued the survivors of the men who had been under siege in the officer's bungalow for 20 hours and recaptured the mountain guns that the Malay State Guides had abandoned.

In the days that followed, reinforcements arrived. Part of the 36th Sikhs was in Singapore, while the balance of the regiment was taking part in the Japanese siege and recapture of German Tsingtau. The 36th and 2nd South Wales Borderers were part of a token British presence at the siege. A force of 200 local men were armed and lent their help. Some local Japanese were named special constables and armed. One hundred and fifty soldiers from the Jahore Military Force were sent to Singapore on 15 February by the Sultan of Jahore. By 17 February, French, Russian, and Japanese warships had pulled into the harbour and sent ashore armed landing parties to reinforce the British.

The mutineers, seeing their cause was lost, broke up into small groups. Some went to the mainland of Malay, just across the narrow Jahore Strait, and others sought sanctuary in local mosques. Most of those on the mainland were rounded up by the Johore Military Force. Johore was a semi-independent state on the Malay Peninsula, much like an Indian state. By Saturday, some 614 sepoys had been killed or captured. The remaining free sepoys, about 200, had fled into the Malay jungle. The authorities brought in Dyak headhunters from Borneo to ensure that all mutineers were tracked down and captured. By the end of March, all but 51 had been captured.

Over 200 sepoys were court-martialled. Most were sent to long periods of transportation (64 for life). Sixty-five were given a death sentence, and 43 of those were executed.

The British seemed to give the regiment collective punishment. It was not sent to Europe or the Middle East. The men had their way on this point. But the regiment was sent back to India, and its remaining personnel were discharged, and new men were enlisted. The regiment was then sent to West Africa, with its high death rate from diseases. It was the only Indian regiment to serve in the West African Theatre.[625]

625 Perry, *Order Part 5B*, p.254; Moberly, *Campaign in Mesopotamia*, vol. 1, pp.444, 449.

When the fighting in West Africa died down in 1917, the 5th LI was transferred to East Africa.[626] There, it played a minor part in the ever-expanding effort to bring von Lettow Vorbeck and his little army to bay. These efforts did not end until 13 November 1918.

In the reorganisation of the Indian army in 1922, the 5th LI was disbanded.[627] Apparently, its actions in Singapore outweighed the regiment's long and distinguished history.

626 Perry, *Order Part 5B*, p.254; W. D. Downes, *With the Nigerians in German East Africa* (London: Methuen and Co., 1919), p.302.

627 Perry, *Order Part 1*, p.128.

# 5

# African and West India Men and Officers

## King's African Rifles

The King's African Rifles (KAR) was formed in 1902 with two battalions from the former Central African Regiment (CARgt; in the Nyasaland, now Malawi, area), one battalion from the East African Rifles (EAR; Kenya), and two from the Uganda Rifles (UR).

**Table 58 KAR Organisation in 1902**

| Battalion | Size in Companies | Former Unit |
|---|---|---|
| 1st | 8 | 1st CARgt |
| 2nd | 6 | 2nd CARgt |
| 3rd | 7 with 1 Camel Company | EAR |
| 4th | 9 | UR (African Companies) |
| 5th | 4 | UR (Indian Contingent) |

The new regiment was given the name 'Rifles' because the founding units had rifles in their titles. None of them were elite units, none used rifle drill, and neither was the KAR. The KAR was under the jurisdiction of the War Office. As of 1901, secondments to it were made for three years and could be extended to five years. The officers went out as subalterns.[1] In 1905, the Colonial Office took over control of the KAR.

The early units all had Indian soldiers of the fighting classes, Sikhs, and so on, from the Punjab in India, Swahilis, and, for the UR especially, Sudanese. All had their drawbacks. The Indians needed a special diet. The Sudanese were born fighters, but their large families, which had to be kept near them, were a nuisance. The Swahili were felt to be only moderate soldiers and deficient in military instincts and spirit.[2] Swahilis are a Bantu native people who lived on the east coast of Africa in the Tanganyika, Zanzibar, and Kenya areas and who have a mixture

1 H. Moyse-Bartlett, *The King's African Rifles: A Study in the Military History of East and Central Africa, 1890–1945* (East Sussex: Naval and Military Press, 2012), vol. 1, p.129.

2 W. Lloyd-Jones, *K.A.R.: Being an Unofficial Account of the Origin and Activities of the King's African Rifles* (London: Arrowsmith, 1926), pp.104–06.

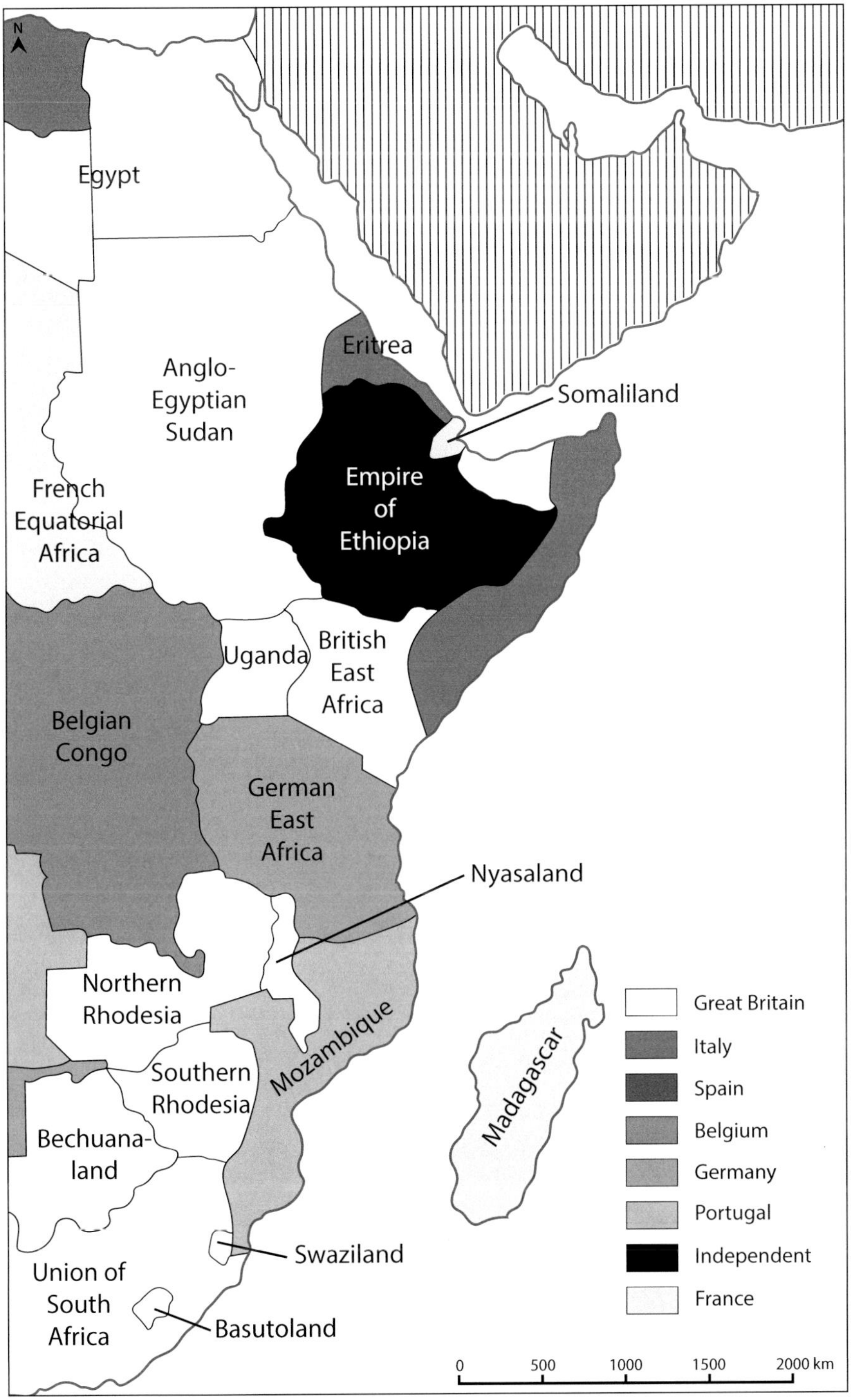


British colonies in East Africa

King's African Rifles (KAR) – native drummer.

KAR – other ranks.

British officer – KAR.

KAR – other ranks in undress uniforms.

of Arab and some Persian DNA from men who came to the east coast of Africa to trade. Their basic Bantu African language is heavily infused with Arab and other loan words.

As time went by, the Sudanese and Swahili elements were reduced. The Sudanese, an ancestor unit of the 4th (Uganda) KAR, had mutinied in 1897. Some of the mutineers were still at large in 1901. In 1900, it was decided to phase out the Sudanese.[3] In 1904, most of the Indians were sent home, but the 3rd (Kenya) Battalion had some Indians in it in 1914.

The predecessor of the 1st Central African Rifles (CAR) had its beginnings in 1891 with 40 Sikh infantry and 30 Muslim cavalrymen from the 2nd Hyderabad Lancers.[4] Since horses do not do well in tsetse fly country, the cavalry fell by the wayside, but the Sikhs stayed on. They and enlisted native peoples spent their time fighting slavers and tribes who did not want to be ruled by the British. In 1896, a second battalion was raised and performed the same duties. In 1899, it had 32 Sikhs out of an other-rank count of 900. It also had 220 wives and 77 children. In 1900, the CAR sent a composite unit of 73 Sikhs and 276 African other ranks to West Africa to help fight the Ashanti in the Golden Stool War.

In Kenya, the British had the EAR, formed in 1892–1895, which consisted of Sudanese, Swahilis, Punjabis, and local tribesmen in equal numbers. Most of the Indians went home in 1900. After they left, the battalion consisted mostly of Sudanese and Swahili men. They spent their time fighting natives who did not want to live under British laws.

As there was less activity by slavers and the tribes saw the futility of resisting the British, there was less fighting for the KAR to do. This led to the 2nd KAR being disbanded in 1911.[5]

The Colonial Office was always interested in saving money. They, therefore, went through bouts of cutting back on the number of men in the KAR and then adding more men.

**Table 59 KAR Strength in 1914**

| Battalion | Size in Companies | Company Ethnic Composition* |
|---|---|---|
| 1st | 8 | 4 Yao<br>2 Atonga<br>2 Nyanja, Ngoni, and Nguru |
| 3rd | 6 | 2 Sudanese<br>1 Ethiopian<br>1 Nandi<br>1 Swahili, Nyamwezi, and Manyema |
| 4th | 7 | 5 Sudanese<br>1 Baganda<br>1 Nyamwezi, Sukuma, Kavirondo, and Swahili |

* See Hordern, *Military Operations in East Africa*, p.559.

As of August 1914, the regiment had 62 officers, two British NCOs, and 2,319 Africans.[6]

3 Malcolm Page, *A History of the King's African Rifles and East African Forces* (Barnsley: Leo Cooper, 1998), p.9.

4 Page, *History*, pp.2–3.

5 A not-insignificant number of the 2nd Battalion's soldiers passed over to the Germans in Tanganyika and enlisted in their colonial forces. The 5th KAR was disbanded when its Indians were all gone.

6 Moyse-Bartlett, *King's African Rifles*, vol. 1, Appendix E.

The most famous and maybe the bravest warriors in East Africa, the Masai, were not in the KAR. They had been recruited for a while and then dropped. While they were brave, they were found to be unreliable and hard to discipline.

The Yao were admired by everyone as courageous soldiers and excellent fighters. They also, unlike the Irish and Sudanese, did not give their officers any problems when not campaigning. They were often called 'the Sikhs of Africa'.

As noted earlier, the Sudanese were admired for their fighting ability. They were 'born to fight'. But they and their families could also cause problems in camp. It was a case of 'can't live with them, can't live without them'. The problem was exacerbated because the British officers came and went at a rapid pace. They had short tours because of the bad climate and high rates of disease.

Drawing on so many different ethnic groups to man the KAR battalions meant that a common language was needed. For the battalions operating out of Uganda and Kenya, the lingua franca was Swahili. The 1st KAR and battalions in Central Africa used Chiyao, the language of the Yaos, as their lingua franca.

The officers were British officers seconded from the British army, and a very few were British officers of the Indian army. They normally served for just a few years, as the local climate was very fatal to Europeans. The officers' motives for joining were a combination of the following: the need for the higher pay offered in Africa; limited career prospects in their present regiments, sometimes from failings on their part; the chance to do big-game hunting; and a zest for adventure and new sights. Just as in India and West Africa, officers were expected to learn the lingua franca of their area and had to pass a test in it within six months of joining. If they failed the test, they would be sent home. If they passed, they got a raise.[7] They had to master it within a year.[8]

The pay must have been attractive. Richard Meinertzhagen of the 3rd KAR, who served in the KAR from 1902 to 1906, noted in his 1903 diary that it was about four times higher than his regular army pay (£108 vs £400 a year; £11,120 vs £41,190 or $13,090 vs $48,470 in current funds) and his expenses were far less. He then claimed for the published version of his diaries that his savings had grown from zero to £3,000 (£308,900 or $363,600 approximate present value) in the four-and-a-half years he spent in the KAR.[9] This is impossible with only his pay.

Having cited statements by Meinertzhagen, it must be noted that everything he said and wrote is suspect. In 2007, a systematic study by Brian Garfield of his statements that could be checked about his life was published. Up to that point, they had been accepted at face value. Almost all of his checkable statements were found to be false.[10]

7 Charles Allen and Helen Fry (eds), *Tales from the Dark Continent* (London: André Deutsch, 1979), p.81.

8 Timothy Bowman and Mark Connelly, *The Edwardian Army: Recruiting, Training, and Deploying the British Army, 1902–1914* (Oxford: Oxford University Press, 2012), p.197.

9 Bowman and Connelly, *Edwardian*, pp.187–88.

10 Brian Garfield, *The Meinertzhagen Mystery: The Life and Legend of a Colossal Fraud* (Washington D.C.: Potomac Books, 2007).

## West African Frontier Force

The military body that attempted to maintain British law and rule in West Africa was the West African Frontier Force (WAFF). The regiment was only formed around 1900 by joining together under one general command, the Royal Niger Company forces and the military police formed in the different areas that were to be served by the new military force: Northern Nigeria, Southern Nigeria, Lagos, the Gold Coast, Sierra Leone, and Gambia.[11]

The responsibility for these areas was moved from the Foreign Office to the Colonial Office. The regiment was under the joint control of the Colonial and War Offices. The regiment was overseen by an inspector from the Colonial Office, but the officers were appointed by the War Office.[12]

The officers went out for a variety of reasons. Probably the main one was that the officer could not afford the expenses involved in being part of their regiment. This was particularly true of the rare men who had been promoted to officer from the ranks.[13] But even officers who had not been promoted from the ranks could face money problems, and they too saw a tour or two in Africa as helpful to their pocketbooks.

The importance of high pay in an officer's decision to come to West Africa is shown by the fact that, at first, the WAFF had trouble obtaining officers and NCOs who were willing to serve with it.[14] The problem was partly solved by offering increased pay, high ranks while with the WAFF, and better pension prospects to regular army officers.[15]

To be eligible for employment, an officer needed to be over 22 and under 36. It was felt that anyone outside that age range could not stand up to the stress of the climate and diseases found in West Africa.[16]

Other reasons drawing officers to West Africa were a mix of lack of prospects at home because of poor character or poor performance in their regiment, seeking adventure and hunting, getting away from the stifling atmosphere of European life, higher status in a colonial society, wanting to start over in a new environment, or using the tour in Africa as a springboard to employment in one of the colonies.

A new officer was expected to learn the local languages within a year and pass a test showing his mastery of them. The standard tour was five years, but some did not last that long. Many others elected to sign up for an extended period of time.

West Africa has long been known as the white man's grave. In the late 1700s, the death rate along the West African coast in the first year was somewhere between 300 and 700 per 1,000 per year. After that, it dropped down to 80–120 per 1,000.[17] By the period 1819–1836, the average annual death rate had fallen to 83 per 1,000 for enlisted white troops. Then, it dropped

11 A. Haywood and F. A. S. Clarke, *The History of the West African Frontier Force* (East Sussex: Naval and Military Press, 2015), pp.7–8, 14.
12 Bowman and Connelly, *Edwardian*, pp.184–85.
13 Lawrence James, *The Savage Wars: British Campaigns in Africa, 1870–1920* (London: Robert Hale, 1985), p.249; Bowman and Connelly, *Edwardian*, p.203.
14 Bowman and Connelly, *Edwardian*, pp.186–87.
15 Bowman and Connelly, *Edwardian*, p.187.
16 Bowman and Connelly, *Edwardian*, p.185.
17 P. D. Curtin, '"The White Man's Grave": Image and Reality, 1780–1850', *Journal of British Studies*, 1:1 (1961), p.95.

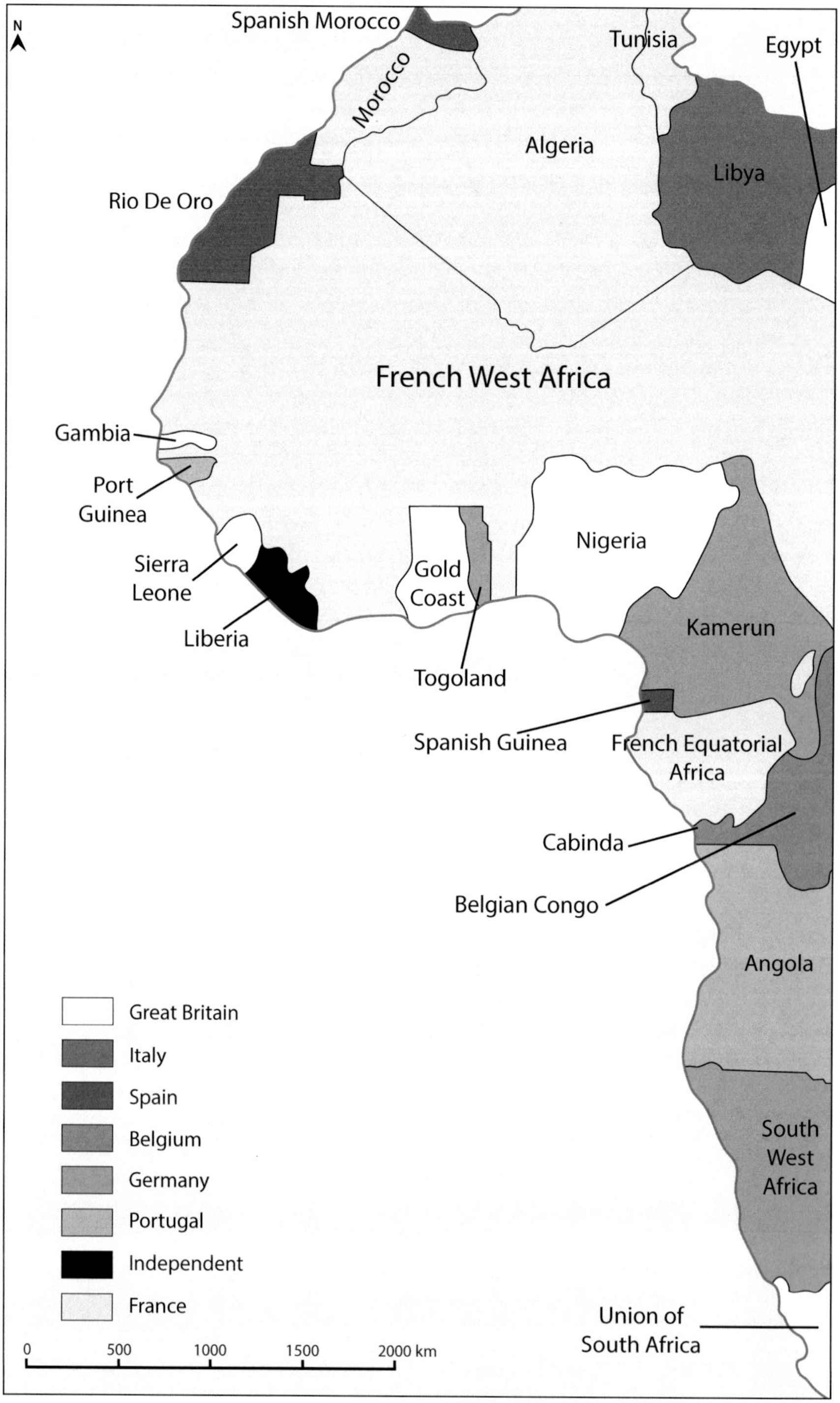


British colonies in West Africa.

NCO West African Frontier Force (WAFF). This man is said to have fired the first British shot of the First World War.

Senior NCO – WAFF.

NCOs – WAFF.

further for the next few years. For the period 1881–1897, it was 76 per 1,000 on the Gold Coast and 53 per 1,000 in Lagos.[18]

By 1909–1913, the death rate had dropped to 5.56 per 1,000, a drop of 98.85 percent from the period 1817–1836, an almost infinite reduction from the first-year rate in the 1700s.[19] The gross numbers of deaths hide wide variations in the death rate. One woman who went out to Nigeria in 1907 in a party of five found that, after a year, she was the only one still alive.[20] While things had improved greatly by the turn of the twentieth century, there were still an impressive number of diseases a person could come down with. Many still died from diseases or were invalided home.[21] In 1907, the official government statistics stated that 20 percent would either be invalided or dead within a year of first coming to Nigeria.[22]

Not only did men get sick and die, but they at times also became mentally unhinged. Hugh Trenchard, who later became the 'father' of the Royal Air Force, was admitted to the hospital with a number of mental problems while colonel of the 1st Northern Nigeria Regiment. He could not complete sentences, was foul-mouthed, had memory loss, and suffered paralysis. In the hospital, he would urinate and defecate against the walls. He suddenly recovered with no memory of his recent actions.[23]

Mental breakdowns seem to have been an occupational hazard that went with service in Africa. A district officer in northern Kenya developed two phobias: that the jackals would eat off his face and that his hut would fall on him as he slept. So, every night, he slept with his head inside the door of his hut and his legs outside.[24] The book *Tales from the Dark Continent*, which is about the British in Africa, has many references to men who became mentally unbalanced.[25]

In 1914, the northern and southern Nigerian regiments were amalgamated. Thus, in 1914, the WAFF consisted of five units.[26]

**Table 60 West African Frontier Force (WAFF) in 1914**

| | Infantry Battalion | Mounted Infantry Battalion | Artillery Batteries |
|---|---|---|---|
| Nigeria Regiment | 4 (30 Companies) | 1 (3 Companies) | 2 (4 Guns) |
| Gold Coast Regiment | 1 (8 Companies) | | 1 (2 Guns) |
| Sierra Leone Battalion | 1 (6 Companies) | | |
| Lagos Battalion | 1* | | |
| Gambia Company | 1 Company | | |

* Not listed with the others.

18 Curtin, 'White Man's Grave', p.110.
19 Philip D. Curtin, *Death by Migration: Europe's Encounter with the Tropical World in the Nineteenth Century* (Cambridge: Cambridge University Press, 1989), pp.6–11.
20 Allen and Fry (eds), *Tales*, p.38.
21 Bowman and Connelly, *Edwardian*, p.200.
22 Allen and Fry (eds), *Tales*, p.34.
23 Bowman and Connelly, *Edwardian*, p.201.
24 Allen and Fry (eds), *Tales*, p.116.
25 See Allen and Fry (eds), *Tales*.
26 Haywood and Clarke, *West African Frontier Force*, p.89.

In 1913, there were 231 white officers commanding the different military units of the WAFF.[27] The force also had British NCOs.

The WAFF regiments and battalions recruited the following ethnic groups:[28]

1. Northern Nigeria – Hausa, Northern Pagans
2. Southern Nigeria – Yorubuas, Ibos
3. Gold Coast – Moshis, Grunshis, Mamprussis
4. Sierra Leone – Timinis, Mendes
5. Gambia – Mandingos, Jollofs
6. Lagos – Mostly Yaruba with a few Hausa and Ibos (formed originally from runaway slaves)
7. Mounted Infantry – Bornu, Zaberma.

## British West India Regiment

This regiment was a regular army regiment. It served mainly in the Caribbean and Africa. In the eighteenth and early nineteenth centuries, the sugar islands were a source of great wealth for the country that controlled them. One sugar island controlled by France produced products worth more money than all of Canada. Because of this, European countries were constantly fighting over who would control a given island. The problem was that the Caribbean, in those days, was a death trap for European soldiers who were sent out to do the fighting. Disease killed so many that it was hard to keep an effective army of Europeans in the area. To cut down on military losses from disease, the British, in the late eighteenth century, began forming regiments of Negros who were thought to be immune from tropical diseases. Over time, the crown had at least 10 different regiments of Blacks, led by British officers.

In the early days, the soldiers were slaves bought from slavers fresh from Africa or purchased from local plantations. It was the custom of England to give these men their freedom when their term of military service was up. Some of the early men in the regiments were former American slaves who had accepted British offers to fight against their former American owners during the Revolutionary War. This changed in 1808, when England abolished the slave trade (but not slavery). She also used her navy to stop slavers from sneaking slaves out of Africa. After 1808, soldiers for the regiment came from African men being carried to slavery on captured slave ships, men captured from enemy colonies during the Napoleonic Wars, and men who volunteered for service in the regiment. As time passed and the wars ended, the first two sources of soldiers dried up, and the regiment became all volunteer. The volunteers would sign up for a long term of service, longer than that used in the regular British army. The men lived in military barracks. Some of the soldiers were allowed to have their wives and children live with them in the barracks. (This was the custom in the regular British as well.)

During the Napoleonic Wars, the regiments fought in battles for control of different islands in the Caribbean. They also served against the Americans in the War of 1812. It was part of the British army that attacked New Orleans in 1814–1815. To defend the city, the Americans stationed their army behind a dirt wall. To defeat the Americans, the British had to climb the

27 Bowman and Connelly, *Edwardian*, p.183, footnote 2.
28 Haywood and Clarke, *West African Frontier Force*, pp.10–14, 16–17, 19, 259.

Other ranks.

Regimental drums.

dirt wall and then fight the Americans. The duty of the West India troops was to place ladders against the wall. Other British regiments would use them to scale the wall. For some reason, they failed to place the ladders. Some commentators have said it was this failure that caused the British to lose. This is unfair. At the other end of the line, a British line regiment, the 44th Foot (in 1914, the Essex Regiment), also failed to place their ladders. It was these twin failures that doomed the British attack.

After the end of the Napoleonic Wars and the War of 1812, the number of men in the regiments was reduced by disbanding many of the regiments. In 1888, the strength was settled at one regiment of two battalions. As peace came to the Caribbean, the regiment(s) served mostly garrison duties. After 1873, men from the regiment began to serve in West Africa. They saw the most fighting after 1885. This was done by having one battalion in Africa and the other in Jamaica. The battalion in West Africa would enrol West Africans to make up for losses from battles and sickness.

The officers of the regiment(s) were British; in later years, some were graduates of Sandhurst. They chose a life of exile and the high risk of death from disease because they wanted to be army officers, and neither they nor their families had enough money to support them while in the army. In the nineteenth and early twentieth centuries, the army did not pay its officers enough to live as officers. Subsidies to their pay from family money were necessary.

## West African Regiment

The British maintained an important naval base in Freetown, Sierra Leone, one of Africa's best ports. It was used as a base for ships to suppress the Atlantic slave trade. Freetown got its name from the fact that it was largely settled by freed slaves who had been living in Canada. There was a high death rate among the British soldiers and sailors living in the area. In 1908, it was decided to form a regiment of native Africans to guard and police the naval base and area. The regiment could also be used to battle the local tribes that objected to the expanding British commercial activity.

The rank and file were largely drawn from the local Mendi people. Many NCOs were British volunteers from the British army. The officers were seconded from the British army as volunteers. The officers and NCOs served for several years and then rotated back to their regular regiments. Both groups volunteered because of the higher pay and the chance for active duty. These, for some, were enough to outweigh the higher chance of death by disease.

The regiment was considered a regular British line regiment.

# Bibliography

## Archival Documents and Government Publications


Army Department [AD], *Army Regulations, India, 1901, Volume 1, Dress* (Calcutta: Superintendent Government Printing, 1901)

Barstow, A. E., *Handbooks for the Indian Army: Sikhs* (Calcutta: Office of the Superintendent, Government Printing, India, 1928)

Betham, R. M., *Handbooks for the Indian Army: Marathas and Dekhani Musalmans* (Calcutta: Office of the Superintendent, Government Printing, India, 1908)

Bingley, A. H., and Nicholls, A., *Caste Handbooks for the Indian Army: Brahmans* (Simla: Government Central Printing Office, 1897)

Bourne, W. F. G., *Handbooks for the Indian Army: Hindustani Musalmans and Musalmans of the Eastern Punjab* (Calcutta: Office of the Superintendent, Government Printing, India, 1914)

'British Army Soldiers up to 1913', *The National Archives*, <https://www.nationalarchives.gov.uk/help-with-your-research/research-guides/british-army-soldiers-up-to-1913/>, accessed 14 Sept. 2022

Christie, R. C., *Handbooks for the Indian Army: Jats, Gujars, and Ahirs* (Calcutta: Office of the Superintendent, Government Printing, India, 1924)

Cole, B. L., *Handbooks for the Indian Army: Rajputana Classes* (Calcutta: Office of the Superintendent, Government Printing, India, 1924)

Committee on Military Education [CME], *Minutes of Evidence Taken before the Committee Appointed to Consider the Education and Training of Officers of the Army* (London: HMSO, 1902)

Committee on Military Education [CME], *Report of the Committee Appointed to Consider the Education and Training of Officers of the Army* (London: HMSO, 1902)

Cunningham, W. B., *Handbooks for the Indian Army: Dogras* (Calcutta: Office of the Superintendent, Government Printing, India, 1932)

Hordern, Charles, *History of the Great War Based on Official Documents by the Direction of the Historical Section of the Committee of Imperial Defence: Military Operations in East Africa, August 1914–September 1916* (London: HMSO, 1941), vol. 1

Moberly, F. J., *History of the Great War Based on Official Documents: The Campaign in Mesopotamia 1914–1918* (London: HMSO, 1923), vol. 1

Mouat, G. E. D., *Handbooks for the Indian Army: Madras Classes* (Calcutta: Office of the Superintendent, Government Printing, India, 1938)

Vansittart, E., *Handbooks for the Indian Army: Gurkhas* (revised by B. V. Nicolay, Calcutta: Office of the Superintendent, Government Printing, India, 1915)
War Office [WO], *Report of the Committee Appointed by the Secretary of State for War to Enquire into the Nature of the Expenses Incurred by Officers of the Army* (London: HMSO, 1903)
War Office [WO], *The Monthly Army List: August, 1914* (London: HMSO, 1914), <https://digital.nls.uk/british-military-lists/archive/103627418>
War Office [WO], *The Quarterly Indian Army List, July 1914* (Calcutta: Superintendent Government Printing, 1914)
Wikeley, J. M., *Handbooks for the Indian Army: Punjabi Musalmans* (Calcutta: Office of the Superintendent, Government Printing, India, 1915)

## Books and Book Chapters

Addison, Albert C., and Matthews, William H., *A Deathless Story: Or, the 'Birkenhead' and Its Heroes: Being the Only Full and Authentic Account of the Famous Shipwreck Extant, Founded on Collected Official, Documentary, and Personal Evidence, and Containing Narratives and Lives of Actors in the Most Glorious Ocean Tragedy in History* (London: Hutchinson, 1906)
Allen, Charles, *Plain Tales from the Raj* (London: Futura Publications, 1978)
Allen, Charles, and Fry, Helen (eds), *Tales from the Dark Continent* (London: André Deutsch, 1979)
Anon., 'Hyderabad, India (State)', in *Encyclopædia Britannica* (Edinburgh: Encyclopædia Britannica, 1911), vol. 14, pp.31–32
Anon., *Regimental Nicknames and Traditions of the British Army* (5th edition, London: Forgotten Books Publishing, 2018)
Asopa, Jai Narayan, *Origin of the Rajputs* (Delhi: Bharatiya Publishing House, 1976)
Bamfield, Veronica, *On the Strength: The Story of the British Army Wife* (London: Charles Knight, 1974)
Bancroft, N. W., *From Recruit to Staff Sergeant* (Essex: Ian Henry Publications, 1979)
Barker, A. J., *The Neglected War: Mesopotamia 1914–1918* (London: Faber and Faber, 1967)
Barnes, R. M., *Military Uniforms of Britain and the Empire* (London: Sphere Books, 1972)
Barnett, Correlli, *Britain and Her Army, 1509–1970: A Military, Political and Social Survey* (London: Allen Lane, 1970)
Barthorp, Michael, *The Old Contemptibles* (New York: Bloomsbury USA, 1989)
Basham, Arthur L., *The Wonder that Was India: A Survey of the History and Culture of the Indian Sub-Continent before the Coming of the Muslims* (London: Sidgwick and Jackson, 1967)
Baynes, John C. M., *Morale: A Study of Men and Courage* (New York: Avery Publishing Group, 1988)
Beckett, Ian F. W., *Discovering British Regimental Traditions* (New York: Bloomsbury USA, 2008)
Beckett, Ian F. W., and Simpson, Keith (eds), *A Nation in Arms: A Social Study of the British Army in the First World War* (Barnsley: Pen and Sword Select, 2004)
Bhagavan, Manu B., *Sovereign Spheres: Princes, Education, and Empire in Colonial India* (Oxford: Oxford University Press, 2003)
Blunt, E. A. H., *The Caste System of Northern India: With Special Reference to the United Provinces of Agra and Qudh* (New Delhi: S. Chand and Co., 1969)

Bonarjee, P. D., *A Handbook of the Fighting Races of India* (Calcutta: Thacker, Spink, and Company, 1899)
Bond, Brian, *The Victorian Army and the Staff College, 1854–1914* (Fakenham: Eyre Methuen, 1972)
Bowling, A. H., *Indian Cavalry Regiments, 1880–1914* (London: Almark Publishing Co., 1971)
Bowman, Timothy, and Connelly, Mark, *The Edwardian Army: Recruiting, Training, and Deploying the British Army, 1902–1914* (Oxford: Oxford University Press, 2012)
Brereton, John M., *The 7th Queen's Own Hussars* (London: Leo Cooper, 1975)
Buchan, John, *The History of the Royal Scots Fusiliers, 1678–1918* (East Sussex: Naval and Military Press, 2015)
Buckland, Patrick, *The Anglo-Irish and the New Ireland, 1885–1922* (Dublin: Gill and Macmillan, 1972)
Cairnes, William E., *The Army from Within* (London: Sands and Co., 1901)
Candler, Edmund, *The Sepoy* (London: John Murray, 1919)
Caplan, Lionel, *Warrior Gentlemen: 'Gurkhas' in the Western Imagination* (Oxford: Berghahn Books, 1995)
Cardew, F. G., *The Bengal Native Army* (London: Leonaur, 2008)
Carew, Tim, *How the Regiments Got Their Nicknames* (London: Leo Cooper, 1974)
Carman, W. Y., *Indian Army Uniforms under the British from the 18th Century to 1947: Artillery, Engineers, and Infantry* (London: Morgan-Grampian Books, 1969)
Caroe, Olaf, *The Pathans, 550 B.C.–A.D. 1957* (New York: St. Martin's Press, 1959)
Chalfont, Alun A. G. J., *Montgomery of Alamein* (New York: Atheneum, 1976)
Churchill, Randolph S., *Winston S. Churchill: Youth, 1874–1900* (Boston: Houghton Mifflin Company, 1966), vol. 1
Churchill, Winston L. S., *The Story of the Malakand Field Force: An Episode of Frontier War* (London: Longmans, Green and Co., 1898)
Clark, Alan, *The Donkeys* (London: Pimlico, 1991)
Clewell, Gladys D., and Thompson, Holland (eds), *Lands and People: The World in Color* (New York: Grolier Society, 1947), vol. 4
Clutterbuck, L. A., Dooner, W. T., and Denison, C. A. (eds), *The Bond of Sacrifice: A Biographical Record of All British Officers Who Fell in the Great War* (London: Anglo-African Publishing Contractors, 1917)
Clyde, Robert, *From Rebel to Hero: The Image of the Highlander, 1745-1830* (East Linton: Tuckwell Press, 1995)
Cohen, Stephen P., *The Indian Army: Its Contribution to the Development of a Nation* (Oxford: Oxford University Press, 2001)
Condon, W. E. H., *Frontier Force Rifles 1849–1946* (East Sussex: Naval and Military Press, 2015)
Connell, John, *Wavell, Scholar and Soldier* (San Diego: Harcourt, Brace and World, 1965)
Cunningham, Hugh, *The Volunteer Force: A Social and Political History 1859–1908* (Hamden, CT: Archon Books, 1975)
Curtin, Philip D., *Death by Migration: Europe's Encounter with the Tropical World in the Nineteenth Century* (Cambridge: Cambridge University Press, 1989)
Davis, Brian L., *British Army Uniforms and Insignia of World War Two* (London: Arms and Armour Press, 1983)

Devi, Gayatri, *A Princess Remembers: The Memoirs of the Maharani of Jaipur* (New Delhi: Rupa Publications, 1995)
Dickinson, Richard J. (ed.), *Officers' Mess: Being a History of Mess Origins and Customs: From a Wealth of Military Records* (London: Midas Books, 1973)
Dixon, Norman F., *On the Psychology of Military Incompetence* (Philadelphia: Basic Books, 1976)
Downes, W. D., *With the Nigerians in German East Africa* (London: Methuen and Co., 1919)
Durant, Will, *The Age of Faith: A History of Medieval Civilization–Christian, Islamic, and Judaic–from Constantine to Dante: A.D. 325–1300* (New York: Simon and Schuster, 1950), vol. 1
Dutt, Devendra Nath, *A Brief History of the Hutwa Raj, with a Genealogical Table of the Hutwa Family* (Calcutta: K. P. Mookerjee and Co., 1909)
Edwardes, Herbert B., and Merivale, Herman, *Life of Sir Henry Lawrence* (3rd edition, London: Smith, Elder and Co., 1873)
Edwards, Thomas J., *Military Customs* (4th edition, Aldershot: Gale and Polden, 1954)
Evatt, J., *Historical Record of the 39th Royal Garhwal Rifles, 1887–1922* (Aldershot: Gale and Polden, 1922), vol. 1
Fallows, Marjorie R., *Irish Americans: Identity and Assimilation* (Hoboken, NJ: Prentice Hall, 1979)
Farwell, Byron, *Armies of the Raj: From the Great Indian Mutiny to Independence: 1858–1947* (New York: W. W. Norton and Company, 1989)
Farwell, Byron, *Mr. Kipling's Army: All the Queen's Men* (New York: W. W. Norton and Company, 1987)
Farwell, Byron, *The Gurkhas* (New York: W. W. Norton and Company, 1984)
Forbes, Rosita, *India of the Princes* (Boston: E. P. Dutton and Company, 1941)
Frederick, John B. M., *Lineage Book of the British Army: Mounted Corps and Infantry, 1660–1968* (Kingston, NY: Hope Farm Press, 1969)
French, David, *Military Identities: The Regimental System, the British Army, and the British People c. 1870–2000* (Oxford: Oxford University Press, 2008)
Frey, Sylvia R., *The British Soldier in America: A Social History of Military Life in the Revolutionary Period* (Austin: University of Texas Press, 1981)
Gardner, Brian, *The East India Company: A History* (London: Hart-Davis, 1971)
Garfield, Brian, *The Meinertzhagen Mystery: The Life and Legend of a Colossal Fraud* (Washington D.C.: Potomac Books, 2007)
Gaylor, John, *Sons of John Company: The Indian and Pakistan Armies, 1903–91* (Gloucestershire: Spellmount, 1992)
Gupta, R. K., and Bakshi, S. R. (eds), *Rajasthan through the Ages: Jaipur Rulers and Administration* (New Delhi: Sarup and Sons, 2008), vol. 4
H. H. The Maharaja of Jaipur, *A History of the Indian State Forces: Their Lineage and Insignia* (New Delhi: Orient Longmans, 1967)
Hamilton, Henry B., *Historical Record of the 14th (King's) Hussars from A.D. 1715 to A.D. 1900* (London: Longmans, Green and Co., 1901)
Hanham, H. J., 'Religion and Nationality in the Mid-Victorian Army', in J. R. Weston and M. R. D. Foot (eds), *War and Society: Historical Essays in Honour and Memory of J. R. Western 1928-1971* (London: Elek, 1973), pp.159–82
Harris, Isadore (ed.), *The Jewish Year Book: An Annual Record of Matters Jewish, #5661, 24th September, 1900 – 13th September, 1901* (London: Greenberg and Company, 1901)

Harris, Isadore (ed.), *The Jewish Year Book: An Annual Record of Matters Jewish, #5663, 2nd October, 1902 – 21st September, 1903* (London: Greenberg and Company, 1902)

Harris, Isadore (ed.). *The Jewish Year Book: An Annual Record of Matters Jewish, #5666, 30th September, 1905 – 19th September, 1906* (London: Greenberg and Company, 1905)

Harris, Isadore (ed.), *The Jewish Year Book: An Annual Record of Matters Jewish, #5668-9, 9th September, 1907 – 31st December, 1908* (London: Greenberg and Company, 1907)

Harris, Isadore (ed.), *The Jewish Year Book: An Annual Record of Matters Jewish, #5674-75, 1st January – 31st December, 1914* (London: Greenberg and Company, 1914), vol. 18

Harris, John, *The Indian Mutiny* (London: Hart-Davis MacGibbon, 1973)

Hart, H. G., *Hart's Annual Army List, Militia List, and Imperial Yeomanry List, for 1914* (London: John Murray, 1914)

Haywood, A., and Clarke, F. A. S., *The History of the West African Frontier Force* (East Sussex: Naval and Military Press, 2015)

Head, Richard, and McClenaghan, Tony, *The Maharajas' Paltans: A History of the Indian State Forces, 1888–1948* (New Delhi: Manohar Publishers, 2013), part 1

Head, Richard, and McClenaghan, Tony, *The Maharajas' Paltans: A History of the Indian State Forces, 1888–1948* (New Delhi: Manohar Publishers, 2013), part 2

Heathcote, T. A., *The Indian Army: The Garrison of British Imperial India, 1822–1922* (London: David and Charles, 1974)

Heathcote, T. A., *The Military in British India: The Development of British Land Forces in South Asia, 1600–1947* (Manchester: Manchester University Press, 1995)

Hennessy, Maurice N., *The Wild Geese: The Irish Soldier in Exile* (London: Sidgwick and Jackson, 1973)

Hochschild, Adam, *To End All Wars: A Story of Loyalty and Rebellion, 1914–1918* (New York: Houghton Mifflin Harcourt, 2011)

Holder, Denzil, *Hindu Horseman* (Chippenham: Picton Publishing, 1986)

Holmes, Richard, *Sahib: The British Soldier in India, 1750–1914* (Hammersmith: HarperCollins, 2005)

Holmes, Richard, *The Little Field-Marshal, Sir John French* (London: Jonathan Cape, 1981)

Hook, Julius N., *Family Names: The Origins, Meanings, Mutations, and History of More Than 2,800 American Names* (London: Collier Books, 1983)

Hope Risley, Herbert, Stevenson Meyer, William, Burn, Richard, and Sutherland Cotton, James (eds), 'Baroda State', in *The Imperial Gazetteer of India* (Oxford: Clarendon Press, 1908), vol. 7

Hope Risley, Herbert, Stevenson Meyer, William, Burn, Richard, and Sutherland Cotton, James (eds), 'Belgaum District', in *The Imperial Gazetteer of India* (Oxford: Clarendon Press, 1908), vol. 7

Hope Risley, Herbert, Stevenson Meyer, William, Burn, Richard, and Sutherland Cotton, James (eds), 'Cochin State', in *The Imperial Gazetteer of India* (Oxford: Clarendon Press, 1908), vol. 10

Hope Risley, Herbert, Stevenson Meyer, William, Burn, Richard, and Sutherland Cotton, James (eds), 'Garhwāl District', in *The Imperial Gazetteer of India* (Oxford: Clarendon Press, 1908), vol. 12

Hope Risley, Herbert, Stevenson Meyer, William, Burn, Richard, and Sutherland Cotton, James (eds), 'Gwalior State', in *The Imperial Gazetteer of India* (Oxford: Clarendon Press, 1908), vol. 12

Hope Risley, Herbert, Stevenson Meyer, William, Burn, Richard, and Sutherland Cotton, James (eds), 'Indore State', in *The Imperial Gazetteer of India* (Oxford: Clarendon Press, 1908), vol. 12

Hope Risley, Herbert, Stevenson Meyer, William, Burn, Richard, and Sutherland Cotton, James (eds), 'Kolhāpur State', in *The Imperial Gazetteer of India* (Oxford: Clarendon Press, 1908), vol. 15

Hope Risley, Herbert, Stevenson Meyer, William, Burn, Richard, and Sutherland Cotton, James (eds), 'Kumaun', in *The Imperial Gazetteer of India* (Oxford: Clarendon Press, 1908), vol. 16

Hope Risley, Herbert, Stevenson Meyer, William, Burn, Richard, and Sutherland Cotton, James (eds), 'Tehri State', in *The Imperial Gazetteer of India* (Oxford: Clarendon Press, 1908), vol. 23

Hope Risley, Herbert, Stevenson Meyer, William, Burn, Richard, and Sutherland Cotton, James (eds), 'Transcore State', in *The Imperial Gazetteer of India* (Oxford: Clarendon Press, 1908), vol. 24

Horn, Pamela, *Life as a Victorian Lady* (Gloucestershire: The History Press, 2007)

Husain, Asad, *British India's Relations with the Kingdom of Nepal, 1857–1947: A Diplomatic History of Nepal* (London: George Allen and Unwin, 1970)

Jabotinsky, Vladimir, *The Story of the Jewish Legion*, as translated by Shmuel Katz (New York: B. Ackerman, 1945)

James, E. A., *British Regiments, 1914–1918* (East Sussex: Naval and Military Press, 2001)

James, Lawrence, *The Savage Wars: British Campaigns in Africa, 1870–1920* (London: Robert Hale, 1985)

Jeffery, Keith, 'The Irish Military Tradition and the British Empire', in K. Jeffery (ed.), *'An Irish Empire'? Aspects of Ireland and the British Empire* (Manchester: Manchester University Press, 1996), pp.94–122

Katz, Nathan, *Who Are the Jews of India?* (Berkeley: University of California Press, 2000)

Keegan, John, and Wheatcroft, Andrew, *Who's Who in Military History: From 1453 to the Present Day* (London: Weidenfeld and Nicolson, 1976)

Keown-Boyd, Henry, *A Good Dusting: A Centenary Review of the Sudan Campaigns, 1883–1899* (London: Leo Cooper, 1986)

Kipling, Rudyard, 'The Young British Soldier', in *Rudyard Kipling's Verse* (London: Hodder and Stoughton, 1921)

Knight, Ian, *Go to Your God Like a Soldier: The British Soldier Fighting for Empire, 1837–1902* (London: Greenhill Books, 1996)

Langley, Michael, *The Loyal Regiment (North Lancashire): The 47th and 81st Regiments of Foot* (London: Leo Copper, 1976)

Leslie, N. B., *Battle Honours of the British and Indian Armies, 1695–1914* (London: Leo Cooper, 1970)

Lewis-Stempel, John, *Six Weeks: The Short and Gallant Life of the British Officer in the First World War* (London: Orion Publishing Group, 2010)

Lloyd-Jones, W., *K.A.R.: Being an Unofficial Account of the Origin and Activities of the King's African Rifles* (London: Arrowsmith, 1926)

Lord, John, *The Maharajas* (New Delhi: Vikas, 1971)

Lunt, James D., *The Duke of Wellington's Regiment (West Riding): The 33rd/76th Regiment of Foot* (London: Leo Cooper, 1971)

Lunt, James D. (ed.), and Norgate, James T. (trans.), *From Sepoy to Subedar: Being the Life and Adventures of Subedar Sita Ram, a Native Officer of the Bengal Army Written and Related by Himself* (Hamden, CT: Archon Books, 1970)

MacMunn, G. F., *The Armies of India* (London: Adam and Charles Black, 1911)

MacMunn, George F., *The Martial Races of India* (London: Low, Marston and Company, 1933)

MacMunn, George F., *Turmoil and Tragedy in India: 1914 and After* (London: Jarrolds, 1935)

Mangan, J. A., 'Social Darwinism and Upper-Class Education in Late Victorian and Edwardian England', in J. A. Mangam and J. Walvin (eds), *Manliness and Mortality: Middle-Class Masculinity in Britain and America, 1800–1940* (Manchester: Manchester University Press, 1987), pp.135–59

Marquess of Anglesey, *A History of the British Cavalry, 1816–1919* (Barnsley: Leo Cooper, 1986), vol. 4

Marquess of Anglesey, *A History of the British Cavalry, 1816–1919* (Barnsley: Leo Cooper, 1986), vol. 6

Marrion, R. J., and Fosten, D. S. V., *The Tradition Book of the Gurkhas* (London: Belmont-Maitland, 1973)

Martin, Ralph G., *Jennie: The Life of Lady Randolph Churchill* (Naperville, IL: Sourcebooks, 2008)

Mason, Philip, *A Matter of Honour* (Austin: Holt, Rinehart and Winston, 1974)

Masters, John, *Bugles and a Tiger: My Life in the Gurkhas* (London: Cassell, 2002)

McCrum, Robert, Cran, William, and MacNeil, Robert, *The Story of English* (New York: Viking Press, 1986)

McNeill, William H., *Plagues and Peoples* (New York: Anchor Books, 1998)

Meredith, George, *Diana of the Crossways: A Novel* (Revised edition, New York: Charles Scribner's Sons, 1900)

Mills, Margaret A., Claus, Peter J., and Diamond, Sarah (eds), *South Asian Folklore: An Encyclopedia* (Abingdon: Routledge, 2003)

Mitchell, B. R., *British Historical Statistics* (Cambridge: Cambridge University Press, 1988)

Mitchell, Sally, *Daily Life in Victorian England* (Westport, CT: Greenwood Press, 1996)

Montague, C. E., *Disenchantment* (London: Chatto and Windus, 1922)

Moore, Lucy, *Maharanis: The Lives and Times of Three Generations of Indian Princesses* (London: Penguin Books, 2004)

Morris, Jan, *Farewell the Trumpets: An Imperial Retreat* (London: Faber and Faber, 2010)

Moyse-Bartlett, H., *The King's African Rifles: A Study in the Military History of East and Central Africa, 1890–1945* (East Sussex: Naval and Military Press, 2012), vol. 1

Myatt, Frederick, *The Royal Berkshire Regiment (the 49th/66th Regiment of Foot)* (London: H. Hamilton, 1968)

Nair, P. T., 'The Growth and Development of Old Calcutta', in S. Chaudhuri (ed.), *Calcutta: The Living City, Volume 1: The Past* (Calcutta: Oxford University Press, 1990)

Nevins, Edward M., *Forces of the British Empire, 1914* (St Petersburg, FL: Vandamere Press, 1992)

Oatts, Lewis B., *Emperor's Chambermaids: The Story of the 14th/20th King's Hussars* (London: Ward Lock, 1973)

Oatts, Lewis B., *The Highland Light Infantry (the 71st H.L.I. and 74th Highlanders)* (London: Leo Cooper, 1969)

Oman, Charles, *A History of the Peninsular War* (Barnsley: Greenhill Books, 1995), vol. 1

Omissi, David, *The Sepoy and the Raj: The Indian Army, 1860–1940* (Houndmills: Macmillan Press, 1994)
Page, Malcolm, *A History of the King's African Rifles and East African Forces* (Barnsley: Leo Cooper, 1998)
Palsetia, Jesse S., *The Parsis of India: Preservation of Identity in Bombay City* (Leiden: Brill, 2021)
Patterson, John H., *With the Judeans in the Palestine Campaign* (London: Macmillan, 1922)
Penslar, Derek J., *Jews and the Military: A History* (Princeton: Princeton University Press, 2013)
Perrett, Bryan, *The Battle Book: Crucial Conflicts in History from 1469 BC to the Present* (London: Arms and Armour, 1992)
Perry, F. W., *Order of Battle of Divisions, Part 1* (Newport, VA: Ray Westlake Military Books, 1988)
Perry, F. W., *Order of Battle of Divisions, Part 5B: Indian Army Divisions* (Newport, VA: Ray Westlake Military Books, 1993)
Phythian-Adams, E. G., *The Madras Regiment, 1758–1958* (Wellington: Defence Services Staff College Press, 1958)
Prasad, Shankar, *The Gallant Dogras: An Illustrated History of the Dogra Regiment* (New Delhi: Lancer Publishers, 2005)
Richards, Frank, *Old Soldier Sahib* (London: Faber and Faber, 1945)
Roberts, Frederick S. R., *Forty-One Years in India: From Subaltern to Commander-in-Chief* (London: Richard Bentley and Son, 1898), vol. 1
Robertson, William, *From Private to Field-Marshall* (Forest Grove, OR: University Press of the Pacific, 2005)
Rosignoli, Guido, *Ribbons of Orders, Decorations and Medals* (New York: Arco Publishing Company, 1977)
Roy, Kaushik, *Brown Warriors of the Raj: Recruitment and the Mechanics of Command in the Sepoy Army* (New Delhi: Manohar Publishers, 2008)
Rubin, Eli, *140 Jewish Marshals, Generals & Admirals* (London: De Vero Books, 1952)
Schollander, Wendell, and Schollander, Wes, *Forgotten Elegance: The Art, Artifacts, and Peculiar History of Victorian and Edwardian Entertaining in America* (Westport, CT: Greenwood Press, 2002)
Shrivastava, V. K., *The Rajputana Rifles* (New Delhi: Lancer Publishers, 2000)
Sibley, J. R., *Tanganyikan Guerrilla: East African Campaign 1914–18* (London: Ballantine Books, 1971)
Simpson, Keith, 'The Officer', in T. Bartlett and K. Jeffery (eds), *A Military History of Ireland* (Cambridge: Cambridge University Press, 1996), pp.63–98
Singh, K. S. (ed.), *People of India: Maharashtra* (Mumbai: Popular Prakashan, 2004), vol. 30, part 1
Singh, R. B., *Origin of the Rajputs* (Oakland: University of California Press, 1975)
Skelley, Alan R., *The Victorian Army at Home: The Recruitment and Terms and Conditions of the British Regular, 1859–1899* (London: Croom Helm, 1977)
Smith, E. D., *Valour: A History of the Gurkhas* (Gloucestershire: Spellmount, 1997)
Smyth, Benjamin, *A History of the Lancashire Fusiliers (Formerly XX Regiment)* (Sheridan, WY: Creative Media Partners, 2017)
Spiers, Edward M., 'Army Organisation and Society in the Nineteenth Century', in T. Bartlett and K. Jeffery (eds), *A Military History of Ireland* (Cambridge: Cambridge University Press, 1996), pp.335–57
Spiers, Edward M., *The Army and Society, 1815–1914* (London: Longman, 1980)

Spiers, Edward M., 'The Regular Army of 1914', in I. F. W. Beckett and K. Simpson (eds), *A Nation in Arms: A Social Study of the British Army in the First World War* (Manchester: Manchester University Press, 1985), pp.37–62

Steel, Flora A., and Gardiner, Grace, *The Complete Indian Housekeeper and Cook* (Oxford: Oxford University Press, 2011)

Streets, Heather, *Martial Races: The Military, Race and Masculinity in British Imperial Culture, 1857–1914* (Manchester: Manchester University Press, 2004)

Sykes, Bryan, *Saxons, Vikings, and Celts: The Genetic Roots of Britain and Ireland* (New York: W. W. Norton and Company, 2006)

Thomas, Bert, *The Best 500 Cockney War Stories: Reprinted from the London Evening News, Early 1920s* (Gloucestershire: Amberley Publishing, 2012)

Tombs, Robert and Isabelle, *That Sweet Enemy: Britain and France: The History of a Love-Hate Relationship* (London: Random House, 2006)

Travers, Tim, 'Learning the Art of War: Junior Officer Training in the British Army from the Eighteenth Century to 1914', in E. Converse III (ed.), *Forging the Sword: Selecting, Educating, and Training Cadets and Junior Officers in the Modern World* (Chicago: Imprint Publications, 1998)

Upton, Emory, *The Armies of Asia and Europe: Embracing Official Reports on the Armies of Japan, China, India, Persia, Italy, Russia, Austria, Germany, France, and England* (Cranbury, NJ: Scholar's Bookshelf, 2006)

Warner, Phillip, *Field Marshal Earl Haig* (London: Bodley Head, 1991)

Wauchope, A. G. (ed.), *A History of the Black Watch (Royal Highlanders) in the Great War, 1914–1918, Volume One: Regular Army* (East Sussex: Naval and Military Press, 2016)

Weller, Jac, *Wellington in India* (Harlow: Longman, 1972)

Wheeler, James, *The History of the Imperial Assemblage at Delhi: Held on the 1st January, 1877, to Celebrate the Assumption of the Title of Empress of India by Her Majesty the Queen, Including Historical Sketches of India and Her Princes, Past and Present* (Jalandhar: R. K. Publishing House, 1982)

Williams, Jeffery, *Byng of Vimy: General and Governor General* (London: Leo Cooper, 1983)

Winter, Denis, *Haig's Command: A Reassessment* (London: Penguin Books, 1992)

Wood, Stephen, *The Scottish Soldier* (Manchester: Archive Publications, 1987)

Woodham-Smith, Cecil, *The Reason Why: The Story of the Fatal Charge of the Light Brigade* (London: Penguin Books, 1958)

Younghusband, George J., *The Queen's Commission: How to Prepare for It, How to Obtain It, and How to Use It: With Practical Information on the Cost and Prospects of a Military Career* (John Murray, 2009, Google Books e-book)

## Internet Resources

'Berar Province', *Wikipedia*, <https://en.wikipedia.org/wiki/Berar_Province>, accessed 31 Dec. 2023

Mokyr, Joel, 'Great Famine', *Encyclopaedia Britannica* (2024), <https://www.britannica.com/event/Great-Famine-Irish-history>, accessed 26 Oct. 2023

'Our Sporting Heroes', *Royal Welch Fusiliers Museum*, <https://www.rwfmuseum.org.uk/downloads/our-sporting-heroes.pdf>, accessed 1 Sept. 2023

## Journal Articles

Barthorp, Michael, 'Disaster at Maiwand, 27 July 1880: Part I', *Tradition*, 64 (n.d.), pp.17–19

Barthorp, Michael, 'Disaster at Maiwand, 27 July 1880: Part II', *Tradition*, 65 (n.d.), pp.18–20, 28

Braithwaite, Walter, 'For the Conduct of an Army Character Weighs More Than Knowledge or Science', *Journal of the United Service Institution of India*, 42 (1913), pp.351–67

Curtin, P. D., '"The White Man's Grave": Image and Reality, 1780–1850', *Journal of British Studies*, 1:1 (1961), pp.94–110

Denman, Terence, '"Ethnic Soldiers Pure and Simple"? The Irish in the Late Victorian British Army', *War in History*, 3:3 (1996), pp.253–73, DOI 10.1177/096834459600300301

Dinwiddy, J. R., 'The Early Nineteenth-Century Campaign against Flogging in the Army', *English Historical Review*, XLVI:CLXXXIII (1931), pp.308–31, DOI 10.1093/ehr/XLVI.CLXXXIII.308

Evans, Nick, '"Sport and Hard Work." Tactics, Reform and Equestrianism in the British Cavalry 1900–1914', *Journal of the Society for Army Historical Research*, 89:358 (2011), pp.139–58, <https://www.jstor.org/stable/44231835>

Gray, Edwyn, 'While World War I Raged in Europe, a Cunning German Naval Officer Touched Off a Bloody Rebellion in Singapore', *Military History*, 15:5 (1998), pp.30–32, 84–90

Karsten, Peter, 'Irish Soldiers in the British Army, 1792–1922: Suborned or Subordinate?', *Journal of Social History*, 17:1 (1983), pp.31–64, <http://www.jstor.org/stable/3787238>

Kosmin, Barry A., Waterman, Stanley, and Grizzard, Nigel, 'The Jewish Dead in the Great War as an Indicator for the Location, Size and Social Structure of Anglo-Jewry in 1914', *Immigrants & Minorities: Historical Studies in Ethnicity, Migration and Diaspora*, 5:2 (1986), pp.181–92, DOI 10.1080/02619288.1986.9974631

Nicholson, J. B. R. (ed.), '10th Queen Victoria's Own Corps of Guides Cavalry (Frontier Force)', *Tradition*, 73:Special Indian Cavalry Issue 2 (n.d.), pp.11–12

Razzell, Peter E., 'Social Origins of Officers in the Indian and British Home Army: 1758–1962', *British Journal of Sociology*, 14:3 (1963), pp.248–60

Stearn, R. T., 'A Great Philanthropist: Sir James Gildea and the Soldiers' and Sailors' Families Association', *Soldiers of the Queen: Journal of the Victorian Military Society*, 142 (2010), pp.3–9

Travers, Tim, 'The Hidden Army: Structural Problems in the British Officer Corps, 1900–1918', *Journal of Contemporary History*, 17:3 (1982), pp.523–44, <http://www.jstor.org/stable/260559>

## Newspapers

*The Illustrated London News*, 50:1289 (20 January 1912)

# Index

## BOOKS IN THIS SERIES:

1. *The Battle of Majuba Hill The Transvaal Campaign 1880–1881* John Laband (ISBN 978-1-911512-38-7)
2. *For Queen and Company Vignettes of the Irish Soldier in the Indian Mutiny* David Truesdale (ISBN 978-1-911512-79-0)
3. *The Furthest Garrison Imperial Regiments in New Zealand 1840–1870* Adam Davis (ISBN 978-1-911628-29-3)
4. *Victory Over Disease Resolving the Medical Crisis in the Crimean War, 1854–1856* Michael Hinton (ISBN 978-1-911628-31-6)
5. *Journey Through the Wilderness Garnet Wolseley's Canadian Red River Expedition of 1870* Paul McNicholls (ISBN 978-1-911628-30-9)
6. *Kitchener The Man Not The Myth* Anne Samson (ISBN 978-1-912866-45-8)
7. *The British and the Sikhs Discovery, Warfare and Friendship c1700–1900* Gurinder Singh Mann (ISBN 978-1-911628-24-8)
8. *Bazaine 1870 Scapegoat for a Nation* Quintin Barry (ISBN 978-1-913336-08-0)
9. *Redcoats in the Classroom The British Army's Schools For Soldiers and Their Children During the 19th Century* Howard R. Clarke (ISBN 978-1-912866-47-2)
10. *The Rescue They Called a Raid The Jameson Raid 1895–96* David Snape (ISBN 978-1-913118-77-8)
11. *Hungary 1848 The Winter Campaign* Christopher Pringle (ISBN 978-1-913118-78-5)
12. *The War of the Two Brothers The Portuguese Civil War 1828-1834* Sérgio Veludo Coelho (ISBN 978-1-914059-26-1)
14. *Forgotten Victorian Generals Studies in the Exercise of Command and Control in the British Army 1837–1901* Christopher Brice (editor) (ISBN 978-1-910777-20-6)
15. *The German War of 1866 The Bohemian and Moravian Campaign* Theodore Fontane (ISBN 978-1-914059-29-2)
16. *Dust of Glory The First Anglo-Afghan War 1839–1842, its Causes and Course* Bill Whitburn (ISBN 978-1-914059-33-9)
17. *Saarbruck to Sedan The Franco-German War 1870–1871 Volume 1* Ralph Weaver (ISBN 978-1-914059-88-9)
18. *The Battle of Lissa 1866 How the Industrial Revolution Changed the Face of Naval Warfare* Quintin Barry (ISBN 978-1-914059-92-6)
19. *The Zulu Kingdom and the Boer Invasion of 1837–1840* John Laband (ISBN 978-1-914059-89-6)
20. *The Fire of Venture Was in His Veins* Major Allan Wilson and the Shangani Patrol 1893 David Snape (ISBN 978-1-914059-90-2)
21. *From the Atacama to the Andes Battles of the War of the Pacific 1879–1883* Alan Curtis (ISBN 978-1-914059-90-2)
22. *The Rise of the Sikh Soldier The Sikh Warrior Through the Ages, c1700–1900* Gurinder Singh Mann (ISBN 978-1-915070-52-4)
23. *Victorian Crusaders British and Irish Volunteers in the Papal Army 1860–70* Nicholas Schofield (ISBN 978-1-915070-53-1)
24. *The Battle for the Swiepwald Austria's Fatal Blunder at Königgrätz, the climactic battle of the Austro-Prussian War, 3 July 1866* Ernst Heidrich (ISBN 978-1-915070-49-4)
25. *British Military Panoramas Battle in The Round, 1800–1914* Ian F.W. Beckett (ISBN 978-1-915113-84-9)
26. *Onwards to Omdurman The Anglo-Egyptian Campaign to Reconquer the Sudan, 1896–1898* Keith Surridge (ISBN 978-1-915070-51-7)
27. *Hungary 1849 The Summer Campaign* Wilhelm Ramming, Christopher Pringle (editor) (ISBN 978-1-915113-80-1)
28. *Line in the Sand French Foreign Legion Forts and Fortifications in Morocco 1900–1926* Richard Jeynes (ISBN 978-1-915113-83-2)
29. *The Republic Fights Back The Franco-German War 1870-1871 Volume 2* Ralph Weaver (ISBN 978-1-915070-50-0)
30. *Controlling the Frontier Southern Africa 1806–1828, The Cape Frontier Wars and The Fetcani Alarm* Hugh Driver (ISBN 978-1-915113-78-8)
31. *The Battle of Magersfontein Victory and defeat on the South African veld, 10–12 December 1899* Garth Benneyworth (ISBN 978-1-915113-79-5)
32. *Too Little Too Late The Campaign in West and South Germany June–July 1866* Michael Embree (ISBN 978-1-804513-77-4)
33. *The Destruction of the Imperial Army* Volume 1: The Opening Engagements of the Franco-German War 1870–71 Grenville Bird (ISBN 978-1-915113-81-8)
34. *Kitchener* The Man Not the Myth Anne Samson (ISBN 978-1-804513-84-2)
35. *From Ironclads to Dreadnoughts* The Development of the German Battleship, 1864–1918 Dirk Nottelmann & David M. Sullivan (ISBN 978-1-804511-84-8)
36. *The Destruction of the Imperial Army* Volume 2: The Battles around Metz Grenville Bird (ISBN 978-1-804511-85-5)
37. *More Work Than Glory* Buffalo Soldiers in the United States Army, 1866–1916 John P Langellier (ISBN 978-1-804513-34-7)
38. *The Spioenkop Campaign* The Battles to Relieve Ladysmith 17–27 January 1900 Robert Davidson (ISBN 978-1-804513-31-6)
39. *The Destruction of the Imperial Army* Volume 3: *The Sedan Campaign 1870* Grenville Bird (ISBN 978-1-804513-32-3)
40. *The Destruction of the Imperial Army* Volume 4: *Sedan, Strasbourg and Metz* 1870 Grenville Bird (ISBN 978-1-804514-59-7)
41. *Memorandum on the Prussian Army in Relation to the Campaign of 1866* Lieutenant Colonel W.E.M Reilly (ISBN 978-1-804516-27-0)
42. *Black Week: The British Army and Defeat in Anglo-Boer War 1899-1900* Quintin Barry (ISBN 978-1-804511-86-2)
43. *War in the East. A Military History of the Russo-Turkish War 1877-78* Quintin Barry (ISBN 978-1-804517-30-7)
44. *The First Schleswig-Holstein War 1848-50* Nick Svendsen (ISBN 978-1-804517-36-9)
45. *The Hundred Thousand Sons of St Louis* Ralph Weaver (ISBN 978-1-804517-37-6)
46. *Bismarck's First War: The Campaign in Schleswig and Jutland 1864* Michael Embree (ISBN 978-1-804517-38-3)
47. *The Honvéd War. Armies of the Hungarian War of Independence 1848-49* Nigel James Smith (ISBN 978-1-804514-60-3)
48. *Radestzky's Marches. The Campaigns of 1848 and 1849 in Upper Italy* Michael Embree (ISBN 978-1-804517-42-0)
49. *The Campaign on the Loire 1870-71: Orléans and Le Mans* Quintin Barry (ISBN 978-1-804517-82-6)
50. *The British Empire's Regulars 1880-1914: Soldiers of Britain, India and Africa* Wendell Scholander (ISBN 978-1-804515-62-4)
51. *The Last Throw of the Dice: Bourbaki and Werder in Eastern France 1870-71* Quintin Barry (ISBN 978-1-804517-78-9)